CROSSING BOUNDARIES

CONSULTANTS

Mildred Bailey	**Teresa Flores**	**Nancy Mayeda**
Rose Barragan	**Charles Hacker**	**Kenneth Smith**
Barbara Burke	**P. J. Hutchins**	**Lydia Stack**
Barbara B. Cramer	**George Jurata**	**Mary Wigner**
Wilma J. Farmer		

Executive Editor: *Sandra Maccarone*

Senior Editors: *Gary W. Bargar, Ronne Kaufman*

Project Editor: *Pamela P. Clark*

Associate Editor: *Jo-Anne Kyriannis*

Editorial Consultants: *Editorial Options, Inc.*

Design Director: *Leslie Bauman*

Assistant Design Director: *Kay Wanous*

Designer: *Thomasina Webb*

Production Director: *Barbara Arkin*

Production Manager: *Trudy Pisciotti*

D.C. HEATH AND COMPANY

Lexington, Massachusetts/Toronto, Ontario

ISBN 0-669-05054-7

1   3   5   7   9   11   13   14   12   10   8   6   4   2

Cover Design: *Thomas Vroman Associates, Inc.* Illustrators: Melanie Arwin, pp. 151-160; Gil Cohen, pp. 227-235; Olivia Cole, pp. 30-35; Pat Cummings, pp. 14-29, 396-409; Diane de Groat, pp. 206-208; Susan Detrich, pp. 370-371; Marian Ebert, pp. 96-97, 174-177, 252-253; Allan Eitzen, pp. 236-250, 358-369; Joy Troth Friedman, pp. 324-333; Will Harmuth, pp. 59-81; Michael Hostovich, pp. 86-95; Yee Chea Lin, pp. 268-285; Bertrand Mangel, pp. 188-190; Sal Murdocca, pp. 265-267; Tom Newsom, pp. 128-139, 180-187; Louis Pappas, p. 110, 117, pp. 304-311; Diane Patterson, pp. 254-264; Howard Post, pp. 118-124; Albert John Pucci, pp. 48-58, 192-205, 218-226; H. Tooter Randall, pp. 142-150, 178-179; Charles Robinson, pp. 380-393; Laurie Simeone, pp. 340-344; Jerry Smath, pp. 161-173, 212-217, 346-355; SN Studios, pp. 36-37, 104-114, p. 116, pp. 125-127, 394-395; Freya Tanz, pp. 288-303; Kyuzo Tsugami, pp. 38-47; Tom Vroman, pp. 378-379; Ron Wolin, pp. 82-83; Lane Yerkes, pp. 98-107.

Photo Research: Elyse Rieder, Tobi Zausner; Photo Credits: Peter B. Kaplan, cover and pp. 1, 8, 9, 11, 12, 13; Flip Schulke, Black Star, pp. 84-85; Tom McHugh, Photo Researchers, p. 112 (top); Russ Kinne, Photo Researchers, p. 112 (bottom); Daniel Brody, Editorial Photocolor Archives, p. 113; Charles Belinky, Photo Researchers, p. 115; Lawrence Schiller, Photo Researchers, pp. 140-141; Frederick Eberstadt, p. 142; Elliott Erwitt, Magnum, p. 143; J. Heffernan, p. 145; Thomas Bloom, Courtesy Opera Company of Boston, pp. 148, 149; Susan McCartney, Photo Researchers, pp. 210-211; Frank Miller, Photo Researchers, pp. 286-287; Museum of the American Indian, Heye Foundation, New York City, pp. 334, 335, 336; Nelson Gallery—Atkins Museum, Kansas City, Missouri (Gift of Mr. Paul Gardner through The Friends of Art), p. 339; U.S. Dept. of Housing and Urban Development, p. 372; George E. Jones III, Photo Researchers, p. 373; U.S. Dept. of Housing and Urban Development, p. 374; Bjorn Bolstad, Photo Researchers, p. 376.

ACKNOWLEDGMENTS

Every reasonable effort has been made to trace the owners of copyright materials in this book, but in some instances this has proven impossible. The publishers will be glad to receive information leading to more complete acknowledgments in subsequent printings of the book, and in the meantime extend their apologies for any omissions.

To the Antioch Press for ''On Watching the Construction of a Skyscraper'' by Burton Raffel. Copyright © 1961 by the Antioch Press. First published in the *Antioch Review*, Volume 20, No. 4. Reprinted by permission of the editors.

To Atheneum Publishers for ''Gravel Paths'' from *Catch Me a Wind* by Patricia Hubbell, copyright © 1968 by Patricia Hubbell; for ''The Lost Umbrella of Kim Chu'' by Eleanor Estes, adapted Chapter Six ''Mae Lee'' from *The Lost Umbrella of Kim Chu* by Eleanor Estes (A Margaret K. McElderry Book), copyright © 1978 by Eleanor Estes; and for ''The Mesa'' from *The Spider, the Cave, and the Pottery Bowl* by Eleanor Clymer, copyright © 1971 by Eleanor Clymer. Used by permission of Atheneum Publishers.

To Brandt & Brandt Literary Agents, Inc. for ''Nancy Hanks'' by Rosemary & Stephen Vincent Benét, taken from *A Book of Americans* by Rosemary & Stephen Vincent Benét, copyright 1933, by Rosemary & Stephen Vincent Benét. Copyright © renewed by Rosemary Carr Benét. Reprinted by permission of Brandt & Brandt Literary Agents, Inc.

To Jonathan Cape Ltd. for ''A Patch of Old Snow'' by Robert Frost from *The Poetry of Robert Frost,* edited by Edward Connery Lathem. Reprinted by permission of the Estate of Robert Frost.

To *The Christian Science Monitor* for ''Unfolding Bud'' by Naoshi Koriyama from *The Christian Science Monitor*, 7/13/57. Reprinted by permission from *The Christian Science Monitor*, copyright © 1957, The Christian Science Publishing Society. All rights reserved.

To Coward, McCann & Geoghegan, Inc. for ''The Mystery of Lyme Regis'' from *Mary's Monster* by Ruth Van Ness Blair, text copyright © 1975 by Ruth Van Ness Blair; and for ''Why Don't You Get a Horse, Sam Adams?'' adapted from *Why Don't You Get a Horse, Sam Adams?* by Jean Fritz, text copyright © 1974 by Jean Fritz. Reprinted by permission of Coward, McCann, & Geoghegan, Inc.

To *Cricket* Magazine for ''Featherwoman'' by Elaine de Bree, reprinted from *Cricket* Magazine, © 1978 by Open Court Publishing Company.

To Thomas Y. Crowell for ''. . . and now Miguel'' adapted text excerpt from *. . . and now Miguel* by Joseph Krumgold, copyright 1953 by Joseph Krumgold; and for ''Where's Robot?'' from *Deep Down: Great Achievements in Cave Exploration* by Garry Hogg, copyright © 1962 by Garry Hogg, a Criterion book. By permission of Thomas Y. Crowell.

To Dodd, Mead & Company, Inc. for ''The Flowering Peach Tree,'' adapted from *Fairy Tales from Viet Nam,* retold by Dorothy Lewis Robertson. Copyright © 1968 by Dorothy Lewis Robertson. Reprinted by permission of Dodd, Mead & Company, Inc.

To Doubleday & Company, Inc. for ''archy hunts a job'' from *Archy Does His Part* by Don Marquis copyright 1927 by Doubleday & Company, Inc.; and for ''The Waking,'' copyright 1953 by Theodore Roethke, from the book *The Collected Poems of Theodore Roethke.* Reprinted by permission of Doubleday & Company, Inc.

To Dresser, Chapman & Grimes, Publishers for ''Tall City'' by Susan Nichols Pulsifer from *The Children Are Poets,* copyright © 1963 by Dresser, Chapman & Grimes. Reprinted by permission of the publisher.
(Continued on page 448)

Contents

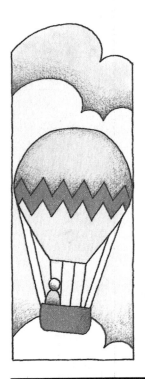

one

two

three

four

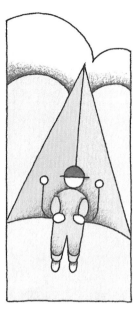

five

six

seven

one

sky garden

up
in the sky
a bouquet of balloons is
blooming   blooming   blooming
and all the people who love spring say
YES
and float up in balloons
and there's a garden in the sky
blooming   blooming   blooming

Bobbi Katz

10

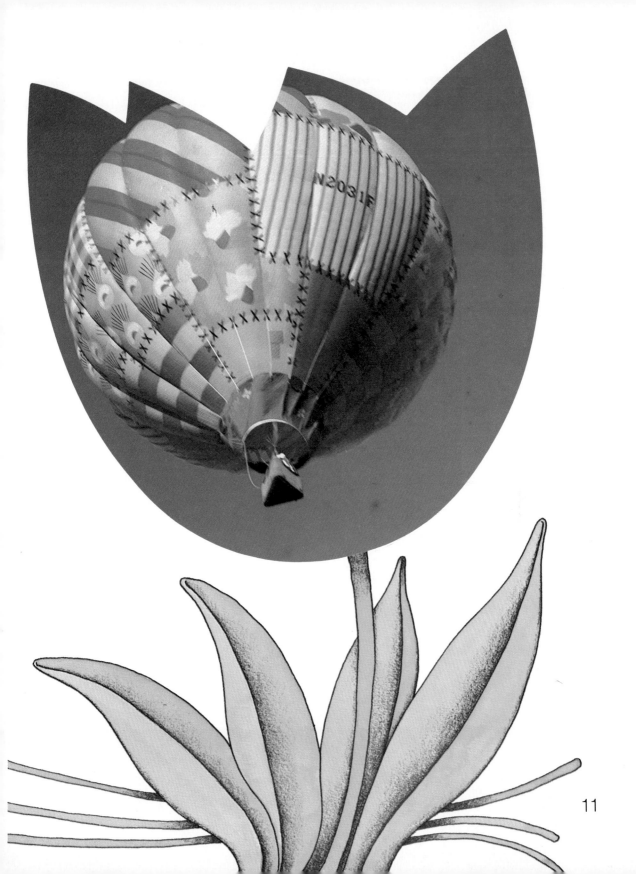

11

13

I remember the morning Rufus got the idea for toothpaste. He had to do some shopping for his mother, and I went along with him. We were in the drugstore, because toothpaste was one of the things on Rufus's list.

I was looking at some eye shadow that was on sale, when I heard Rufus say, "Kate, look at this! 79¢! 79¢ for a six-inch tube of toothpaste. That's crazy!"

"It's better than 89¢," I said, pointing to some 89¢ tubes farther down the shelf.

"That's even crazier," Rufus said. "What can be in those tubes anyway? Just some peppermint flavoring and some paste."

"Maybe the paste is expensive to make," I said.

"Paste!" Rufus said. "You don't need powdered gold to make paste. Paste is made out of everyday ordinary stuff. Didn't you ever make paste?"

"Toothpaste?" I said.

"I mean just plain paste for pasting things together," Rufus said. "My Grandma Mayflower showed me how to make paste when I was four years old."

"How do you do it?" I asked.

"Simple," Rufus said. "You just take a little flour and starch and cook them with a little water till the mixture has a nice pasty feel.

Then you can use it to paste pictures in a scrapbook. Or paste up wallpaper."

"But you couldn't brush your teeth with *that*," I said.

"Well, I don't know," Rufus said. "I never tried. But I bet toothpaste isn't any harder to make. Anyway, I'm not paying any 79¢ for a tube of toothpaste."

Rufus crossed toothpaste off his mother's shopping list.

"But your mother said to get toothpaste," I said. "You can't help it if it's expensive."

"I'll make her some," Rufus said. "I bet I can make a gallon of it for 79¢."

"Maybe even for 78 ⅛¢," I said.

Rufus laughed. "Maybe," he said.

"Hey," I said. "Do you think you could make eye shadow, too?"

It suddenly struck me that 69¢ for a smidgen of eye shadow about as big as a nickel was a little bit expensive, too. And that was the cut-rate price!

"Eye shadow's a kind of pasty stuff," I told Rufus. "Maybe if you just added coloring to toothpaste . . ."

"Maybe," Rufus said. "But what's the point? Nobody really needs eye shadow. If people are crazy enough to pay 69¢ for something they don't *need,* I can't be bothered about them. But people have to brush their teeth. If I could make a good, cheap toothpaste, that would be worth doing."

I decided not to buy any eye shadow. Rufus was right. Who needed it?

"Rufus," I said, as we rode our bikes home. "It just occurred to me that if I never buy any eye shadow for the rest of my life, I'll probably save at least $10 a year. If I live till I'm eighty, that's $700."

"Great!" Rufus said.

"And if I could save money on toothpaste, too . . ." I said. "Wow!" I was thinking about how easy it would be to get rich just by not buying things the stores want you to buy.

"How much do you think it would cost us to make our own toothpaste?" I asked Rufus.

"I don't know," Rufus said. "But I just thought of something else. You know what I used to brush my teeth with when I stayed with my Grandma Mayflower?"

"What?" I asked.

"Bicarbonate of soda," Rufus said. "Just plain old baking soda. You just put a little of the soda powder on your toothbrush."

"*Bicarb?*" I said. "That's the stuff my mother gives me when I feel sick to my stomach. Bicarbonate of soda in water. I can't *stand* the taste."

"Really?" Rufus said. "To me bicarb has a nice refreshing taste. Sort of like a soft drink but without the flavor."

"But who wants to drink a soft drink without the flavor?" I said. "That's the whole *point*!"

"I guess you're right," Rufus said. "I guess that's why more people don't brush their teeth with bicarb."

The next afternoon when I stopped by Rufus's house to borrow his bike pump, he had about fifty bowls and pans scattered around the kitchen.

"What are you making?" I asked.

"I already made it," Rufus said.

He handed me a spoon and a bowl with some white stuff in it. I took a spoonful.

"Don't eat it," Rufus said. "Just taste it. Rub a little on your teeth."

I tried a little.

"How does it taste?" Rufus asked.

"Not bad," I said. "Better than the kind my mother buys in the pink-and-white striped tube. How'd you get it to taste so good?"

"A drop of peppermint oil," Rufus said. "But I've got other flavors, too."

He pushed three other pots of paste across the table. The first one I tried had a spicy taste.

"Clove-flavored," Rufus said. "You like it?"

"I don't know," I said. "It's interesting."

"Try this one."

The next sample had a sweet taste. "Vanilla," I guessed.

"Right," Rufus said.

"I like vanilla," I said. "In milkshakes. Or ice cream. But it doesn't seem quite right in toothpaste. Too sweet."

"This one won't be too sweet," Rufus said, handing me another sample.

"*Eeegh*," I said and ran to the sink to wash out my mouth. "What did you put in *that*?"

"Curry powder," Rufus said. "You don't like it? I thought it tasted like a good shrimp curry."

"Maybe it does," I said, "but I don't like curry."

Rufus looked disappointed. "I don't suppose you'd like it almond-flavored, either," he said. "I made some of that, too, but I decided not too many people would like it."

"What flavor is in that big plastic pan?" I asked.

"That's no kind yet," Rufus said. "That's just 79¢ worth of stuff that goes in the paste. I didn't want to flavor it till I figured out the best taste."

"What does it taste like plain?" I asked.

"Well," Rufus said, "mostly you taste the bicarb."

"Bicarb!" I said. "You mean all this stuff I've been tasting has got bicarbonate of soda in it?"

Rufus grinned. "Yeah," he said. "It's probably good for your stomach as well as your teeth."

I forgot to mention another nice thing about Rufus. The afternoon when Rufus let me sample his first batch of toothpaste, he was also trying to figure out how many tubes of toothpaste it would make.

We looked at a medium-sized tube of toothpaste.

"You must have enough for ten tubes in that plastic bowl," I guessed.

"More, I bet," Rufus said.

"Why don't you squeeze the toothpaste in the tube into a measuring cup and then measure the stuff in the bowl," I suggested.

"That would be a waste of toothpaste," Rufus said. "We couldn't get it back in the tube." Rufus hates to waste anything.

"I have a better idea," he said. "I'll pack into a square pan the toothpaste I made. Then I can figure out how many cubic inches of toothpaste we have. And you can figure out how many cubic inches of toothpaste are in the tube."

"But the tube is round, Rufus," I said. "I can't measure cubic inches unless something is cube-shaped."

Rufus thought a minute. "Maybe we can squeeze the tube into a cube shape," he said.

I thought that was brilliant. But then I had another idea.

"Rufus," I said. "It says on the tube that it contains 3.25 ounces of toothpaste. Why couldn't we just weigh your paste and divide by 3.25 to see how many tubes it would make?"

"Hey—we could!" Rufus said. "You are *smart,* Kate. I'm always doing things the hard way."

That's what is really so nice about Rufus. It's not just that he gets ideas like making toothpaste. But if *you* have a good idea, he says so.

Anyway it turned out Rufus had made about forty tubes of toothpaste for 79¢.

Before I finished breakfast the next morning, there was a knock on the door. It was Rufus. He was very excited.

"Kate!" he said. "Do you know what the population of the United States is?"

"No," I said. I never know things like that. My mother looked up from her paper. "According to the most recent census—over

24

200,000,000," she said to Rufus. My mother always knows things like that.

"You're right," Rufus said, "and by now, it must be even bigger."

"Probably," my mother said, "but why do you want to know? What are you thinking about, Rufus?"

"Toothpaste, Mrs. MacKinstrey," Rufus said. "I was just trying to figure out something. I was thinking that everybody in the United States probably uses about one tube of toothpaste a month."

"Probably," my mother said.

"And if they do," Rufus said, "how many tubes of toothpaste are sold in a year?"

My mother thought for a second. "Roughly two-and-a-half billion tubes."

"Right!" Rufus said.

This was the first of several math problems that Rufus came up with that day. The next ones caused me more of a problem than just trying to do the arithmetic.

There I was sitting in math class when Mr. Conti, the math teacher, said "Kate MacKinstrey, would you please bring me that note you're reading."

"Well, it isn't exactly a note, Mr. Conti."

"I see," said Mr. Conti. "I suppose it's another math problem."

"It looks like a math problem, Mr. Conti."

The message from Rufus that Mr. Conti got to read that day said:

> *If there are 2½ billion tubes of toothpaste sold in the U.S. in one year, and 1 out of 10 people switched to a new brand, how many tubes of the new brand would they be buying?*

The right answer is 250 million. It took the class a while to figure that out. Some people

have trouble remembering how many zeros
there are in a billion.

Then there was a second part to the note:

*If the inventor of the new toothpaste made
a profit of 1¢ a tube on the toothpaste,
what would the profit be at the end of a
year?*

It turns out that the inventor of this new
toothpaste would make a two-and-a-half million dollar profit!

To mix up a batch of good tasting bicarbonate of soda may not be difficult. But to turn that bowl of paste into a million dollar business takes a lot of "know-how" and a bit of good luck. Find out if Rufus has enough of both to make his dream come true. Read the whole story in The Toothpaste Millionaire. After all, who knows when you might have a brainstorm of your own, just like Rufus!

1. Why did Rufus decide to try to make his own toothpaste?

2. What was the main ingredient in the toothpaste that Rufus made? What were some of the different flavors that Rufus added?

3. How much profit did Rufus think he could make selling toothpaste? How did he figure out his profit?

4. From whose point of view is this story told? Why do you think the author chose to tell the story this way?

5. What problems might arise as Rufus tries to sell his toothpaste? How do you think Rufus will solve those problems?

6. Kate considered Rufus to be a very special friend. Why do you think she felt this way? What do you think of Rufus?

7. Tell about an idea you've had for making or selling something.

No More "No Money" Blues

Meet Wayne and Linda. They've got the "no money" blues. They'd like to have coins in their pockets, but they don't. They'd like to buy two tickets to the new movie in town, but they can't. They've got the "no money" blues. And it's too bad, because there are lots of ways that they could make money. Kids all over are doing things to earn their own spending money.

Take Fred, for example, who's got a way with plants. Everyone in the neighborhood says he's got the greenest thumb around. There was a time when

his whole house was covered with dozens of philo-
dendrons, coleuses, and spider plants. But no more.

The day Fred's parents tripped over an immense
rubber tree, they put their foot down. The greenery
would have to go. That's when Fred got his bright
idea.

He wrote different prices on index cards: 25¢,
50¢, 75¢, $1.00. Then he set up a card table
outside, lined up all his plants on the table, and
placed an index card at the front of each row. Before
the day was over Fred had sold over a dozen of his
prized plants and earned himself $5.50!

Well, Fred was on his way. That evening he took
cuttings from all the plants he had not sold. He put
the cuttings in two jars of water and set the jars in a
sunny spot.

For the next two weeks Fred set up his plant
stand every day after school. By the time Fred had
sold all his large plants, the cuttings had taken root.

Fred bought rich potting soil with his first profits. He then planted his new cuttings in used milk cartons and set up the card table again.

After three months Fred had the best nursery in the neighborhood. Both he and his parents were delighted!

Jennifer is one of Fred's best friends. She likes plants, but she doesn't have much of a green thumb. Jennifer loves to run and ride her bike, so she decided to earn extra money by running errands.

Jennifer realized that many times people need one or two items from a store. But they don't always feel like going out themselves. Jennifer asked around and found out that her neighbors would be happy to pay her from 25¢ to 50¢ to run simple errands.

Jennifer was off and running. She named her new business *The Flying Feet Delivery Service*. Then she advertised with special cards that told who she was, what she did, when she worked, and what her telephone number was. Jennifer got permission to post the cards on bulletin boards in nearby stores. She also told her friends and their parents about her new enterprise.

Business was slow at first, but soon word got around. Once people knew they could count on her, they started using her service regularly.

The best part about Jennifer's errand service was that she didn't need any of her own money to begin with. The 25¢ or 50¢ she received for each trip was pure profit.

There's that word *profit* again. It keeps coming up. And it's no wonder. People usually start a business with the idea of making a profit.

Jennifer Watts
Flying Feet Delivery Service
555-1234
Monday, Tuesday
Saturday afternoons

Both Jennifer and Fred keep track of their profits by carefully recording all their income and expenses. Each time they earn money from their business, they write the amount, the date, and the customer on the front of an envelope. Each time they spend money, they write the amount, the date, and the reason on an index card. They keep the envelopes and the cards in a special box. At the end of each week or month, they add up all the money they've earned from the business. Then they add up all the money they've spent on the business. They subtract the money spent from the money earned. The remainder is their profit. After all the adding and subtracting is done, the index cards go inside the envelopes as a permanent record.

As you can see, it's really very easy to get rid of the "no money" blues. And it's fun, too. By the way, if you happen to see Wayne or Linda in your neighborhood, tell them about Jennifer and Fred. These success stories might give Wayne and Linda some ideas of their own.

Income

Amount:	Date:	Customer:
$1.50	2/11	Mr. Jones
$3.00	2/13	Ms. Allen
.75	2/13	Mrs. Grodin

Expenses
Amount: $1.75
Name: Green's Plants
Date: 2/15
Reason: Potting Soil

1. What does it mean to have the "no money" blues?

2. What did Fred decide to do to earn extra money?

3. How did Fred grow new plants to sell? After the cuttings had taken root, what did Fred do with them?

4. What did Jennifer decide to do to earn extra money?

5. How did Jennifer advertise her services? How much did she charge?

6. How did both Fred and Jennifer keep track of their profits?

7. Why do you think it's so important for people who have their own businesses to keep careful records?

8. Think about the ways Fred and Jennifer earned extra money. How are their money-making schemes similar?

9. Have you ever had the "no money" blues? What did you do to solve the problem? Tell about some ideas you've had for earning extra money.

The Ins and Outs of Money

Ask grownups what they read every week, and the answers might surprise you. They might say the newspaper, bills, a checkbook, and a paycheck. Many people read almost as many numbers as words.

You just read how Fred and Jennifer kept track of their profit by recording their income and expenses. Many adults keep track of their spending money by keeping a budget. It's easy to keep a budget. You just have to know how to read numbers. Here's a budget that a student made. Read it carefully. Then answer the questions that follow on page 37.

Weekly Budget

Income		*Expenses*	
For lunches and school supplies	$5.00	School lunches	$3.25
		Snacks	$1.00
Dog-walking		School supplies	$1.50
Monday to		Entertainment	$1.75
Friday	$5.00	Miscellaneous	$1.50
TOTAL	$10.00		$9.00

Weekly Savings
$1.00

1. The budget is divided into two main parts. What are they? Which part means money coming in and which part means money going out?
2. How much are the student's expenses each week? How much income does the student have weekly?
3. How much does the student spend on snacks in a week? How do you know?
4. How much is spent on lunch each week?
5. At the end of a week is there any money left over? What part of the budget tells you this?
6. Suppose one week the student made an extra dollar walking dogs. How would the extra dollar affect the income side? Would it affect the expense side? How will it affect savings?

   Now make up a real budget for yourself. List all your income on one side and your expenses on the other side. The budget may help you spend your money more wisely!

...and now Miguel

All year long Miguel Chavez* waits for summer, the time of year his family's sheep go to pasture in the Sangre de Cristo Mountains. But before leaving the farm in the flatlands of New Mexico, there is much work to do. In this selection from . . . *and now Miguel,* Miguel learns how the ewes and their lambs are paired by number.

*Miguel Chavez (mē gel' chä'ves)

The best of all the different ways to get a lamb and a ewe to be mothered-up, my father told me, was the lambing pens.

These were built all over, in the corners of the corrals or any place. In the corner you would put up some planks and block off a place just big enough for a sheep. In this space you would put the ewe and the lamb and leave them for a day or even longer. During this time the ewe can't run away and in the end the mother and the lamb get to know each other and like each other. Then there is no more danger letting them go off by themselves. There were more than a dozen of these lambing pens all around, and they were always filled up with a family that was settling down to live together.

So that at the last, whether with lambing pens or by one of the other ways, the whole flock was taken care of and everybody was happy.

Except for the orphans.

I don't care how good you are thinking up things that are sad, there is nothing sadder than a lamb that is an orphan.

We call them tramps, such orphans. But it isn't their fault, like they ran away from home or something. It isn't even because the mother dies, most of the time. An orphan comes most of the time when there are twins, and the mother cannot feed both. Or when a lamb gets lost from its

mother for two or three days, and she doesn't recognize it even by the smell anymore. This doesn't have to be our fault or anybody's fault. It could be there's a storm and the sheep get separated. Or they get frightened by a wolf or another kind of animal and they go rushing around.

However it happens, an orphan is one unlucky animal. And the reason for this is that a ewe will have absolutely nothing to do with any lamb except her own lamb. She won't feed it or lick it or anything. What's worse, when the orphan comes hanging around looking for a meal, nosing this way and that to see what he can get, the ewe beats it up. A ewe can butt almost as hard as a nanny goat. And when she takes off and butts at one of these orphans that's trying to get friendly

with her, it's like the orphan got hit by a truck.

We had two orphans this year. And for a little while we let them hang around to give them a chance to find their mothers by themselves. But they never did. They were like a couple of big zeros, going this way and that way in the middle of a lot of numbers that were happy together in pairs. Two 1's, two 2's, two 3's, all the way up into the hundreds. All the orphans got all day long was ewes butting them from the right and the left until you'd think they were black and blue, only lambs don't get black and blue, just dirty.

But then it happened that one of the lambs that did have a mother died. This was bad, without doubt. But it gave my father a chance to fix up at least one of the orphans with a mother.

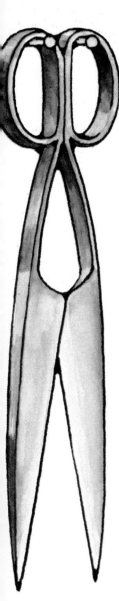

The way he did this was a kind of a trick. He
got the dead lamb—its number was 86—from
where it was laying on the ground at the feet of
the ewe that was its mother. The ewe just stood
there hour after hour, baaing and bleating because the lamb wouldn't get up and feed itself
and go walking around like it did before it died.
My father took the body of the lamb around to
the other side of the shearing shed where the ewe
couldn't see. And here he stripped off its coat with
a hunting knife. Then he fitted the little sheepskin of the dead lamb over one of the orphans. It
didn't fit so good, about the way one of my
father's coats fit me. But at least it stayed on the
lamb and gave the little animal a number, 86.

"The ewe will smell the skin of her own dead
lamb." My father looked up at me watching him
work. "She'll think the orphan is her child. She'll
let the orphan feed and stay together with her as
a family."

"It's like a trick?"

My father, working, nodded his head, yes.

"Is it right? I mean to do it?"

"Is what right?"

"To fool the ewe."

He stood up with the orphan in his arms and
shook his head. "When anyone must believe
something the way a ewe must believe she has a
child, you don't fool her when you help. Watch!"

42

When he went around back to the ewe with the orphan, the sheepskin hanging on it with the number 86, it was interesting. First the ewe looked suspiciously at the orphan standing there. Then it sniffed a little in front and behind, then it went off and turned around and came back. The orphan didn't do anything. I guess it was so beat up trying to be friendly with ewes, it was scared to do anything. It just stood there, wrapped around in a blanket with the number 86 on it. Then the ewe gave a different kind of a cry—happy—and shoved the orphan with its nose. This was some kind of signal. The orphan went right for its dinner, and the ewe looked down as if this was the smartest thing anybody ever did.

43

"See?" said my father.

"I see."

They walked off together, the ewe number 86 and the lamb with the coat 86 dragging by one corner on the ground. "The ewe is happy," said my father. "It believes it has a lamb. And the lamb is happy. It believes it has a mother. And this is what they must believe if they are to live happy. This is not fooling anybody, is it?"

I said, "I guess not."

"And in a day or two it will be true, without doubt. Soon the smell of the skin from the dead lamb goes away. At the same time, the ewe gets used to the smell, the real smell, of the orphan. She will recognize the new smell to be the smell of her child. When that happens we will take the sheep skin off the lamb. You will put 86 on this lamb to match its new mother and they will be a ewe and a lamb together."

"I'll watch out," I said, "and have the 8 and the 6 ready."

But, thank goodness, not so many lambs die. You can't work this trick for all the orphans. We couldn't do it this year for even the second orphan. All the other ewes have lambs.

This one was given to my older sisters, Tomasita and Leocadia, to keep. Between them the girls had five orphans to take care of last year. They fed each one milk out of a bottle. Then after a while they showed the orphans how to eat grass and alfalfa from around the farm. My sisters did all right. At the end of the summer they sold the lambs they raised and made much money. Fifteen dollars for each one.

The orphan they have now they call Jimmy. It is like a pet for my sisters, walking behind them wherever they go. This is the way it is with lambs, if they don't have a ewe they'll follow anything around. Once I heard a poem called "Mary had a little lamb." I don't know whether it is a good poem or a bad poem. But it's true, I know that. The way the lamb followed this girl Mary when she went to school, that's the way it happens. Not only does a lamb follow someone called Mary around, but even a truck or a tractor or, if nothing else, an old tire that someone might be rolling along.

To be taken care of by my sisters an orphan is at least lucky. It won't die. But it can't be very happy. It never becomes part of the regular flock. It's always off by itself. What's more, it stays with the girls on the farm all summer. It never goes with the flock to the summer pasture. It never climbs with the rest when they go up there, up into the mountains of the Sangre de Cristo.

Unless I put a number on the sheep, one that matches the number of a ewe, one of the numbers that is part of the flock, it gets left behind.

You can see how all I had in my head these days was numbers. And to see that no one got left out, and to put numbers on them. Eights and twos and sixes and threes. Numbers all day long. And even when I got into bed at night and I would answer my brother's questions, even then I couldn't forget numbers. And numbers would be still in my head, the very last thing when I would take a look at the mountains before turning over.

Once I even thought I saw up there, on the Sangre de Cristo Mountains, the number 12—it must have been a shadow or something from a cloud. And I, too, was 12.

I went to sleep thinking that the mountain and I were mothered-up like the sheep.

1. What are lambing pens? How are lambing pens used by sheepherders?

2. Why do some lambs become orphans? Why did Miguel Chavez feel that an orphaned lamb was such an "unlucky animal"?

3. How did Miguel's father manage to pair up the ewe numbered 86 with one of the orphans?

4. On the Chavez sheep farm, what happened to the lambs that could not be mothered-up?

5. Why do you think Miguel questioned whether or not it was right to trick the ewe into thinking that the orphan was her lamb? What convinced Miguel that it was all right to do this?

6. What did Miguel mean when he said, "the mountain and I, we were like mothered-up"? Why do you think Miguel was so eager to go with the others up into the Sangre de Cristo Mountains?

7. From whose point of view is this story told? How does the author make you think that a twelve-year-old boy is telling the story?

8. Tell about a time when you've been told that you must "wait until you are older" to do something. How did you feel?

The story you are about to read is the first chapter in a book called *The Spider, the Cave, and the Pottery Bowl.* In "The Mesa," you will meet Kate, her brother Johnny, and their grandmother, with whom they spend each summer. But this year the visit to Grandmother did not begin as Kate had expected. On the following pages, Kate herself will tell you how the summer *did* begin.

THE MESA

In a certain place in the desert there is a cave, and sometimes outside the cave you can see a spider in its web. And on the shelf in my grandmother's house there is a pottery bowl. All these things are connected, and this is what I am going to tell about. But first I must tell about myself.

I am Indian. My name is an Indian word meaning One Who Dips Water. But in school they call me Kate. In winter I live with my father and mother and brother in a town near the edge of the desert. My father works in a store. There is a garage next to the store and he helps there, too. We have a garden and peach trees. We have a wooden house. We have running water and electricity. We aren't rich, but we have those things.

But in summer I go back to the mesa where my grandmother lives. We used to live there too, but we moved away. Grandmother's house is part of a village built of stone, with many small rooms, all connected, like a wall of houses around an open place. It's a small village. Some of the houses have other houses that were built on top of them when more rooms were needed. The village is very old, many hundreds of years old. When you drive across the desert you can see the mesa, like a high wall of rock ahead of you. And on top is the village.

I love it on the mesa. It is windy, hot in the sun but cool in the shade of the houses, and you can see far out over the desert—the Painted Desert they call it, because it looks as if it were painted. It is beautiful on the mesa, but it is hard to live there. There is no water. The people must carry water up from springs down below. They must carry up everything they need, and they must go down to tend their gardens, and walk a long way through the desert to find grass or plants for their sheep to eat. It is hard work.

That is why some people moved away. My father doesn't mind hard work, but he needed to earn money for us. So we had to go away to the town.

But every summer we come back, my mother and my brother and I. We stay in my grandmother's house. My mother helps Grandmother with the summer work. And I help, too. We go down below and work in the garden, and we

dry the corn and squash for the winter. We gather peaches from the orchard at the foot of the mesa, and we dry them. My brother plays with his friends and rides the burros that live in the corral.

We gather firewood for the stove and fireplace and pile it up for the winter. We plaster the walls to make the house look clean. And we go a few miles away and bring home clay for the pottery.

The pottery is what I love most of all. I love to work the cool wet clay between my hands. When I was little, my grandmother gave me pieces of clay to play with, and I made things out of them. I made little animals: sheep and donkeys and birds.

Then when I got bigger, I watched my grandmother make bowls and jars. She made a flat piece for the bottom. Then she rolled pieces of

clay into long rolls between her hands and coiled them on top of the flat piece till she had built up a jar. She smoothed it with a stone or a piece of shell and shaped it in beautiful curves. When it was dry, she painted it with lovely designs. I watched her hand holding the brush of yucca

leaves, slowly painting birds and leaves around the curving sides of the bowl. When she had enough bowls and jars, she built a fire and baked them hard.

People came to buy them, and my father took some to sell in the store where he works. But one bowl was never for sale. It stood on the shelf in the corner. It had been there for as long as I could remember.

The other women in the village made pottery, but I liked the things my grandmother made. There's nothing I wanted more than to make pottery like hers. So I was always happy when summer came and we could go to the mesa.

But this summer was different. My mother did not come. She had to get a job.

For many days I heard my parents talking. There had been no snow during the winter, and all spring it had not rained. The springs did not give much water. The gardens were not growing well.

Where we live, everything depends on water. We are careful not to waste it. The people plant their gardens with little walls around them to save every drop that might run off. We have dances and prayers and music that help to bring rain. Even our names are like prayers for rain. That is why my name is One Who Dips Water. My brother's name is a word that means Clear Water, but his school name is Johnny.

Anyway, Mother and Father knew they would need money to buy food next winter. There are jobs in summer when the tourists come to stay in the hotels, and my parents decided that my mother should get such a job to earn extra money.

I said, "But what will we do? Won't we go to the mesa? What will Grandmother do?"

Mother said, "Kate, you are big, you will help Grandmother. Johnny will do his share. He is big enough to bring wood and water. Perhaps the neighbors will help with Grandmother's garden. But if the mesa springs are as dry as ours, perhaps there will not be much of a garden. We will need money to help Grandmother, too. When the summer is over and we come to get you, perhaps Grandmother will come with us and live here."

I did not think she would, but I did not say so.

So my father drove us to the mesa in the truck. It is about forty miles. We rode across the desert, between red, black, and yellow rocks and sand dunes covered with sage and yellow-flowered rabbitbrush. I was thinking about the work I would do. I don't mind the work, because it's important. Some day Grandmother's house will be Mother's, and then it will be mine. So I ought to know how to do everything.

At last we saw the houses and the store and the school at the foot of the mesa. We took the narrow rocky road up the side of the mesa, and at last we came out in the open space on top.

My grandmother was waiting for us in the doorway of her house. When I saw her I was surprised. She looked much older than the last time I had seen her. I had always thought of Grandmother as a strong, plump woman with black hair. This year she looked smaller, thinner, and her hair was gray.

Father noticed, too. He said to her, "Are you all right?"

Grandmother said, "Yes, I am well."

Father carried in the basket of food we had brought, and the boxes with our clothes. He explained why Mother had not come.

Grandmother turned quickly in surprise. But she only said, "Well, if that is the way it is, it will have to be."

I said, "I will help you, Grandmother."

She nodded and said, "Yes, you are a big girl now."

And the neighbors who had come in said, "We will all help."

Father asked about Grandmother's garden. But she said she had not planted a garden this year. Then he asked if she had any pottery for him to take back, and she said, "No, I have not made any."

"Do you need clay?" he asked.

She said, "No, I don't need any clay."

Father said good-by then. As he was leaving, he said to me, "Remember, if you need Mother or me, go down to the store and telephone, and we will come."

Then he went away, and there we were.

I did not know what to do at first. I thought Grandmother would tell me, but she did not. So I made a fire in the stove and made coffee. We drank some. Johnny went to find his friends.

I said, "Is there something you want me to do?"

Grandmother said, "Later. Now I think I will sleep a little." And she lay down on her bed.

I went outside. It was strange for my Grandmother to be sleeping in the morning. I thought, "Well, after she has a rest, we will do things."

Later I went back to our house. It was nearly dinnertime. Mother had sent some stew, so I warmed it up and cut the bread. Then I called Johnny and we ate.

Grandmother did not eat much. After dinner she went out and sat in the sun.

What do you think is wrong with Kate's grandmother? How do you think Kate will deal with her condition? To discover what happens, read the rest of *The Spider, the Cave, and the Pottery Bowl.*

THINK ABOUT IT

1. Who is telling this story? Why does she have two names?

2. Where does Kate's grandmother live? What is her home like?

3. How does Kate feel about the mesa? Why does she want to learn all she can about running her grandmother's house?

4. How had Kate's grandmother changed since the last time the family had seen her?

5. Why do you think Kate's grandmother decides to remain in her mesa home rather than move to town? Do you think she will ever want to leave the mesa? Why or why not?

6. Why do you think the one bowl was never for sale?

7. How is life in the mesa village different from life in the place where you live? Would you like to visit the mesa? Why or why not?

The Boy Who Voted for Abe Lincoln

Part One

Sam Adams climbed to the wagon seat and clucked to the yoke of oxen. His father was out of sight now, over the hill, heading for the wheatfield. As the wagon rattled down the road, Sam looked back and waved to his mother. She was standing in the farmyard, her yellow hair and gray calico skirt blowing in the brisk wind.

She waved anxiously. "Hurry now, Sam!" she called. "You know how important that wheat is. If those cattle get in before the fence is up—!" She left the sentence unfinished.

"I'll get there, Ma," he called back reassuringly. "Don't worry."

But Sam couldn't help worrying himself. A
herd of cattle roving over the hills had already
destroyed the Hills' cornfield and the Moores'
oats. It was Mr. Moore who had ridden over to
warn Sam's father that the cattle were headed
that way.

Sam gritted his teeth. If anything happened to
the wheatfield, next winter would be a barren one
with food scarce and money scarcer. Sam could
remember two years ago, when he had been only
ten. All winter there had been an empty ache
where his stomach should have been. No, he
didn't want another winter like that.

He tried to get the oxen to move faster, but the

road was narrow and full of deep ruts. It was
muddy, too, from yesterday's rain.

Bumping and sliding, the wagon loaded with
fence rails finally came in sight of the field. Sam
gave a glad shout. He was almost there, and the
wheat was rippling in the wind, still untrampled.
He could see his father riding along the far edge.

But Sam's shout had stopped the oxen. To
them it had sounded like a call to halt. Sam tried
to urge them forward but it was too late. The
right wheels were sunk up to the hubs in the
sticky mud.

"Giddap," Sam cried desperately, but it was no
use. The wagon was stuck, glued to the slimy
ruts. Sam lifted his head and opened his mouth to
call for help, but the shout died in his throat.

Thronging the hill beyond the wheatfield were moving cattle, a hundred head or more. They were coming steadily on toward the precious wheatfield.

It was no use now to call his father. They would never get the wagon out in time, nor would they get the fence up. If his father could head the cattle off alone it would be a miracle.

Sam choked. He had tried to be brave, but now tears came to his eyes. There was nothing he could do to stop the cattle from ruining the wheat. Eyes blinded with tears, he slid from the wagon seat.

As he did so, he heard the familiar beat of a horse's hoofs behind. Someone was coming down the road!

Shouting hoarsely, Sam waved his arms and pointed to the wheatfield. Tears blurred his vision so that he could not tell if the man approaching was friend or stranger.

He backed against the wagon as the horse galloped forward, spurting mud toward him.

"Don't worry, son! Block up your wheels and put the rails under them. I'll help your father head off the cattle."

Sam hadn't had time to see what the man looked like, but now, brushing the tears away, he stared after him in relief. The wheatfield had a chance now, maybe.

Sam noticed that the man on the horse was long and lanky, but in heading off cattle, he was clever and successful. Soon he and Sam's father had managed to herd the steers away from the wheat. The cattle thundered off, bellowing, in the direction they had come.

Sam's heart hammered gratefully, as he watched the stranger dismount and talk with his father. Then he remembered the man's instructions for getting the wagon out of the mud.

Sam started to work busily. The cattle had been headed off for the time being, but no telling how soon they might come back again. The sooner he got the fence rails to the field, the better.

When he looked up again, the stranger had climbed on his horse and was riding off down the road at a canter, his lean form swaying awkwardly.

Mopping his brow with a large handkerchief, Mr. Adams crossed the field toward his son.

"That was sure a close shave, son," he said, coming up to the wagon. "If it hadn't been for Abe, we'd have lost the wheat, for sure. I never could have headed those steers off alone."

"Abe who?" asked Sam. "A friend of yours, Pa?"

"Why, that was Abe Lincoln, son. He was on his way back to Springfield after making a speech. As for being a friend of mine, I guess Abe's just about everybody's friend."

"He sure was our friend," said Sam gratefully. "What does this Abe Lincoln do, Pa?"

"He's a lawyer, son; in politics, too. In fact, he's just been nominated for the presidency of the United States, on the new Republican Party ticket. Don't know as he's got much of a chance, though."

"Why not?" asked Sam loyally. "I guess we'd be lucky, wouldn't we, Pa, to get a man as good as he?"

"You bet we would, but you see, he's up against some pretty smart folk. Educated folk like Stephen Douglas, for instance."

"But you're going to vote for Mr. Lincoln, aren't you, Pa? You'd like for him to be President, wouldn't you?"

"You bet I'll vote for him, Sam. Nothing can stop me from polling my vote for Abraham Lincoln, come November."

But something did stop Hank Adams from voting for Abraham Lincoln. In early July he was thrown from a horse and seriously injured. Judith, his wife, and his son, Sam, were beside him when he died.

"Don't—forget—the—wheat, Sam. Take—it into—Springfield." He sighed, closed his eyes. "I—meant—to—take—it—in Election Day. When—I—voted—for Abe. Too bad."

Two weeks later Sam answered a knock at the door and found two men standing outside.

"This the Adams farm?" asked one.

"Yes, sir. Will you come in?" Sam answered.

"Who is it, Sam?" called his mother.

"I'm Joe Winship," said the taller of the two strangers. "And this is my partner, Jerry Hogan. We've brought a letter from Mr. Abe Lincoln."

"From Abe Lincoln?" She took it wonderingly. "Why, it's addressed to both of us, Sammy."

"To me, too?" asked Sam eagerly. "Open it, Ma. What does it say?"

She looked up at the two men whom, in the excitement of the letter, she had almost forgotten. "Oh, I'm sorry. I—I guess I've clean forgot my manners, gentlemen. Sammy, push up some chairs for Mr. Winship and Mr. Hogan."

"Oh, don't mind us. We're just—just part of the letter, you might say," said Mr. Hogan, flushing.

But Sam ran for some chairs anyway. When he came back, his mother had the letter and was looking up from it, her face glowing.

"Bless Abe Lincoln," she said softly. "It's a beautiful letter."

"He's a kind man, ma'am," said Mr. Winship fervently. "There aren't many lawyers who would let Jerry and me work out a debt like this, instead of paying straight cash."

"What does it say, Ma?" asked Sam eagerly.

"It says," replied his mother gently, "that Mr. Lincoln is deeply sorry to learn of your pa's going. And he hopes we'll be kind enough to let these two friends of his, Mr. Winship and Mr. Hogan, work out their debt to him for legal work by helping us with the farm work for a spell."

"Ma!" said Sam. "That means we'll have help threshing the wheat."

"You sure will," said Mr. Hogan, grinning widely. "You'll have all the help you need."

"I-I don't know what to say," said Mrs. Adams, choking. "We can sure use the help. Sam's been doing fine, but he's a long way from being grown. How can I thank Mr. Lincoln?"

"We'll just tell him about the look on your face when you read the letter, Mrs. Adams. That'll be thanks enough for Abe."

"Is that all the letter, Ma?" asked Sam. "Didn't he say anything about me? You said the letter was addressed to me, too."

"Why, yes, Sam. There is a note for you."

The boy took the page eagerly and read:

Sam,
I used to hear your father talk about what a fine good boy you were. He was very proud of you and I know he's glad you're there to take care of your mother. Don't ever give up if you should get stuck in the mud again because there's always a way out.

Sam put the letter down. "Ma! Abe Lincoln's just got to be elected President. Why, I reckon he must be the best man in the whole world."

Part Two

In November, Sam Adams took the wheat into Springfield to sell. Joe Winship and Jerry Hogan had told him where to take it in order to get the best price.

It was good to know that his mother would not have to worry about money all winter long. They'd have enough to eat now. He wished he could keep her from missing Pa too much. Maybe if he bought her something . . . something with the money she'd said he could have for his very own.

It was still early morning when he rolled into Springfield. There were a lot of people going to town—more than he'd ever seen before. The streets of the little town hummed with excitement. There was something in the air, something in the way people gathered in groups on street corners,

that set young Sam Adams's pulse throbbing.
Unusual happenings today, sure enough, he reck-
oned, maybe it was a parade or a fair.

Then a group of men bearing banners marched
down the street to the beat of the blaring band
music. Printed in large letters across the banners
were the words: "Elect Stephen Douglas President."

Sam sat bolt upright, shocked to see the sign in
favor of Mr. Douglas. Why, it was Abe Lincoln
they should be voting for, just like his own pa had
been going to do.

He knew then why there were so many people
here in Springfield today. It was Election Day—
the day the people voted for President of the
United States. He wondered why his mother
hadn't told him, but they'd been working so hard
lately that she must have forgotten.

Well, he was here now, luckily. He'd go sell the wheat first, then he'd come back.

Sam sold his wheat for an even better price than he'd expected. Mr. Salford, the man who bought the grain said that he knew about Sam from Joe Winship and had been expecting him.

"Too bad your mother couldn't come in to town, too," said Mr. Salford, helping unload the bags of wheat.

"I reckon she'll be mighty sorry, too, when she hears it's Election Day," said Sam, "but someone had to stay and take care of the farm. There are only two of us now."

"Well, you're a fine, strong lad," Mr. Salford said. "I'm sure your mother depends on you a good deal."

Sam asked the way to the nearest polling place. The town hall was closest, Mr. Salford said, waving good-bye.

The street outside the town hall was crowded. The sidewalks were clotted with groups of people, all talking in loud voices or speaking in low confidential asides.

Sam nudged a man with a very red nose and fierce, black beard. "Where do folks go to vote?" Sam asked timidly.

"Just follow the crowd," answered the man, waving a hand. "Just follow the crowd." Then, getting a good look at Sam for the first time, he stared in disbelief. "Are you planning to vote, son?" he said, bursting into peels of loud laughter. "Well, if you do, don't vote for that scarecrow, Abe Lincoln!" A group of people nearby then joined in the loud laughing. Sam felt his ears get hot as he hurried past them to the voting room.

There were little booths in the room where people voted. As soon as one man left one of the booths, another man went in.* Sam waited patiently for his chance and at the first opportunity went into a booth.

*Only men could vote in Lincoln's day.

"Hey!" said a voice. "A kid went in that booth! Yank him out."

As Sam was being pulled out of the voting booth, he pleaded, "But—but I want to vote. I want to vote for Mr. Lincoln."

A man laughed at Sam. "But you're not old enough to vote, kid. You have to be twenty-one in order to vote." He gave Sam a shove and shouted, "On your way, son!"

"But please, mister—I'm voting for my pa. He aimed to cast his ballot for Lincoln."

"Well, he'll have to come himself," said the man impatiently. "Now go on—get out of here. You're just taking up floor space needed by legal voters."

"But my pa can't come himself," pleaded Sam. "Honest, mister, why isn't it all right for me to—"

The man beckoned two burly-looking men over to his side. "This youngster's stubborn. I reckon you'd better show him the way out."

The two men took hold of Sam and lifted him squirming from the floor.

Two minutes later he picked himself up from the street outside. His best pants were torn, his hat had fallen into the gutter, and his knees and one elbow were skinned. But worst of all was the way he felt inside. He'd failed—failed both his pa and Mr. Lincoln.

Sam got up and picked his crumpled, muddy hat out of the gutter. His eyes filled with tears. He tried to choke back the sobs.

Suddenly a heavy hand fell on his shoulder; Sam looked up, startled.

"Please, mister. I'm not doing anything. I'm going now."

"What's the trouble, son?"

Sam looked up into the face of a man so homely, so gaunt that, despite the kindness of his tone, the boy's fright returned. Maybe they'd sent this man to come and put Sam in jail.

"Please, mister," he sobbed, "I didn't know it was wrong. I was just trying to help make Mr. Lincoln President."

"Were you now? And what makes you think he ought to be President?"

"Because he's so good," Sam said. "That's why I wanted to vote for him."

The long arm went around his shoulder and held it tightly. "You mean—you tried to cast a vote for Abe Lincoln, son?"

Sam nodded and looked up proudly. "I was going to vote for my pa, mister. You see, my pa knew Mr. Lincoln. But he can't vote for Mr. Lincoln like he said he wanted to, because—because—he's dead, mister."

The eyes that looked down at him were warm and pitying. All at once the man's face didn't look homely to Sam any more. The hollow cheeks and deep creases gave it strength, warmth, understanding. Sam relaxed.

"What was your father's name, son?"

"Henry Adams, mister. We live out by Apple Creek. There's just my ma and me now, though. But Mr. Lincoln sent some men out to help us thresh our wheat, and so we won't have to worry all winter about having enough. My pa said Mr. Lincoln was always doing nice things like that and that he was everybody's friend."

"I knew your father, son. He was a fine man and I'm glad you got the wheat crop threshed all right."

"I'm glad, too," said Sam, but his face clouded again. "But I feel awful bad, on account of not casting my pa's vote for Mr. Lincoln."

"Then I reckon we ought to do something about that," said the man softly. "You know, I haven't voted yet myself. I was kind of debating about the matter because I'm not completely convinced that Abe Lincoln is the man for President."

"But he is, mister. Honest he is. Pa said so."

"Well," the tall man drawled, rubbing his chin, "I don't know that I can sincerely cast my vote for Abe on my own account. But I'll tell you what I'll do. I'll go in and vote for Lincoln for your father's sake."

"Mister!" Sam's face glowed, "that's sure fine of you. I'm mighty grateful."

He watched the tall, thin figure mount the steps. He seemed to know a great many people, for he spoke to nearly everyone, nodding and smiling.

"I wonder who he is," thought Sam. "He's a mighty nice man, even if he wasn't quite sure about voting for Mr. Lincoln. I reckon that since he knew my pa, I should have found out his name to tell Ma."

It was getting late and he'd have to hurry if he wanted to get that present for Ma. He hastened along the street to the general store. The store was so crowded that Sam had to wait a long time before he got waited on. But when he came out, his arms were full of packages. Thank goodness the team and wagon were still patiently waiting where he had left them.

Sam climbed to the seat quickly and clucked to the horses. He'd have to hurry to get home before Ma began to worry about him.

As he started up, there was a commotion on the street, people cheering and shouting. Towering above the crowd was the man Sam had persuaded to cast his father's vote.

Quickly he leaned down and called to a boy his own age, who was standing near the wagon.

"Say, can you tell me what that man's name is there? That tall one?"

The boy stared up at Sam, unbelieving. "You must be from the country. Everybody in Springfield knows Abe Lincoln!"

1. How did Abe Lincoln help save the Adams wheatfield from the herd of cattle?

2. Why was Hank Adams not able to cast his vote for Abe Lincoln on Election Day?

3. Why wasn't Sam Adams able to cast a vote for his father?

4. Who finally did cast a vote for Hank Adams? How did Sam find out who this person was?

5. Sam Adams had met Abe Lincoln before. Why didn't he recognize him when he saw him again in Springfield?

6. When does this story take place? Do you think that it is a true story? Why or why not?

7. What do the events of the story tell you about Abe Lincoln's character?

8. Would you like to have lived during the time of Abe Lincoln? Why or why not?

9. How could you find out if Abe Lincoln won the election?

If Nancy Hanks
Came back as a ghost,
Seeking news
Of what she loved most,
She'd ask first
"Where's my son?
What's happened to Abe?
What's he done?

"Poor little Abe,
Left all alone
Except for Tom,
Who's a rolling stone;
He was only nine
The year I died.
I remember still
How hard he cried.

Nancy Hanks
(1784-1818)

"Scraping along
In a little shack,
With hardly a shirt
To cover his back,
And a prairie wind
To blow him down,
Or pinching times
If he went to town.

"You wouldn't know
About my son?
Did he grow tall?
Did he have fun?
Did he learn to read?
Did he get to town?
Do you know his name?
Did he get on?"

*-Rosemary and
Stephen Vincent Benét*

two

MEET
THE
AUTHOR
Jean Craighead George

Sometimes a robin hops across the desk in Jean George's study. It is a tame bird, one that the George family raised when its mother was killed by a cat. Not long ago, the author's son counted all the animals in the George household. There were 173!

Most of these animals stay awhile and then disappear. While they are with the family, however, they are likely to become characters in one of Jean George's stories.

Like the story you are about to read, most of Jean George's books have a nature theme and are told from firsthand experience. The author was born into a family of naturalists.

"When we were children," says Ms. George, "our home was filled with owls, falcons, raccoons, crickets, and turtles. We watched them with great curiosity as they went about their lives.

"Every weekend of our childhood was an adventure. Our father would take us along the Potomac River to canoe and fish and swim. We

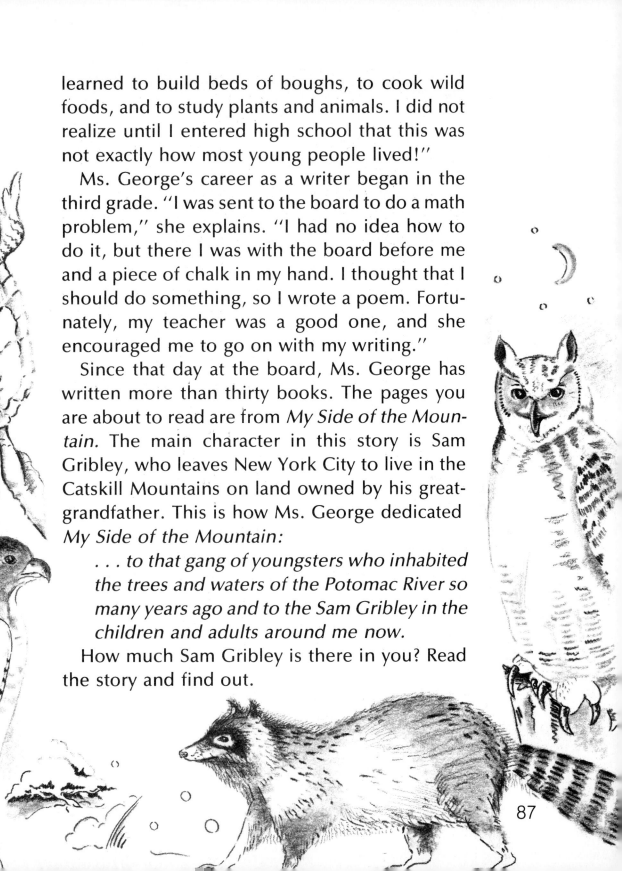

learned to build beds of boughs, to cook wild foods, and to study plants and animals. I did not realize until I entered high school that this was not exactly how most young people lived!"

Ms. George's career as a writer began in the third grade. "I was sent to the board to do a math problem," she explains. "I had no idea how to do it, but there I was with the board before me and a piece of chalk in my hand. I thought that I should do something, so I wrote a poem. Fortunately, my teacher was a good one, and she encouraged me to go on with my writing."

Since that day at the board, Ms. George has written more than thirty books. The pages you are about to read are from *My Side of the Mountain.* The main character in this story is Sam Gribley, who leaves New York City to live in the Catskill Mountains on land owned by his great-grandfather. This is how Ms. George dedicated *My Side of the Mountain:*

> *. . . to that gang of youngsters who inhabited the trees and waters of the Potomac River so many years ago and to the Sam Gribley in the children and adults around me now.*

How much Sam Gribley is there in you? Read the story and find out.

My Side of the Mountain

I am on my mountain in a tree home that people have passed without ever knowing that I am here. The house is a hemlock tree six feet in diameter and must be as old as the mountain itself. I came upon it last summer and dug and burned it out until I made a snug cave in the tree that I now call home.

My bed is on the right as you enter and is made of ash slats and covered with deerskin. On the left is a small fireplace about knee high. It is of clay and stones. It has a chimney that leads the smoke out through a knothole. I chipped out three other knotholes to let fresh air in. The air coming in is bitter cold. It must be below zero outside, and yet I can sit here inside my tree and write with bare hands. The fire is small, too. It doesn't take much fire to warm this tree room.

It is the fourth of December, I think. It may be the fifth. I am not sure because I have not recently counted the notches in the aspen pole that is my calendar. I have been just too busy gathering nuts and berries and smoking venison, fish, and small game to keep up with the exact date.

The lamp I am writing by is deer fat poured into a turtle shell with a strip of my old city trousers for a wick.

It snowed all day yesterday and today. I have not been outside since the storm began, and I am bored *for the first time since I ran away from home eight months ago to live on the land.*

I am well and healthy. The food is good. Sometimes I eat turtle soup, and I know how to make acorn pancakes. I keep my supplies in the wall of the tree, in wooden pockets that I chopped myself.

Every time I have looked at those pockets during the last two days, I have felt just like a squirrel. That reminds me, I didn't see a squirrel one whole day before that storm began. I guess they are holed up and eating their stored nuts, too.

I wonder if The Baron—that's the wild weasel who lives behind the big boulder to the north of my tree— is also denned up. Well, anyway, I think the storm is dying down because the tree is not crying so much. When the wind really blows, the whole tree moans right down to the roots, where I am.

Tomorrow, I hope The Baron and I can tunnel out into the sunlight. I wonder if I should dig the snow. But that would mean I would have to put it somewhere, and the only place to put it is in my nice snug tree. Maybe I can pack it with my hands as I go. I've always dug into the snow from the top. I've never dug up from under the snow!

The Baron must dig up from under the snow. I wonder where he puts what he digs? Well, I guess I'll know in the morning.

When I wrote that last winter, I was scared and thought maybe I'd never get out of my tree. I had been scared for two days—ever since the first blizzard hit the Catskill Mountains. When I came up to the sunlight, which I did by simply poking my head into the soft snow and standing up, I laughed at my fears.

Everything was white, clean, shining, and beautiful. The sky was blue, blue, blue. The hemlock grove was laced with snow, the meadow was smooth and white, and the gorge was sparkling with ice. It was so beautiful and peaceful that I laughed out loud. I guess I laughed because my first snowstorm was over, and it had not been so terrible after all.

Then I shouted, "I did it!" My voice never got very far. It was hushed by the tons of snow.

I looked for signs from The Baron Weasel. His footsteps were all over the boulder, also slides where he had played. He must have been up for hours, enjoying the new snow.

Inspired by his fun, I poked my head into my tree and whistled. Frightful, my trained falcon, flew to my fist, and we jumped and slid down the mountain, making big holes and trenches as we went. It was good to be whistling and carefree again, because I was sure scared by the coming of that storm.

I had been working since May, learning how to make a fire with flint and steel, finding what plants I could eat, learning how to trap animals and catch fish—all this so that when the curtain of blizzard struck the Catskills, I could crawl inside my tree and be comfortably warm and have plenty to eat.

During the summer and fall I had thought about the coming of winter. However, on that third day of December, when the sky blackened, the temperature dropped, and the first flakes swirled around me, I must admit that I wanted to run back to New York. Even the first night that I spent out in the woods was not as frightening as the snowstorm that mushroomed up over my mountain.

I was smoking three trout. It was nine o'clock in the morning. I was busy keeping the flames low so they would not leap up and burn the fish. As I worked, it occurred to me that it was awfully dark for that hour of the morning. Frightful was leashed to her tree stub. She seemed restless and pulled at her tethers. Then I realized that the forest was dead quiet. Even the woodpeckers that had been tapping around me all morning were silent. The squirrels were nowhere to be seen. The juncos and chickadees and nuthatches were gone. I looked to see what The Baron Weasel was doing. He was not around. I looked up.

From my tree you can see the gorge beyond the meadow. White water pours between the black wet boulders and cascades into the valley below. The water that day was as dark as the rocks. Only the sound told me it was still falling. Above the darkness stood another darkness. The clouds of winter, black and fearsome. They looked as wild as the winds that were bringing them. I grew sick with

fright. I knew I had enough food. I knew everything was going to be perfectly all right. But knowing that didn't help. I was scared. I stamped out the fire and pocketed the fish.

I tried to whistle for Frightful but couldn't purse my shaking lips tight enough to get out anything but "pfffff." So I grabbed her by the hide straps that are attached to her legs, and we dove through the deerskin door into my room in the tree.

I put Frightful on the bedpost and curled up in a ball on the bed. I thought about New York and the noise and the lights, and how a snowstorm always seemed very friendly there. I thought about our apartment, too. At that moment it seemed bright and lighted and warm.

A long time ago, Dad had told me about Great-Grandfather Gribley, who owned land in the Catskill Mountains and felled the trees and built a home and plowed the land—only to discover that he wanted to be a sailor. The farm failed, and Great-Grandfather Gribley went to sea.

As I lay with my face buried in the sweet greasy smell of my deerskin, I could hear Dad's voice saying, "That land is still in the family's name. Somewhere in the Catskills is an old beech with the name *Gribley* carved on it. It marks the northern boundary of Gribley's folly—the land is no place for a Gribley."

"The land is no place for a Gribley," I said. "The land is no place for a Gribley, and here I am three hundred feet from the beech with *Gribley* carved on it."

I fell asleep at that point, and when I awoke I was hungry. I cracked some walnuts and got down the acorn flour I had pounded with a bit of ash to remove the bite. Then I reached out the door for a little snow, and stirred up some acorn pancakes. I cooked them on top of a tin can, and as I ate them, smothered with blueberry jam, I knew that the land was just the place for a Gribley.

THINK ABOUT IT

1. Where had Sam Gribley come from?
2. Who were some of the "friends" that Sam made in his mountain home?
3. Where did Sam stay during the snowstorm? What had Sam done to prepare himself for the storm?
4. Compare how Sam felt during the blizzard with how he felt when he emerged from his tree and saw the snow all around him.
5. What kind of person do you think Sam Gribley was? Give reasons for your answer.
6. Did Sam Gribley agree with his father that "the land is no place for a Gribley"? Why or why not?
7. Have you ever gone camping? What did you enjoy about living outdoors?

The Waking

I strolled across
An open field;
The sun was out;
Heat was happy.

This way! This way!
The wren's throat shimmered,
Either to other,
The blossoms sang.

The stones sang,
The little ones did,
And flowers jumped
Like small goats.

96

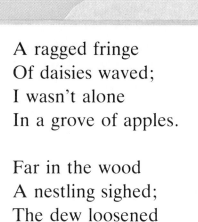

A ragged fringe
Of daisies waved;
I wasn't alone
In a grove of apples.

Far in the wood
A nestling sighed;
The dew loosened
Its morning smells.

I came where the river
Ran over stones:
My ears knew
An early joy.

And all the waters
Of all the streams
Sang in my veins
That summer day.

Theodore Roethke

97

Other People's Weather

Febold Feboldson was out on the prairie holding on to a kite string when Big Steve came walking by. Daisy, his rock hog, was at his heels.

"Howdy, neighbor!" Febold called out.

"Howdy," answered Big Steve. "Nice day for flying a kite."

Febold laughed till his hat fell off. He pointed up to the string in the sky. "That look like a kite to you?" he asked.

Big Steve squinted up at the sky. "Looks more like a young tornado," he said.

"That's just what it is!" Febold cried triumphantly. "I'm experimenting. Here, help me tie the string to this cottonwood tree."

So while Febold held on to the tornado, Big Steve tied the loose end of the string to the tree with a double square knot.

"I'm trying to see if I can do something about the Nebraska weather," explained Febold.

"What's the matter with it?" asked Big Steve.

"Colder'n blazes in winter, hot in summer. What I'd like to do is get some of that good Florida weather here, at least in the winters," answered Febold.

Big Steve said, "You can always pipe it in."

"Well, well!" shouted Febold, slapping his thigh. Then he looked at Big Steve. "Who's going to lay all that pipe?"

"Don't need any pipe. Just bore a tunnel. . . ."

"What business did you say you're in, mister?" interrupted Febold.

"I'm a tunnelman," said Big Steve.

"Well, well!" cried Febold. "You're just the man for me!"

That night, in Febold's hut on the prairie, Big Steve studied a map of the U.S.A.

"This is our big chance for a double-quick beeline job, Daisy," he said.

Daisy barked and thumped her tail earnestly.

"Just a minute," said Febold. "What kind of tunnel is this double-quick beeline tunnel? I want nothing but the best."

Big Steve straightened up and looked at him. "That's what you're getting—the best tunnel you'll see in a month of Sundays. Daisy'll start from this end. I'll start from the Florida end. We'll meet in the middle—somewhere south of Poplar Bluff in Missouri."

Febold was shaking his head. "You'll never make it," he declared. "You'll never in the wide world meet in the middle."

All evening long, from time to time, Febold would shake his head and say, "They'll never make it! Never!"

In the morning, Big Steve took Daisy to the point where the Nebraska end of the tunnel would start. He set her nose in the exact direction she was to tunnel. Then after waiting to see that she had a good start, he hurried down to Florida to begin his end of the tunnel.

He started just south of St. Augustine.* He tunneled up through Florida, Georgia, Alabama, Tennessee, and finally into Missouri.

When he got that far, he began to get anxious. What if Daisy had got her nose off the beeline? What if she was chasing gophers somewhere in Kansas?

Then who should come tunneling toward him but Daisy herself. She almost knocked him down with her joyous greeting.

*Augustine (ô′gə stēn′)

Big Steve shouted, "Daisy, you old rock hog, you did it! You did it!"

When they'd both calmed down a bit, they started walking through Daisy's part of the tunnel back to Febold's place. The fine weather had already started moving up from Florida through the tunnel. All the way back to Nebraska they walked in warm sunshine to the songs of mockingbirds and the rustling of palm trees. Why, they could even hear the boom of the Atlantic Ocean!

When they finally walked out of the Nebraska end of the tunnel, they found a big crowd waiting for them. Febold Feboldson was right out in front to greet them. He stuck his face into the tunnel and sniffed loudly. "Mmmmm!" he exclaimed. "Smell that good, that delicious, that nutritious Florida weather!"

Febold threw a big party for the crowd. He had glasses of icy apple juice, big tubs of beef stew, and lots of corn on the cob. He even had home-made honey ice cream.

A few Kansans had come to Nebraska for the big event. They stood basking in all that fine Florida weather that was pouring out of the tunnel. Finally they asked if they could have a little of it piped into their state.

"Nope," Febold said. "Nebraska can use all the Florida weather it can get."

That winter turned out to be a record one.

In Nebraska, from October 2 on, the snow lay thirteen feet, five and a half inches deep. Big Steve and Daisy had never seen such a winter. But Febold thought nothing of it.

"It's going to take a lot of that Florida weather to have any effect on this winter," he said. "Another month, and we'll see the snow start to melt. Then we'll get the balmy weather. We should've started sooner. We shouldn't have let the Nebraska winter get a chance to catch hold. That's the trouble."

One day Big Steve glanced at a calendar. It was already the third of March! The Florida weather had still not arrived. "I ought to burrow through that snow and look at the tunnel," he said. "It may be clogged up."

"Good idea," Febold answered gloomily. "Stove's not drawing so good—snow must be over the chimney by now."

Big Steve opened the door and started burrowing through the solid wall of snow. When he got to the weather tunnel, he found that the mouth was indeed clogged up. He burrowed two miles into the tunnel, but there was still no sign of Florida weather.

He walked underground clear across Nebraska and into Kansas, and that's where he found the trouble. The Kansans had opened a vent in the tunnel. All that good Florida weather was pouring out into Kansas!

Big Steve plugged up the vent good and tight and then hurried back to tell Febold. Febold was beside himself with rage. He'd show those Kansans! He had two guards patrol the tunnel to see to it that the Kansans left it strictly alone.

The fine Florida weather began coming through at last. The snow thawed rapidly. People were beginning to say that Nebraska had the best weather in the world.

One day, shortly after this, Febold was sitting on the banks of the Dismal River, fishing near the tunnel opening. Suddenly the two guards he had posted in the tunnel came whirling out on a terrific gust of wind.

They barely had time to yell "Hurricane!" before they shot past him up into the air. Febold dropped his fishing pole and ran for the tunnel opening. He tried to slam the door shut, but there was a hundred-mile wind roaring through. He couldn't budge the door. In all his praise of Florida weather, Febold had never once thought of hurricanes.

Well, that hurricane came roaring through Big Steve's tunnel and came rampaging out over Nebraska. Rain came down in such torrents that it almost floated Nebraska into neighboring Iowa. The hundred-mile wind tore the state line to shreds. For a while everybody had a hard time telling what was Nebraska and what was someplace else.

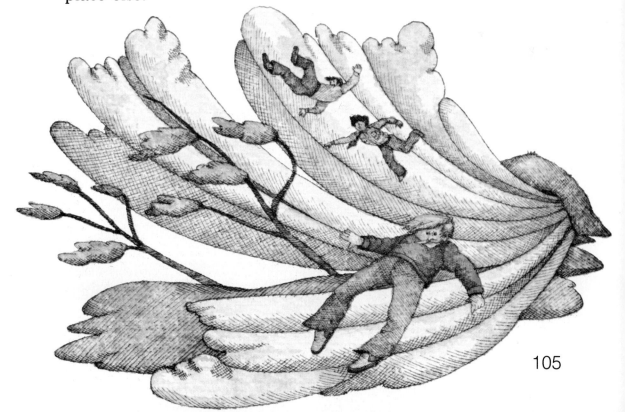

As soon as the hurricane was over, some of Febold's neighbors came to see him. They thanked him for all he had done for Nebraska in the past. They would now thank him to stop importing other people's weather into the state.

When they left, some people from Florida came to see Febold. They said, "This past winter we had hardly any weather at all on account of you piping it out of the state. We're telling you here and now: Florida weather is not for export. If you want some of our weather, come down and use it on the premises."

So Big Steve plugged up the tunnel. He felt sorry for Febold and tried to cheer him up. But Febold only shook his head. "It's all right, Steve. None of it's your fault. Well, there's nothing more I can do here, so I'm off for California. No hurricanes there, no tornadoes—just a little earthquake now and then."

THINK ABOUT IT

1. What did Febold Feboldson have at the end of his kite string? What was Febold trying to accomplish?

2. How did Big Steve plan to build a tunnel from Florida to Nebraska? How was Daisy to help?

3. Was Big Steve's tunnel a success? What were some of the problems that resulted?

4. How did the Nebraskans feel about the tunnel after the hurricane? How did the Floridians feel?

5. What finally happened to the tunnel? What happened to Febold Feboldson?

6. What examples of exaggeration can you find in this story? Which detail do you think is the hardest to believe?

7. How does the saying, "The grass is always greener on the other side of the fence," apply to this story?

8. Have you ever thought about trying to change the way something is? What did you want to change? How did you plan to do it?

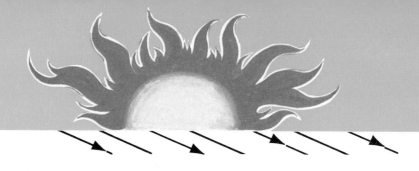

SUPER POWER

The Sun's Energy

The sun, the super power of our solar system, is just a big ball of energy. To get a picture of how much energy the sun gives off, imagine that gasoline flows over Niagara Falls instead of water. Think of all the gasoline that would have passed over the Falls during the last twenty million years. Imagine that the gas collected in a huge container. If the gas in that container were burned, it would give off about the same amount of energy as the sun gives off in *just one hour.*

Not all the sun's energy reaches the earth. But every forty minutes, enough sunlight shines here to meet the world's energy needs for a whole year. On a clear day every square meter of the earth receives about one thousand watts of solar energy. Imagine how much energy is hitting your school playground right now.

Collecting Solar Energy

If there is so much solar energy, what's the energy crisis all about? Why are we still bothering with coal, gas, and oil?

The answer is simple. When solar energy reaches the earth, it is very spread out. It cannot be put to use

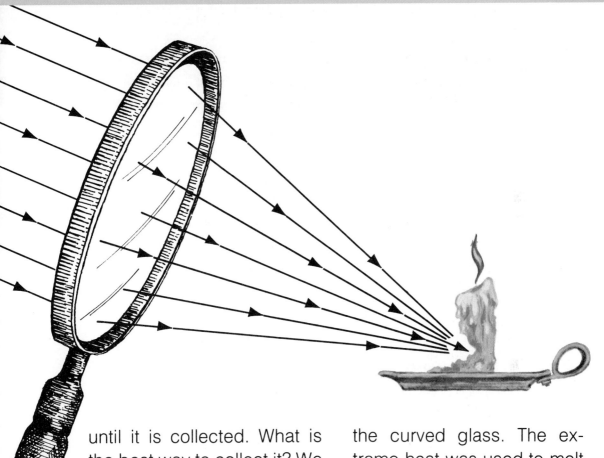

until it is collected. What is the best way to collect it? We are not yet sure.

For thousands of years people have been trying to collect the sun's rays. They started by using a magnifying glass. Sunlight was caught and concentrated in the curved glass. The extreme heat was used to melt wax and burn paper.

More serious attempts to collect the sun's energy were made in the 17th century by Salomon de Caus. He was a French engineer. He figured out a way to concentrate sun-

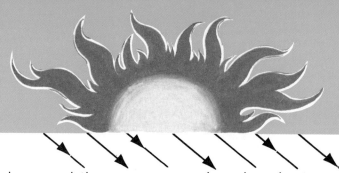

light. Then he used the sunlight to run a small pump.

One hundred years later, Antoine Lavoisier built a solar furnace. Two huge lenses caught the sun's rays and sent them into the furnace. There temperatures reached two thousand degrees Fahrenheit.

Charles Wilson's 1871 solar plant was one of the biggest. He built it in the Andes Mountains of northern Chile. It was used to change salt water into fresh water. Wil-

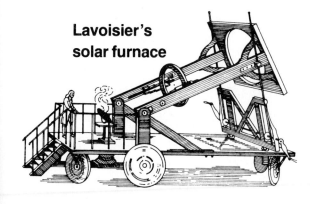

Lavoisier's solar furnace

son's solar plant successfully gave out 6000 gallons of fresh water every day.

Until 1912, however, most solar projects were small. Frank Shuman, an engineer from Pennsylvania, changed all that. By 1912 he had built a solar boiler. It produced 52 horsepower. That's enough power to run a large outboard motor.

Shuman took his solar plant to Egypt. There he set to work along the Nile River. Soon Shuman's solar-powered pump was irrigating the dry desert land.

Shuman's boiler worked well in Egypt. In fact, it worked better there than it had in Pennsylvania where he had first tried it out. The reason is no mystery. There is more sunshine in Egypt than in Pennsylvania.

110

Types of Solar Collectors

So far there are two basic types of solar collectors. It is difficult to figure out which one is better. The difference between them is their shape. One type has a curved surface. The other type has a flat surface.

Curved mirrors or shiny metal have been used to make solar stoves. The sun's rays hit the curve and bounce off it. The rebounding rays are focused on one spot. This spot becomes very hot. It gets hot enough to boil water, cook meat, or fry eggs. So that's where a pot or pan is placed.

Solar stoves really work. In fact, they have already been mass-produced in India.

A solar furnace may work in almost the same way, but

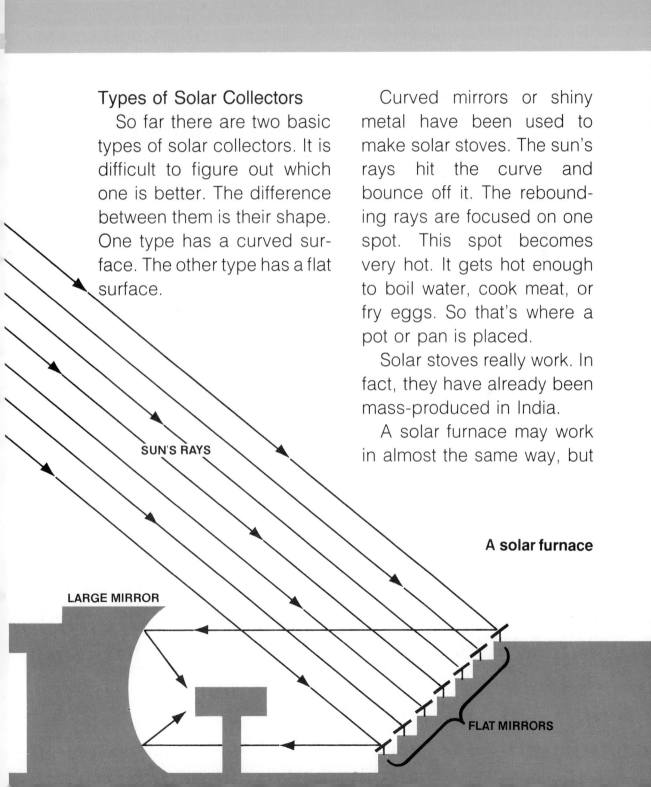

SUN'S RAYS

LARGE MIRROR

A solar furnace

FLAT MIRRORS

on a much bigger scale. The set of flat-surfaced solar mirrors for a furnace at Font-Romeu, France, is housed in an eight story building!

A curved solar collector of that size is very expensive. Flat collectors are much cheaper. They're made of a flat metal sheet or plate and a system of pipes. The metal plate is painted black. The dark color helps it soak in as much sunlight as possible.

As the metal plate absorbs the sun's rays, it becomes hot. Pipes under the sheet circulate cool water. The water absorbs heat from the metal. As the liquid moves, it becomes warmer and warmer. By the end of its journey, it is hot enough for use in household radiators.

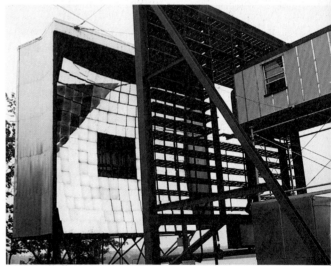

Top: Flat solar collectors
Bottom: Curved solar collector

112

The Future

Today there are few solar-heated homes. There are even fewer solar-run factories. But tomorrow, who knows? We can only guess at what the future of solar energy will be.

Someday huge tracts of empty land may be turned into solar farms. Thousands of energy collectors will soak up the sun's light. They will turn it into electricity and send it along to distant cities and towns.

Someday we may not have to worry about where our next watt is coming from. With solar energy, the sky is the limit.

Home with flat solar collectors

1. On a clear day, about how much solar energy does a square meter of earth receive?

2. At the present time, why aren't we able to depend completely on solar energy?

3. What was the earliest method used to collect solar energy?

4. How did Frank Schuman use the solar power he harnessed? Why did his solar boiler work better in Egypt than in Pennsylvania?

5. What is the basic difference between the two kinds of solar collectors?

6. How does a solar stove work?

7. What might solar farms of the future be like?

8. Why do you think it's important to continue research on solar energy?

9. Would you be willing to heat your home with solar energy? Why or why not?

10. Do you think the use of solar energy will become more widespread in the future? Why or why not?

COOKING WITH THE SUN

Imagine this: you and your friends are at the beach for a picnic. There's not a cloud in the sky; the sun is shining straight overhead. It's time to eat. You take out your homemade solar stove, and the cooking begins. Provided, of course, that you actually did build your own solar stove.

To do that, you will need some heavy cardboard, two large sheets of poster board, one roll of aluminum foil, and some glue.

The cooker is circular in shape and about three feet (one meter) in diameter. Its center has a shallow curve to it.

The frame of a solar stove is made of sixteen strips of heavy cardboard. Each strip is a little more than a foot and a half (fifty centimeters) long. Each is wider at one end than at the other end. The thicker side helps form the curve of the cooker bowl.

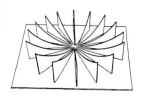

The cardboard strips, standing on their sides, are glued onto a large flat piece of cardboard. The thinner end of each rib is placed at the center of the cardboard base. The ribs fan out from one spot to form a circle. When all the ribs are glued in place, they look almost like a pin wheel or the spokes of an old-fashioned wagon wheel.

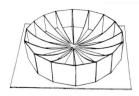

The ribs divide the cooker bowl into sixteen sections. Each section is covered over with a piece of poster board. This gives the stove a smooth surface. Finally, the whole bowl is covered with aluminum foil.

Now you have a solar stove. But you're not quite ready to cook.

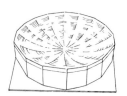

So far your stove can only lie flat on the ground. This is fine if you want to cook at noon. The sun is high in the sky then. It will shine directly on the stove, and there won't be any shadows. (Shadows take away the cooker's heat.)

But once the sun starts to go down, the stove will cast shadows on itself. In order to keep your stove hot, you'll have to set it on its edge. A simple stand will be a big help. It's easy to make one out of a board and a pole. The board should be as large as the stove itself. The pole can be an old broomstick or curtain rod.

First, push the pole several inches into the ground. Then rest the solar stove on the board, and lean the board against the pole.

To get the most heat from your stove, experiment with different angles. Start by placing the stove flat on the ground. Lift one side of it little by little, and pass your hand over the foil surface. Stop when you feel the most heat. Rest the stove against the pole at that angle.

Find a stand to hold the pot, similar to the one shown below. Then place the pot or grill at the hottest point and begin taking orders. You'll be eating sooner than you think.

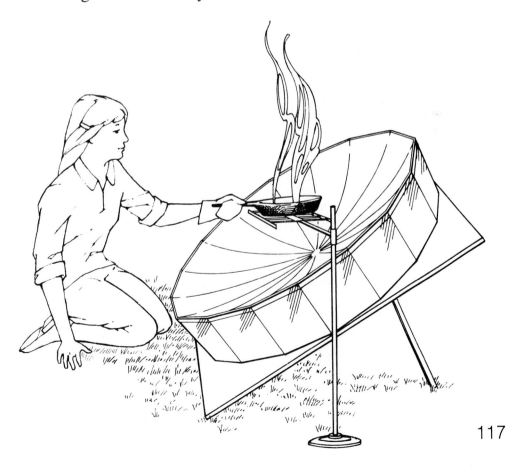

The Mystery of Lyme Regis

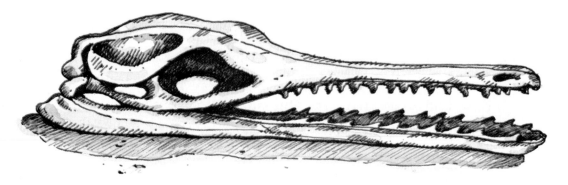

"The Mystery of Lyme Regis[1]" is from a book called *Mary's Monster*—the true story of Mary Ann Anning, who lived in Lyme Regis, England, in the early 1800's.

Mary shared an interesting hobby with her father. Together they hunted for curious stone shells buried on the beach and in the cliffs of Lyme Regis. During bad storms, great chunks of earth would break away from the cliffs, uncovering new earth and bare rocks. The Annings found many of their best shells in these bare rocks. Mary and her father called these shells "curiosities." Scientists call them "fossils."

As "The Mystery of Lyme Regis" begins, Mary's father has just died. In this part of Mary's story, you will also meet her brother Joseph as well as Henry, one of her friends.

[1]**Lyme Regis** (līm rē′jəs)

After a time, Mary became used to working without her father. Slowly her store of curiosities grew larger and more interesting. Among them was a strange skull over two feet long. It had a long mouth of sharp teeth. Joseph found it, quite by accident, and gave it to her.

"I think the rest of it is somewhere in the cliff near Charmouth,[2]" he said.

Mary thought the skull was that of a crocodile. She put it away on a shelf with some other strange bones she had found.

One night after Mary went to bed, the wind blew and blew. It rained hard. The waters of the bay crashed high on the beach and even splashed over the highest part of the Cobb. As Mary listened to the wild storm, she said to herself, "Tomorrow morning, I'll go to the cliffs near Charmouth. The storm will have washed away earth and stone from them. Perhaps I can collect some large curiosities that will fetch me a good price."

The next morning, Mary got up early and set out for the cliffs. She noticed that the cliffs had lost great chunks of soil and rock which now lay in piles at their base. Very carefully she began to search for curiosities, keeping an eye out for loose rocks that might fall on her.

As Mary peered at the cliffs, something unusual

[2]**Charmouth** (chär′məth)

caught her eye. She saw what seemed to be bones lying in the rock in front of her.

She tapped the crumbling rock with her hammer. Chunks of it fell away. Mary tapped again. More bones appeared. She backed away for a better look. "What is it?" she thought.

With her chisel, Mary carefully lifted away pieces of the splintered rock. Underneath lay other bones. Finally, a huge backbone, with large curving ribs attached, stood out as the soft earth and rock continued to fall away.

Mary's heart pounded with excitement. What had she found?

She walked along the cliff face a few feet, tapping as she went. At every tap, more bones appeared, until the skeleton of a strange, unknown animal began to take shape. Even though its head was missing, Mary was quite sure this creature was no crocodile.

"It's a monster," Mary cried. "A monster curiosity—trapped in the rock exactly like the smaller curiosities! But what can it be? Where is its head?" Then Mary remembered. The skull that Joseph gave her—could that be it? She would find out as soon as she could remove all of the huge curiosity from the cliff wall.

Curiosities must be handled with care. Mary knew that. But how in the world did a person handle a curiosity as big as this one?

As Mary stood there wondering how she could
get the monster safely out of the cliff, Henry ran
down the beach toward her.

"What is that?" he yelled.

"I don't know."

"What are you going to do with it?"

Mary thought a bit. "I'll hire workers from the
quarry," she said. "With their help, we can cut it
out of the cliff without harming it."

"I'll fetch them," Henry cried as he darted away.

"Wait," said Mary. "Tell Joseph to bring the
head he gave me."

"The head! What head?"

"Just tell him to bring it. He'll know."

While Henry was gone, Mary took her hammer

and chisel and began to peck out an outline around the skeleton. Now the quarry workers would know where to cut.

It was almost an hour before Henry and Joseph came running back with the quarry workers lumbering after them. Joseph carried the "crocodile" skull in his arms. As soon as he saw the bones in the cliff he shouted, "You found it, Mary. You found the rest of it!" He ran to the skeleton and held the skull at the end where the head should have been.

What a fearsome thing the creature became when the ugly head was added. Now it was a monster twice as long as Joseph was tall. It had short flippers or feet. Its sharp teeth looked ready to bite. And its enormous eye socket seemed to glare at those who stared at it.

The group of workers stopped in astonishment when they saw the strange skeleton with its monstrous head.

"Mercy," one of them yelled. "What terrible creature is that?"

"I won't go near it," shouted another. "It's the work of the devil!"

One man laughed. "It's only bones," he cried. "Bones can't hurt you!"

It took most of the afternoon for the workers, with the help of Joseph and Henry, to remove the monster from its resting place. Mary gave directions as the skeleton was carefully cut into pieces small enough to lift.

"What can it be?" she wondered. "Is it a fat crocodile, or a thin whale?"

By the time the skeleton was removed from the cliff, people had gathered from everywhere to see what was going on.

"What is it? What can it be?" they cried as they crowded closer. "Is it a crocodile? Is it a dragon?"

Henry pushed them aside. "I'll go fetch Dr. Everard Home," he said. "He is the king's physician and is visiting in Lyme Regis. He knows a great deal about human bones. Perhaps he can tell us what Mary's creature is."

When Henry returned with Dr. Home in tow, the doctor hurried up to the skeleton. He examined it carefully from head to tail.

"Is it a crocodile?" Mary asked.

"No," Dr. Home replied. "But it may be another type of reptile, or perhaps a member of the whale family. Whatever it is, it's the first of its kind I have ever seen. This is a great discovery you have made, lass."

Mary sighed. "Will anyone know what it is?"

"I will consult with other scientists at once," said Dr. Home. "Together we should come up with an answer. But in the meantime, for want of a better name, we'll simply have to call the skeleton 'The Mystery of Lyme Regis.'"

For a long time Mary Anning's monster was called "The Mystery of Lyme Regis." Finally the head of the British Museum said: "Everyone agrees that the monster is a sea-going reptile with the shape of a fish. Let us call it 'ichthyosaur[3]' after the Greek words *ichthyo* meaning 'fish,' and *sauros* meaning 'lizard.'"

And that is what Mary's discovery is called to this day.

[3]**ichthyosaur** (ik'thē ə sôr')

THINK ABOUT IT

1. Who was Mary Ann Anning? What hobby did she and her father share an interest in?

2. Why did Mary decide to go to the cliffs near Charmouth after the rainstorm? What did she find as she started to chisel away at the cliff?

3. What did the monster that Mary found look like? Why do you think Mary's discovery was so important?

4. What proof is there in the selection that Mary took a scientific approach to things?

5. Have you ever seen a fossil? What did it look like? What do you think you would do if you discovered a fossil?

Find the Ichthyosaur

Do you think you might run into an ichthyosaur today? It's not likely, except, of course, in a museum. You discovered in "The Mystery of Lyme Regis" that ichthyosaurs lived long ago. But do you know exactly when they roamed the earth? Or what they looked like? To answer these questions, you might turn to a science book. Here, scientists present, as fact, events they believe to have happened.

You'll find that reading a science book is quite different from reading a book of stories. Science books give facts and explain how different facts fit together. The following paragraph is from a science book. Read it and see what facts you can find on the ichthyosaur.

Reptiles flourished during the "Age of Reptiles," which is called the Mesozoic Era. Some reptiles, like the dinosaur, lived on land. Others lived in the sea. Among the reptiles that lived in the sea was the ichthyosaur, or fish lizard. Ichthyosaurs sometimes grew to be 50 to 60 feet (15 to 18 meters) long. Instead of legs, they had small paddlelike limbs and a well-developed tail.

Science books also may include charts to make written words and ideas easier to under-stand. The chart below was included alongside the paragraph you just read. The chart helps make the information in the paragraph clearer. Study the chart closely. Then see how well you can answer the questions on the next page.

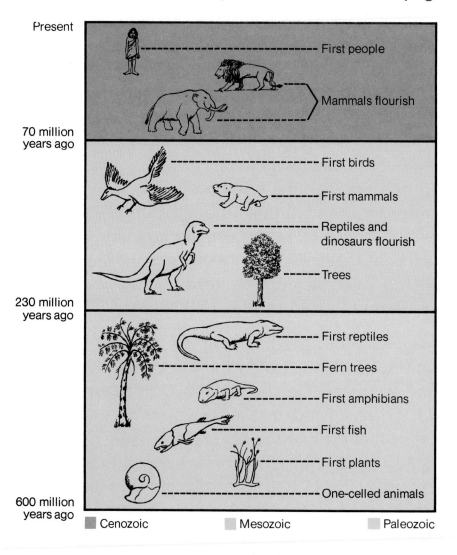

Present

70 million
years ago

230 million
years ago

600 million
years ago

First people

Mammals flourish

First birds

First mammals

Reptiles and
dinosaurs flourish

Trees

First reptiles

Fern trees

First amphibians

First fish

First plants

One-celled animals

Cenozoic   Mesozoic   Paleozoic

Now use facts given in the paragraph and the chart to answer these questions:

1. The chart shows things that scientists believe to have happened in the past. What part of the chart shows the oldest time period? How do you know?
2. If you want to read from the earliest time to the present, do you start at the top or bottom?
3. How can you tell which part of the chart is called the Paleozoic Era? the Mesozoic Era? the Cenozoic Era?
4. According to the chart, which age lasted longest? How do you know?
5. Now look back at the paragraph on the ichthysaur. According to the science book, in what era did the ichthyosaur live? Find it on the chart. About how long ago did the ichthyosaur live? What else developed around that time?
6. How big was an ichthyosaur? Did you learn this from the chart or the paragraph?
7. Which came first, reptiles or fish? Did you learn this from the chart or the paragraph?

DAR TELLUM

Ralph Winston is an ordinary fifth grader with an extraordinary friend from the planet Sidra. Dar Tellum "visits" inside Ralph's head every day. They communicate by thought.

Dar Tellum has taught Ralph a special skill—telekinesis. Telekinesis is the ability to move objects by thinking hard about them. This skill and Dar Tellum's superior intelligence are about to save the planet Earth.

When our story begins, Earth is in the midst of a big crisis. Cars and factories have polluted the Earth's atmosphere with carbon dioxide. The carbon dioxide acts as a one-way "lid" on the Earth: it lets the sun's rays in, but it won't let much heat out. Therefore, the polar ice caps are melting, causing

the oceans to rise. Coastal cities are in danger of terrible flooding.

Scientists and engineers, including Ralph's father, are trying to solve the problem. But they're not succeeding. That's where Dar Tellum comes in. He communicates the solution to Ralph. Dar Tellum knows of a special kind of algae that can survive in the upper atmosphere. Algae take carbon dioxide and turn it into oxygen. If these algae could be shot up into the atmosphere, the "lid" on Earth would be removed.

Ralph invents a way to tell his father about Dar Tellum's idea. He manages to write it down and slip the paper into his father's briefcase. Will the idea work? Read on to find out.

The fact that I was staying up pretty late talking to Dar Tellum must have showed.

"Ralph, you really look tired," Mom said one morning. That's when I made a big mistake. I started to tell Mom and Dad about Dar Tellum.

"Mom, I guess I am. It's sort of . . . well . . . that I'm visiting with someone every night," I said eagerly.

Mom shot a worried look at me so I felt as though I had to go on talking. "Well, you see . . . this friend of mine and I, we sort of get together. He's from another planet and . . . I think he is, anyhow."

By this time I was stumbling along, trying to make it sound better and getting more confused by the second. That's when Mom felt my forehead. I stopped right then. It wasn't going to work. I made up my mind never to mention Dar Tellum to anybody again.

When Dad came home that night, I knew something was wrong. He gave me a strange look, but he didn't say anything until after dinner. "Ralph, I'd like to talk with you," he finally said. When you hear those words, you know something's coming.

"Anything important, Dad?" I asked, being as carefree as I could.

Dad got straight to the point. "Ralph, did you ever put anything in my briefcase?" That's all he said, too, but I knew he meant business. I also knew I better say something soon.

"Ugg . . . err . . . just once, Dad," I managed to mutter. Then I decided that I better tell him something—even if I didn't tell about Dar Tellum.

"Dad, I got this idea in a dream. And I knew it might help so I wrote it out and put it in your briefcase. Did you get into trouble, Dad?" I asked.

"No, Ralph, no trouble. Some scientists I work with tested the idea about shooting algae into the atmosphere," he said. "It's the only idea we've found that might save Earth's cities. I think you'll be visited by an important person soon. And he'll want to know how you got your idea," he added, looking at me in a funny kind of way.

I realized then that Dad suspected more than what I told him. I felt I had to say *something*. "Uh . . . well, Dad, probably the old family genius at work, huh?" I said cheerily. Dad didn't laugh.

I got out of the room as fast as I could. It wasn't until I was in bed that I realized something. Dar Tellum's idea would probably save Earth! Suddenly, I was very happy.

The next week passed quickly. Dar Tellum and I contacted each other at least once a day. Then one afternoon, when I got home from school, I found my father and another man waiting for me.

"Ralph, this is Dr. Wheeler, from the office where I work," Dad said. I nodded and said hello.

"Ralph," Dr. Wheeler began, "how did you get the idea of sending algae into the atmosphere?"

If I told him about Dar Tellum, he'd think I was crazy. . . "Well . . . ah . . . it just came in a dream. That's about all, Dr. Wheeler," I stuttered.

Dr. Wheeler and Dad looked at me strangely. "Another reason I came, Ralph," said Dr. Wheeler, "is to invite you to the launching tomorrow of the first algae-carrying rocket."

"WOW! A chance to see a rocket launching." I shouted. I got so excited that they both smiled.

That night I contacted Dar Tellum as soon as I could. I told him I was going to see a rocket launching.

"What's a rocket launching?" he asked.

"Don't you have rockets on Sidra?" I asked.

"What are rockets, Ralph?" Dar Tellum answered. Once Dar Tellum wanted to know something, he just kept asking about it. If I asked a

question in return, he'd just ignore it and ask one of his own.

I told Dar Tellum all I knew about rockets. When I finished, Dar Tellum seemed to be thinking.

"Rockets seem wonderful, Ralph. We on Sidra live a completely different way," he said. After talking a few more minutes, we broke contact, and I went to sleep, thinking about tomorrow.

"Hurry up, Ralph. You don't want to be late," was the next thing I heard. Dad was shoving me gently by the shoulder. The launching!

Once I remembered that, I didn't have any trouble waking up. It was still dark outside, but soon Dad and I were in a car heading for the launching site. After an hour or so, we arrived. Practically nothing was around except some cement buildings. And the rocket, of course. It was tall, thin, and silvery.

We met Dr. Wheeler, and then entered one of the buildings—launching headquarters. Inside, a large glass window looked into a big, white room.

"That's where we grew the algae, Ralph," Dr. Wheeler told me. "The room is sealed so that germs from outside can't get in to spoil the algae," he explained. "Right now a container is being filled with algae. Then it will be put right into the rocket and shot into the atmosphere."

Then he spoke to my Dad. He said that some scientists weren't sure that the type of algae Dar Tellum named would work. So they grew another kind, too. And on the table in the big room were both kinds—each kind in a different container.

Dr. Wheeler told my Dad that they had made some tests, and they had picked the type of algae to be shot into the air. *But not the kind that Dar Tellum named.* My Dad shook his head. I could tell he wasn't happy about the choice.

Then I had a suggestion. "Why not shoot both types into the air?" I said.

Dad answered. "Because, if the experiment is a success, we won't know which kind of algae is responsible. We'd have to waste time growing both kinds, and time is too short for that."

Right then I decided to check with Dar Tellum. It's a lucky thing for Earth that I did. The others were talking about the launching and not paying attention to me. I closed my eyes. "Dar Tellum, can you contact me now?" I called out in my mind.

Dar Tellum answered right away. "Yes, Ralph, I can hear you."

I didn't waste any time. I told him the name of the algae they were going to shoot.

Dar Tellum sounded excited. "That's the wrong type, Ralph," he said. "It won't work well, I know."

At that moment, the only thing on my mind was how to switch containers. I decided to use telekinesis. I asked Dar Tellum if he'd help, and he said he was willing to try.

I kept watching through that big glass window. I saw a man in the white coat put a container in a small tray. Then he left the room. I guessed that container was the one to go in the rocket. If I was going to switch them, now was the time.

I clenched my hands together and Dar Tellum and I began telekinesis. The container on the tray was heavy. Both of us strained with all our might. Luckily, we had to lift it only an inch or so to clear the edge of the tray.

Sweat dripped down my back. My hands ached. At last I felt the container lift. Quickly, we moved it right beside the other one.

The next step was moving the container with the correct algae onto the tray. But I was tired, and so was Dar Tellum. Telekinesis is a lot of work.

We strained hard but we found we could only slide the container. It skidded slowly across the table until it reached the edge of the tray. We tried a last effort to lift it on. But no good. We couldn't make it move, much less lift it. Then a woman in a white coat came into the room. I figured that we had lost.

I watched the woman in the white coat walk toward the tray. She stared at it for a second or so. Then she slowly shook her head looking from one container to the other.

Just then Dr. Wheeler called in through an intercom system, saying that everybody was waiting. The woman in the white coat picked up the container that Dar Tellum and I had just moved and put it on the tray. Then she carried the tray out of the room. It was just pure luck that she didn't double check the markings on the containers.

It didn't take long to put the algae into the rocket. In a half hour the countdown began. I watched the launching through another window. When they reached zero, I heard a roar. The rocket rose slowly at first and then gained speed. It turned a

red silvery color when it went high enough for the sun to shine on it more. Then it gradually disappeared into the sky, getting smaller all the time.

That night in my room I contacted Dar Tellum.

"I think it will be a success, Ralph," Dar Tellum said. "I'm sure the algae in the atmosphere will soon cure your planet of its troubles."

Dar Tellum was right. A month or so later, Dad told me that more rockets loaded with algae were being sent into the atmosphere. By the time they had found out the wrong container—but really the right one—was in that first rocket, it was too late. Then they found that the algae they did send up turned carbon dioxide back into oxygen faster than anyone expected. Earth's crisis was over.

I soon got to know Dar Tellum a lot better. I'll tell you about that sometime, including my visit to Sidra. But I've written this down so you know Dar Tellum is real and how his idea saved Earth, and how it almost didn't work.

Don't bother telling any grown-ups about him, because they won't believe you. And if you ever meet Dar Tellum yourself, or a friend of his, I can tell you another thing for certain.

Keep it a secret.

1. Who was Ralph Winston? Who was Dar Tellum? How did Ralph and Dar Tellum communicate?

2. How did Dar Tellum help the people on Earth solve the problem of the melting polar ice caps?

3. How did the scientists feel about the idea Ralph placed in his father's briefcase? Why did they decide to send up algae that was different from the kind Dar Tellum suggested?

4. Why did Ralph use such an unusual method to communicate Dar Tellum's idea to his father? Why didn't he come right out and tell his father about Dar Tellum?

5. Why do you think Dar Tellum was so willing to try to help the people on Earth?

6. Which events in the story do you think could actually happen? Give reasons for your answer.

7. If you had been in Ralph's place, would you have revealed more about Dar Tellum? Why or why not?

three

Sarah Caldwell: Magician of Opera

Sarah Caldwell was born in 1928 in Maryville, Missouri, and grew up in Arkansas. When she was four years old, she began studying the violin. As a child, she was also very talented in mathematics. At age fourteen Sarah graduated from high school. After going to college in Arkansas, Sarah traveled to Boston where she "fell in love"

with opera. Before she was twenty, Sarah Caldwell had staged her first opera. In 1957, at age twenty-nine, Sarah began what is now the Opera Company of Boston, one of the finest opera companies in America. In 1976, she became the first woman ever to conduct at the Metropolitan Opera House in New York City.

The Opera Company of Boston has not always had its own theater. For a stage, Sarah has often had to use a school gym, and even a hockey rink.

For this reason, Sarah has sometimes had singers enter through the audience. Sarah became famous because she uses what she has and makes operas fun for the people in the audience and the people on stage. Performers may be children, real animals, or even the world-famous clown Emmett Kelly. In a hunt scene, Sarah once had a real waterfall. Sarah invents ideas as she rehearses. Sometimes she keeps coming up with new ideas until the curtain goes up for the show. No one is really sure what she will think of next.

In the following interview, Sarah Caldwell talks about opera and young people.

Q. *What is a good opera performance?*

A. Well, it should be tremendously exciting as theater. As a member of the audience, you should be able to get deeply involved in a story—in what's happening to the characters on stage. You should understand why they're reacting and feeling the things they do. You should get tremendous pleasure out of the music you hear and the way it relates to what's happening in the play.

Q. *When you do an opera, you try to learn as much as possible about it before you put it on stage. When*

*you did Montezuma, you went to Mexico to travel
the same trails the Spanish explorer Cortez traveled
on his way to see the great Mexican Indian chief
Montezuma. You even had special flutes carved like
the ones Montezuma's musicians would have used.
Many people wouldn't go to all this trouble. Why do
you work so hard?*

A. Because I enjoy it. Because I find that every opera I do takes me into a new world that otherwise I wouldn't enter. I think that the research and preparation we do for each opera is really fun. It's stimulating. And it's one of the best reasons I know for producing opera.

Q. *You gave a special name to the children who like to watch your rehearsals. You call them the "knothole gang." Tell us more about the knothole gang. Who are they? How did they get that name? Why are they important to your work?*

A. The name "knothole gang" came, I think, from children who watched baseball practices through holes in the fence. At first, the children who watched our rehearsals were children of people in our opera company. We found that there are many things in opera to interest a young person. Some children are more excited by the scenery. Some are excited by the musical instruments in the orchestra. Some are excited by the performers. Some get excited by all of it. But we found that children who were members of our knothole gang have grown up to be real opera fans.

Q. *Why did you decide to do the opera* Hansel and Gretel? *How did your ideas about* Hansel and Gretel *influence the person who designed your stage set?*

A. Oh, we decided to do it because it's an opera that I love very much. It is always a great deal of fun to produce for young people. And it can involve some audience participation. I think that my ideas influenced the designer of the set somewhat and his ideas influenced our production, too. You see, the lovely thing about theater is that it's really a partnership if it's done well. And the most interesting part of it is to work with really gifted designers and actors and singers. Then it becomes something we do together. We get involved in really, really trying to make the piece come alive. When we reach together for an idea that seems to be a good one, no one quite remembers whose idea it was. It just seems like a really splendid idea. That was one of the special joys of working with David Sharir, who's a very gifted young designer.

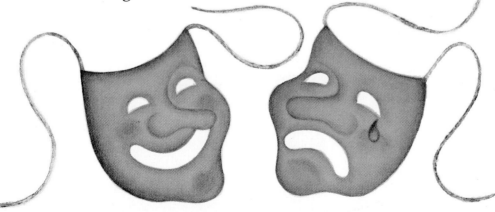

Q. *For* Hansel and Gretel, *you had an edible house of real gingerbread. Could you give us a little information on this?*

A. The house was not all edible, but there were many, many edible candies and cookies and things. At the end of the performance, the children in the audience came up on the stage and ate them.

Q. *And why did you do that?*

A. I think that many children were seeing their first opera. It seemed like a fun thing to do and like a very nice introduction to opera. We also had gingerbread smells that we put in the air circulating system. When the gingerbread began

to bake, we could smell it as we came into the auditorium.

Q. *Many people feel that there is a special "magic" in your operas. What is the magic? Where does it come from?*

A. The "magic" comes as a result of very careful rehearsal of many, many things. One has to get everything right. The music must be right. The singing actors must be doing a convincing job of theater. If the music and the theatrical parts are working smoothly together, then at that moment something seems to happen. The music seems more beautiful. The theater seems more exciting. That's what opera is all about.

1. Who makes up the "knothole gang" that Sarah Caldwell described?

2. According to Sarah Caldwell, what is a good opera performance? What provides the special "magic" in the operas that Sarah Caldwell directs?

3. What kind of person is Sarah Caldwell? Why do you think people respond with such enthusiasm to her and to her operas?

4. Do you think that the title of this selection, "Sarah Caldwell: Magician of Opera," is a good one? Give reasons for your answer.

5. This selection is written in the form of an interview. What kinds of things can you learn about a person from a personal interview that you might not learn from an article about the person?

6. Have you ever been to an opera? Have you ever seen one performed on TV? Do you think you would enjoy seeing an opera produced by Sarah Caldwell? Why or why not?

The Magic Guitar

The teacher was talking about something, but Juan wasn't listening. He sat in the first row in a seat by the window. With a sigh, Juan looked out the window at the school yard and at the buildings that surrounded it. Buildings, buildings, and more buildings. Buildings and streets. That was the city.

As Juan stared out the window, he no longer saw buildings. He saw white sand and green-blue water.

He saw tall trees and blue sky and a barefoot boy walking along a dirt road to the beach. The boy had a guitar slung across his back. The boy was Juan. He was home again—home in Puerto Rico. The sun was warm and the beach was empty. He sat under a tree and began to play his guitar. The music mixed gently with the sounds of the sea.

"Read the part of the story you liked best," the teacher said. "Juan, will you please read first?"

There was no answer. Juan did not hear Mrs. Marks. Juan heard only the music of his guitar, blending with the sounds of the sea.

"Juan," Mrs. Marks said again. "Will you please start?"

Again there was no answer.

"Juan!"

Finally Juan awoke from his daydream. He no longer heard the music and the sea. He no longer saw the beach of white sand or the green-blue water. He saw only the school yard, and beyond the high-spiked fence, he saw the buildings.

"*Sí?*" he said at last.

"Juan, please pay attention. And also please try to remember to speak English in class."

"Yes, *Señora*—I mean Mrs. Marks," said Juan. "I will speak English." Juan knew English. He had learned English in school in Puerto Rico. But sometimes, when he was pretending to be on the beach, he forgot. And sometimes, because he didn't want to leave his pretend beach, he pretended to forget English.

"Now, let's try again."

"*Sí.* Oh, I'm sorry." He'd done it again! He really hadn't meant to. It had just slipped out.

"That's all right, Juan. Now do you have the place in the book?"

"Yes," he said. Just as Juan started to read, the bell rang. Its shrill sound broke the late afternoon stillness. The girls and boys gathered their books and papers together. Juan closed his reader. At last another terrible day was over.

"Hurry up," Sally Smith called to a group of boys and girls. "Let's get out on the field." Some of the children had baseball gloves, and Sally carried a bat. Outside, everyone hurried toward the empty lot on the corner.

"Come on, Juan!" someone called. But Juan walked in the other direction to the bus stop. He didn't want to play baseball. He had something better to do.

Juan lived uptown on the top floor of a six-story apartment house. He was out of breath when he finally reached the top. He unlocked the door and went in. The apartment was empty, for his father, mother, and older sister all worked. They wouldn't be home until around five-thirty.

Juan was glad to have the small apartment to himself. Later, when his family got home, there would hardly be room to breathe. He threw his books down on the couch, which became his bed at night. Then he took his guitar from the corner, where it stood next to his father's.

The guitar felt good in his hands. The brown wood glowed in the late afternoon sun. Juan held the guitar for a moment and then began to play. The music filled the room, shutting out the sounds of the street. As the notes drifted one after another from the guitar, Juan was back on the beach. The sun was warm on his face, and the sea washed up on the sand.

That night Mrs. Marks thought about Juan. She had tried to help him to be happier in school, but nothing she did seemed to help. She remembered the talk she'd had with Juan's mother.

"He's homesick," Juan's mother had said. "All he likes to do is play his guitar. I guess it reminds him of Puerto Rico."

Then Mrs. Marks had an idea. "Well," she thought, "nothing else has worked. I might as well try this."

The next day Mrs. Marks announced to the class that they were going to have a contest. Each child was going to do something—sing, dance, tell a story, play an instrument, or tell jokes.

"I think Barbara might tell some funny stories," Mrs. Marks said. "She's always telling jokes, anyway." The children laughed. There would be time for only five children to perform at the end of each day. Then on Friday the class would vote to decide which girl or boy performed best.

The first day Sally sang a song, and Betty told a story. Billy played the drum, Barbara told jokes, and Joe did a Greek dance.

Juan's turn came on Friday. He didn't want to play for the class, but Mrs. Marks said that everyone had to do something. He brought his guitar to school and kept it by his desk. He decided that he would play a short piece and get it over with. All too soon it was time for the Friday group to perform.

When Juan's turn came, he got up and went to the front of the class with his guitar. He played fast. His fingers jumped over the strings. As the notes followed one another, the sound of loneliness filled the classroom. It was as if Juan were saying with his music, "I am lonely for Puerto Rico."

When Juan had finished, the children clapped their hands long and loud. "Please play something else, Juan. Please!"

Juan thought, "Do they really like my music that much?" He looked at Mrs. Marks.

"Yes, Juan, we have time for more music. Maybe you could play something a little slower. Do you know a slower piece?" she asked.

"*Sí.*" This time Mrs. Marks didn't notice that he hadn't said "Yes." Juan played again—a slow, soft piece.

The song ended. There was no sound for a moment. Then everyone clapped. Juan went to his seat and sat down.

When the votes were counted, Juan had won. Almost everyone had voted for him. There were two votes for Barbara and her jokes.

"I voted for myself," Barbara said, "but I did it as a joke. I really wanted Juan to win. But who's the joker who voted for me?"

"I did," Juan said. "I liked your jokes." Then he asked, "Do you really like my music?"

"Of course, we do," Barbara answered. "Why shouldn't we like your music?"

Just then the bell rang. School was over. The girls and boys gathered up their books and started to leave the room. Mrs. Marks heard Sally say, "Hey, Juan, you play a pretty good guitar. Can you play ball? Can you hit?"

Juan looked at Sally. There was a friendly smile on Sally's face. The smile said, "Come on if you want to. We'd like to have you play with us."

"Yes," Juan said, "I can play ball, too." Walking to the empty lot with the other boys and girls, Juan began to smile. "I will never forget Puerto Rico," he promised himself. "But here—here is home, too."

THINK ABOUT IT

1. What did Juan often daydream about while he was in school? Why did he sometimes pretend to forget English?

2. Why didn't Juan go with his classmates to play baseball? Where did Juan go? Why?

3. What plan did Mrs. Marks develop to help Juan feel happier at school?

4. How was Juan's new home different from his home in Puerto Rico? Why do you think Juan was so homesick for Puerto Rico?

5. How did winning the contest help change Juan's feelings about his classmates and new home?

6. What kind of teacher was Mrs. Marks? Give reasons for your answer.

7. Have you ever moved away from a place that you liked? Were you homesick for a while? What did you miss most about your old home?

8. What are some things that you could do to make a new classmate feel welcome?

The Sultan's Perfect Tree

There was once a sultan who loved perfection. In his palace he would allow only the most perfect things. Each fruit that he ate had to be without blemish. Each cup that he drank from had to be without flaw. Everything, in fact, was perfect.

One day in the fall, the sultan was looking out at his perfect garden. Seven gardeners saw to it that only the most beautiful plants were allowed to grow. Each day they would trim off broken branches or dying leaves. Then they would replace any flower that was in danger of drooping.

In the center of the garden grew a tree. It had been planted by the grandfather of the sultan. The tree was tall and straight and was kept perfectly shaped.

As the sultan gazed out his window at the garden, his eyes most naturally fell on the tree at its center. Suddenly, a swift wind blew into the garden, more savage than any wind before it. The tree bowed and swayed. Its leaves shook and shivered, turning up first the red side, then the gold. As the sultan watched, many of the leaves were ripped loose from their stems and blown to the ground. Soon the tree looked patchy, as if painted in by a trembling hand.

"It is not perfect," the sultan said angrily to himself. Then more loudly he cried out, *"It is not perfect!"*

At his cry, the servants came running. "What is it, O perfect one," they asked, for so they had been instructed to address him.

"That!" the sultan answered angrily, pointing out the window at the offending tree.

"It is but a tree," said the newest serving girl, daughter of the chief steward. Though she tried as she could, she was not yet perfect in her conduct.

"But it is no longer perfect," said the sultan. "I want a perfect tree. A perfect autumn tree."

"How is that to be done?" inquired the chief

steward, for he knew well enough to let the sultan give instructions.

"Call the gardeners!" ordered the sultan.

The seven gardeners came at a run. They caught the falling leaves in willow baskets and carried them out of sight. They plucked the remaining leaves from the tree, climbing to the top on shaky wooden ladders. But they were not quick enough for the sultan.

He turned away from the window and cried, *"It is not perfect.* Take down the tree."

The chief steward was so shocked, he forgot for a moment to be perfect. "But it is your grandfather's tree," he stammered. "It was planted on the day your father was born."

And because his grandfather had been perfectly wise in all that he did, the sultan thought
again. Then he said, "I shall not cut it down."

"What shall be done, then?" asked the chief
steward, once again the perfect servant.

"Close up my window to the garden," said
the sultan. "And send for the best painter in
my kingdom. Have him paint me a perfect
autumn tree on a screen. Set the screen before
the window. Then when I let my gaze fall that
way, I shall always see a perfect tree."

So it was done. The best painter in the kingdom was sent for. He labored seven days until

he had painted a perfect autumn tree, upright, tall, and completely red-gold.

"Perfect," said the sultan when the painter was done.

Two servants set the screen before the window. The painter was rewarded handsomely.

For many months the sultan was delighted. Often he would remark to his chief steward, *"There* is a perfect autumn tree."

Meanwhile, outside it had grown cold. The winter snows came swirling down from the far mountains. The world lay still and white— everywhere but on the sultan's autumn tree.

One day, as the sultan sat drinking his tea, the newest serving girl came into the room. She carried a bowl of winter branches perfectly arranged and set in hard-packed snow.

"O perfect master," she said, "pray accept this representation of the season."

The sultan looked from the bowl to the screen, where his perfect autumn tree stood, splendid and red-gold. His face grew thoughtful. Then it grew angry.

"My tree is no longer perfect!" the sultan cried out. "For if it were, it would be blanketed in snow."

At his cry, the other servants came running, the chief steward in the lead. "What is it, O perfect one?"

"That!" the sultan said angrily, pointing to the screen.

"But that is your perfect autumn tree," said the young serving girl, with only the hint of a smile on her face.

"Perfect autumn tree, yes," said the sultan. "But now it is winter."

"Do not be upset, O perfect master," said the chief steward. "We shall make it perfect."

Again the painter was summoned. He labored yet another seven days to paint a perfect winter tree blanketed with snow.

And for several months the sultan was delighted with his perfect winter tree.

But while the sultan gazed with satisfaction at his tree, the world outside had begun to change once more. Little shoots of green were pushing through the brown cover of earth. The trees were wearing buds like delicate green beads.

One day as the sultan sat deep in thought, the young serving girl again entered the room. This time she came bearing a vase with branches that were covered with young buds and tender green leaves.

"What is this, child?" asked the sultan.

"O perfect master," she said, "pray accept the gardeners' gift of the season."

Again the sultan saw that his tree was no longer perfect, and he cried out in anger. Again

the chief steward summoned the painter to
paint a new scene. And again, for a few months
the sultan was happy.

But one day, as the sultan sat in perfect con-
tentment, the young serving girl brought him
yet another vase. This one was filled with fully
green boughs and ripe fruit. The branches in
the vase bobbed and swayed under the weight
of the fruit.

Neither the sultan nor the girl exchanged a word this time. But when she had gone, the sultan looked over the screen, his heart heavy in his breast. With several sharp claps of his hand, he called the chief steward to him.

"The tree on my screen is no longer perfect," the sultan said sadly. "It is not fully green and laden with fruit. It does not bend and sway like the boughs on my table. Its imperfection rests heavily on my heart," he confided. "I will not eat or drink until I have a perfect tree."

The chief steward sent for the painter at once. "The tree you painted is no longer perfect," he explained. "This time, our perfect sultan requires a tree that will bend and sway with the weight of its ripe fruit. Only then will it be perfect."

The painter looked downcast. "What you ask, alas, I cannot do. I am a painter, not a god. With my paints, I can make a perfect tree—perfect *for the moment*. But I cannot make it live. I cannot make it grow. I cannot make it change."

"Then what shall we do?" cried the chief steward, as much to himself as to the painter. He sat down by the sultan's great bed and wept, his face in his hands.

"If we cannot make a perfect tree, the sultan will not eat or drink. And if he does not eat or drink, he will surely waste away and die."

The painter sat down by his side and wept

likewise. He too loved the perfect sultan and did not wish to see him waste away and die.

One by one, as they heard the weeping, the serving men and women came into the room. They listened silently to the sad tale. Then they too sat down beside the chief steward and cried. Soon there was a whole row of them, sitting and sighing and weeping for want of a perfect tree.

At last the new young serving girl came in and saw the rows of weeping servants. When she, too, had heard the tale, she said. "Oh, you perfect sillies! I know how to make such a tree. It is perfectly simple."

"How can you know?" the chief steward asked his daughter sharply. "The sultan who is the perfect master, the painter who is the perfect painter, and we who are the perfect servants do not know."

"Perhaps it is because I am not yet perfect," said the young girl, "for to be perfect means the end of growing. Close your eyes and you shall see."

They all did as they were told—even the chief steward—and the young serving girl went over to the window. Carefully, she took down the folding screen. Outside, the real tree at the garden's center was covered with fruit. With every passing breeze, its leaves fluttered and its branches bent and bowed.

"Now you may open your eyes," she said.

The servants opened their eyes and gazed at the place where the screen had been. They saw out into the garden and looked upon the real tree. "Oh!" they all cried.

The chief steward and the painter opened their eyes and saw the tree. "Aah!" they both sighed.

At that, the sultan opened his eyes. He sat up in his bed. Slowly, he rose and went over to the window. For a long, long time he gazed out at the tree. He saw how some of the branches were nearly full and some nearly empty. He

saw how some of the branches were short and some long. He saw how some of the branches were almost all green and how some were almost all brown.

"It is not perfect," he said softly.

The servants began to murmur worriedly. The chief steward looked over at his daughter. An angry scowl began to crease his handsome brow. But the sultan cut all this short with a wave of his hand.

"It is not perfect," he said, "but it is living, and growing, and changing. That is better than perfect!"

Then he took the young serving girl by the hand. Together they went out of the palace into the garden to enjoy the fruit of the tree.

THINK ABOUT IT

1. What was it that the sultan demanded of everything and everyone?

2. Why was the sultan displeased with a certain tree that grew in his garden?

3. How did the sultan think he could solve the problem of the not-so-perfect tree?

4. Why wasn't the painter able to create the perfect tree that the sultan required?

5. Who showed the sultan the error of his ways? How did she do it?

6. What did the young serving girl mean when she said "to be perfect means the end of growing"?

7. By the end of the story, how had the sultan changed?

8. Have you ever owned something you thought was perfect? Explain your answer.

Surprises

Have you ever thought of a poem as being full of surprises? As you read the poems on the next few pages, look for surprises. The surprise may be a clever use of words. Or it may be a special way of talking about a very ordinary thing. It may even be a description of something you just experienced yourself!

Unfolding Bud

One is amazed
By a water-lily bud
Unfolding
With each passing day,
Taking on a richer color
And new dimensions.

One is not amazed,
At a first glance,
By a poem,
Which is as tight-closed
As a tiny bud.

Yet one is surprised
To see the poem
Gradually unfolding,
Revealing its rich inner self,
As one reads it
Again
And over again.

Naoshi Koriyama

173

Seal

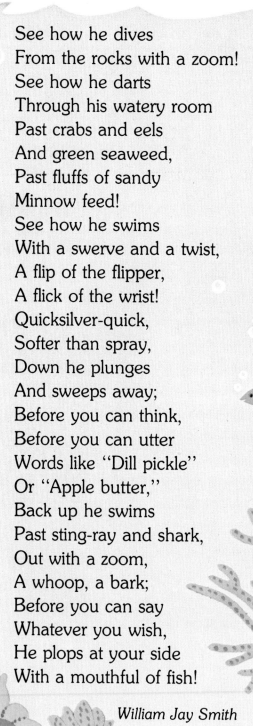

See how he dives
From the rocks with a zoom!
See how he darts
Through his watery room
Past crabs and eels
And green seaweed,
Past fluffs of sandy
Minnow feed!
See how he swims
With a swerve and a twist,
A flip of the flipper,
A flick of the wrist!
Quicksilver-quick,
Softer than spray,
Down he plunges
And sweeps away;
Before you can think,
Before you can utter
Words like "Dill pickle"
Or "Apple butter,"
Back up he swims
Past sting-ray and shark,
Out with a zoom,
A whoop, a bark;
Before you can say
Whatever you wish,
He plops at your side
With a mouthful of fish!

William Jay Smith

A Patch of Old Snow

There's a patch of old snow in a corner,
  That I should have guessed
Was a blow-away paper the rain
  Had brought to rest.

It is speckled with grime as if
  Small print overspread it,
The news of a day I've forgotten—
  If I ever read it.

Robert Frost

"4th of July," I

The ship moves
but its smoke
moves with the wind
faster than the ship

—thick coils of it
through leafy trees
pressing
upon the river

William Carlos Williams

175

In the Car

In the car
I steer straight
and race the moon.
The clouds don't know—
they come between us.
The dark trees don't know—
they scrape the moon.
The people in houses don't know—
they pull the shades.
My father doesn't know—
he keeps whistling.
Only the moon and me.

Richard J. Margolis

Gravel Paths

I feel crinkled when I walk on gravel paths.
The gravel crinkles me
And I become gravel,
Crunched under five thousand footsteps.
I know what it is to be gravel,
Pecked at by pigeons,
Searching for crumbs of park picnics.
Gravel gets tired,
Being poked at by sparrows and pigeons,
Being squashed under grown-up feet,
Being combed by park men's tickling rakes.
Gravel would rather play,
Explode in skittery sprays under running sneakers.
At least I think it would,
And I should know,
Having run crinkled
And sneaker-shod
Up many gravel paths.

Patricia Hubbell

HUNTING FOR CLUES

See how he swims
With a swerve and a twist,
A flip of the flipper,
A flick of the wrist!

This isn't the way people talk or the way they write a story. Poetry is different from prose. It should be read differently, too. You can look for clues in poetry to help you read it. Read these lines from the poem "Unfolding Bud" again.

One is not amazed,
At a first glance,
By a poem,
Which is as tight-closed
As a tiny bud.

Look for the punctuation in the poem. The only period is at the end. This means all five lines are *one* sentence. Many times sentences run over from one line to the next in a poem. To understand the meaning, you have to read the whole sentence. The punctuation clues help you tell where the sentence ends.

Look again at the first four lines of poetry on page 178. How many sentences are there? How do you know? When you read a poem, don't stop at the end of each line. Read the sentences in the poem and pause where you'd pause in a sentence. Read this sentence:

See how he swims with a swerve and a twist, a flip of the flipper, a flick of the wrist!

Did you pause at the commas? Did you pause after *swims*?

Stanzas are another clue that can help you read a poem. A stanza is a group of lines divided from the other lines by space. A stanza often expresses a whole thought.

1. Look back at the poem "Unfolding Bud" on page 173. How many stanzas are there? Does each stanza express a whole thought?
2. Now find a book of poetry and pick a poem to read. What clues does the poem contain? What does the punctuation tell you? How many stanzas are there? Read the poem aloud.

Where's Robot?

In a small village in southwestern France, five schoolboys met in 1940 to discuss how to spend the hot summer afternoon.

"I am bored," said Queroy.[1]

"Me too!" Estréguil,[2] Coencas,[3] and Marcal[4] were quick to agree with Queroy.

They turned to Ravidat,[5] the oldest of their little group. He might have a suggestion to make. Be-

[1] **Queroy** (kə rwo′)
[2] **Estréguil** (es′trā gē′)
[3] **Coencas** (kō′an käs′)
[4] **Marcal** (mär käl′)
[5] **Ravidat** (rä′vē dä′)

tween his knees Ravidat held his small wirehaired terrier, Robot.[6] The dog was panting from the heat.

"It might be cooler up on the hill," Ravidat said slowly. "There's usually a breeze up there."

"It's much too hot to climb the hill," Coencas grumbled.

"We couldn't be any hotter," Estréguil said. "I think it's a good idea, don't you, Marcal?"

Before Marcal could answer, Ravidat got to his feet. "Come on," he said. "Robot wants to go. Look! He's off already!"

The rest of them, grumbling a little, got up, too. Soon the boys and the wirehaired terrier had left the last houses in the village behind them. If they had been told that the expedition they were embarking on was to make history, they would have laughed at the idea.

The two sides of the Vézère[7] Valley rise to a great height and, for the most part, steeply. They are not smooth, grassy slopes so much as enormous masses of whitish rock piled one on top of the other. As the region is known to be very old, archaeologists searched here for records of primitive people. They found plenty of relics, including the skeletons of three men, a woman, and a child. These early people came to be known as Cro-Magnon.[8] They had roamed the district as long ago as twenty-five thousand years!

---

[6] **Robot** (rä′bō)   [7] **Vézère** (vā′zer′)   [8] **Cro-Magnon** (krō mag′nən)

181

The five boys threaded their way through the vineyards that covered the lower slopes of the rocky hillside, Robot bounding eagerly ahead of them all the time. They had no thoughts of finding relics; they were out to find a breeze.

Beyond the vineyards, the hillside steepened. Every now and then one of the boys would loosen a stone and send it bounding down the track. "Watch out!" he would call to those behind him. Robot bounded ahead of them taking short cuts too steep for them to follow on two legs!

The section of the hillside they were on was called Lascaux.[9] A year or two before, a donkey had been left alone there to graze. When its owner returned to fetch it, it had vanished. The owner thought that it had probably fallen into a hole in the ground where the roots of a tree had been torn out. A rough fence of sticks and branches was erected around the hole in case some other animal strayed that way. "Trou de l'Âne,"[10] it came to be called: Donkey's Hole. It was best to avoid it altogether; an unlucky hole, that Trou de l'Âne!

[9] **Lascaux** (lä skō′)   [10] **Trou de l'Âne** (trü′də län′)

Panting and out of breath from their climb, Queroy, Coencas, Marcal, Estréguil, and Ravidat dropped to the ground when they reached the shade of the trees. They had plenty of time on their hands. There was, as Ravidat had said, a little breeze up there. Enough to fan them gently. They relaxed in the shade and shut their eyes.

It was not until an hour had passed that anyone noticed that Robot was missing. It did not surprise any of them, for Robot was a restless creature and always up to something. However, Ravidat was not entirely happy; it was unlike the little terrier to stay away so long. Ravidat put two fingers to his lips and let out a piercing whistle that could be heard right across the valley.

When he had repeated the whistle half a dozen times without any result, Ravidat became worried. "I'm going to look for him," he announced to the others.

Some unknown fear took him in the direction of the Trou de l'Âne. He began to run. At last, there it was in front of him: a low fence of twisted branches. But there was a hole in it! The hole had

been made by a small animal, low on the ground, moving fast! Ravidat knew at once who that animal was.

"Robot! Robot!" he called out, throwing himself down so that his head was almost in the hole. "Robot!"

This time there was an answer. From far, far away and deep down below the ground, there came a muffled yelping. It was Robot!

Ravidat was really alarmed now. Although he had never seen the Trou de l'Âne at close quarters, he knew that it must be deep; otherwise the owner would have found his donkey. Ravidat shouted to the others to come and help. Then he began feverishly tearing at the matted branches to clear a passage large enough to take his shoulders. Robot was down there; he must be rescued. He might even have been injured by his fall. Ravidat went cold at the very thought.

By the time the other boys had joined him, the hole was large enough for Ravidat to wriggle through. Marcal followed him, and the two boys stared downward at what confronted them. A long slope of rubble, loose rocks, stones, and rock dust led from the lip of the hole and vanished into the darkness. It looked dangerous.

"I shall go down and find him," Ravidat said firmly.

Digging his toes in hard—and his elbows too—Ravidat did his best to check the speed of his descent. It was difficult, for the rubble and stones were loose. All the time he was sliding down the slope he had but one thought in mind: Was Robot injured? He would soon know.

Suddenly his feet touched solid ground. He straightened his arms and then stood upright. His knees and elbows hurt. Suddenly there was a wild scampering behind him, and he felt Robot's wet tongue licking his legs. He gathered him up and carefully felt him all over. No broken bones, thank goodness! Good old Robot! What a game terrier he was!

Luckily Ravidat had a small flashlight in his pocket. It had been given to him as a gift. The light revealed that he was in a cave with walls of solid rock. Ravidat's next thought was to call his friends down to see what he had found.

"Come quickly!" he shouted up to them.

They did not need a second invitation. Soon all five boys were standing shoulder to shoulder on the gritty floor, with Robot jumping excitedly about between their feet. They saw that the cave was at least twice as long as it was broad. Its roof of solid rock rose above their heads in a great arch like the curved roof of a church.

The small light could not dispel all the shadows in the cave; some remained here and there on the cave's walls. Something about those shadows—if they were in fact shadows—aroused Ravidat's curiosity. He made for the nearest wall, beckoning to the others to come, too. What they saw took their breath away!

They were not shadows at all! Right up to the curved roof over their heads the walls of the cave were covered with animals painted in black and brown and yellow and red! There were large and small animals. There were fighting, charging,

resting, leaping animals. There were animals in all positions. There were single animals and animals in large and small groups.

The drawings and painting were unlike anything else the boys had ever seen in their lives. Some of them were as much as fifteen feet (4.5 m) in length. Some were outlined in bold black lines and colored red or yellow or brown inside. Others had no outlines but were made up of two or more colors. All of them seemed to shine in the faint yellow light of the flashlight, almost as though they had been glazed over. Queroy touched one of the painted figures. It was as smooth as glass.

Soon the boys decided they would come back tomorrow for a more serious exploration. Planting their feet carefully along the slippery rubble slope, the boys began their ascent. Holding Robot, Ravidat was glad when he and his friends finally reached the lip of the hole.

The next day the boys were back, complete with torches, spare batteries, and rope. Quickly they anchored one end of the rope to a good sound root and threw the loose end down the slope. Then they scrambled one after another down it, descending deep into the cavern.

They investigated the cave foot by foot. At the far end there was an opening in the floor which clearly led somewhere.

They dropped to their knees around the opening and pointed their torches into the darkness. They saw a staircase of loose stones slanting downward, at a guess, as much as thirty feet (9 m) or more. They could not see the end of it from where they were kneeling. Ravidat and Estréguil looked at one another; this was something too good to miss.

Ravidat went first. After thirty feet or so he found himself on a level rock floor again. He called to the others to join him. Then they flashed their torches around this new cavern-beneath-a-cavern. Here, too, paintings of animals covered the walls all the way to the arched roof above their heads, trans-

forming the cave into an underground museum. They could hardly contain their excitement.

They returned the next day, and the next, and the day after that. They explored every nook and cranny of the network of underground chambers and passages. Finally Ravidat decided it was time to tell someone about their discovery. Their teacher, the boys decided, was the person who would know what to do. Excitedly, they talked about their find.

One week later, about ten days after the small wirehaired terrier had tumbled into the Trou de l'Âne, a party of archaeologists descended on the sleeply little village. They were led by the greatest French archaeologist of his day—one of the greatest scholars of prehistory, Abbé Breuil.[11]

They knew at once that what they were looking at was among the most important archaeological discoveries ever made. The only other wall paintings that began to compare with these at Lascaux were those found in a cavern in northern Spain.

[11] **Abbé Breuil** (a′bā bre′ē′)

Above all, the archaeologists were excited by the very last of the paintings the boys had discovered. It was an action picture — the oldest ever discovered.

An action picture tells a story. The cave painting at Lascaux shows a bison, a man, and a rhinoceros. On the right of the painting, the magnificent bison is about to collapse from a great wound in its belly. Near the bison's head is a long, straight stick figure such as those drawn by young children. The figure is falling stiffly backward, apparently having been gored to death by the bison in its own death agony.

A triple-horned rhinoceros can be seen lurching away in the left of the picture. It is obviously the rhinoceros that has ripped the powerful bison's belly with its cruel horns. A hunter's spear would not have been capable of making such a terrible wound.

Abbé Breuil and his team of experts were able to establish that these rock paintings were the work of the Cro-Magnon. Other prehistoric paintings had, of course, been found elsewhere; but none of them offered an action picture such as this. The ability to portray animals in action established that the Cro-Magnon were much more highly developed than had once been believed.

The paintings also proved that, as well as being great hunters, the Cro-Magnon were considerable artists. They lived at a time when one of the Ice

Ages was blotting out much of Europe. The Cro-Magnon fought wild animals for living space, survived the bitter cold, and left deep underground these paintings of a way of life.

None of these paintings might have been discovered if five schoolboys had not been bored on a hot summer afternoon, and if one of them had not asked, "Where's Robot?"

THINK ABOUT IT

1. When and where does this selection take place?

2. What relics had some archaeologists already found in the Vézère Valley? What name had archaeologists given to the primitive people who had lived in this area? How long ago had these people roamed the valley?

3. What happened to Ravidat's dog, Robot? What did Ravidat discover when he crawled down to save Robot?

4. Why do you think Ravidat's discovery was so important?

5. If you visited the caves at Lascaux, what questions would you like to ask your guide?

The Lonely Silence

Sabina Hall ran up the front steps and reached for the doorbell.

The doorbell was not like other doorbells. Nor were Bina's parents like her classmates' parents. The button controlled a lever that dropped a heavy weight to the floor with a thud. The thud vibrated so that Bina's parents could "feel" the doorbell "ring." Her parents could not hear or speak. They were deaf-mutes. The only way they could communicate between themselves and with others was with sign language. With the various hand gestures that formed words and phrases, they got along very well indeed.

Bina hesitated before she rang the bell. Perhaps her mother was resting after work. She didn't expect Bina home until after her duty at the hospital. Bina worked as a Candystriper, a volunteer who helped the nurses. Perhaps she should just drop off her books and not disturb her mother.

When she put her key in the lock and opened the door, she was drawn to the kitchen by the delicious smell of roasting meat. She only had time for an apple before leaving for the hospital.

As Bina put her books down on the desk in the living room, a piece of paper fell to the floor. She stooped to pick it up and recognized her mother's handwriting. It was a half-finished letter to Mrs. Gibson, head of the Candystripers:

Dear Mrs. Gibson:
Sabina's birthday is on the nineteenth. I would like to give a surprise birthday party for her, but I do not know the names of her friends who work with her at the hospital. Please be kind enough to send me a list of the other Candystripers so that I may send invitations

The letter broke off suddenly, as though her mother had remembered something she must do in the kitchen.

Fear rose in little waves as Bina crumpled the letter into a tight ball. This couldn't happen. She put her hands over her ears to shut out the cruel voices she remembered all too well. They were voices from her childhood—teasing voices reminding her that her parents were deaf-mutes.

Closing her eyes, she could see the ring of mocking children as they danced around her. They were wiggling their fingers at her and clapping their hands, pretending to speak the sign language that Bina and her parents used.

It was Caroline, who lived next door, who had made up the verses and led the teasing first-graders. By the time Bina moved away some years later, they had forgotten their childish game. But Bina hadn't. She would never forget those voices.

Uncle Jack had found their present house here in Martinsville. Bina went to a new school and met new classmates. In school and on the street she did not use the sign language she had learned almost before she had learned to speak. She never invited friends home. None of her classmates knew that her parents were deaf-mutes.

A handclap brought her attention to the kitchen doorway. Her mother stood there staring at the crumpled letter in Bina's hand. She was angry, but Bina was angry, too. Bina spoke sharply.

"Why? Why do you want to spoil everything for me? After I've tried so hard." A sharp fold of the paper dug into Bina's palm as she clutched it. "If you send this letter and invite people here, I won't come to the party. I won't be laughed at anymore. I won't go back to being the deaf-mutes' daughter."

Her mother's fingers moved rapidly in protest, but Bina would not look at them. It was the first time she had ever mentioned the cruelty of her playmates. She had spoken quickly. She knew that her mother had had

difficulty lipreading all her words. Her mother's look, however, showed that she understood the meaning of Bina's outburst.

"I've got to catch the bus," Bina said. "I'm late now." She hurried toward the door, ignoring the clapped command to stop and turn around. She did not want to hurt her mother, but she could not bear to be hurt anymore either. Why couldn't her parents let her lead her own life?

It wasn't so hard for them. Dad worked with his brother, Jack, in Grandfather's printing business. Mom worked at the school for the deaf. They both had attended the school and had met many friends there. Sometimes Bina watched them entertaining their friends, laughing at each other's silent jokes and arguing with rapid fingers. Bina thought glumly that she suffered more from their handicaps than they seemed to. She was the one who could not ask her friends home.

She tried to push her worries away when she reached the hospital. Today was her turn in the Children's Ward with Nancy Graham. As they entered the elevator, a woman in a gray pants suit smiled at them. Bina could see approval in her eyes for the Candystripers' crisp red-and-white striped uniform over the short-sleeved white blouses.

"I like the Children's Ward, don't you?"
Nancy asked as they stepped off at the third
floor. "It may be noisy, but it's never dull."

Bina grinned back. From the large ward
room came all sorts of noises, from moans and
giggles to howls of temper. "Yes, I think we
will be able to keep busy."

They gave their pink slips to the head nurse
at the desk. She would mark the number of
hours they worked, along with any comments
about how they performed their duties. The
slips were then dropped into a box when their
hours were over.

"It's going to be a busy three hours,"
thought Bina as soon as they entered the ward.
The student nurse's face was already tired as
she looked up from the crib where she was

trying to calm a little boy. He seemed determined to batter his head on the bars of the crib.

"Glad to see you girls," the nurse said wearily. "I have to get these beds finished in a hurry. Any suggestions on how to quiet this one?"

Nancy went forward to try to help her, but Bina stopped short. Her heart seemed to stop, too. In the crib by the door a boy was twisting his thin hands weakly. He was using sign language to send a silent plea to the mother who was not there. Bina paused beside his crib. Her hands curved almost automatically to signal an answer to him. But the head nurse spoke behind her. "This little fellow can't speak, and no one on duty knows sign language."

Bina let her hand drop to her side. She had come so close to giving away her secret! Anger swept through her. She had come here to escape her problem, if only for a few hours. But here she was, face to face with it again. It wasn't fair.

The nurse took the small, pleading fingers in both her hands. "It will be all right, Carl. Your mother is here in the hospital, too. You will see her soon." She looked up at Bina. "If only I could make him understand. His mother is sleeping and cannot be disturbed, but the doctor is sure she will be all right. She was driving an out-of-state car when they had an accident. The police are trying to get in touch with relatives." She sighed. "Poor boy. He is frightened because he cannot understand."

A little blond girl in the next crib fussed a bit and Bina turned to her. She was afraid to be near Carl. She was afraid to help him.

Nancy would not let her ignore him. "It must be terrible not to be able to understand or to make yourself understood."

Bina busied herself picking up the crayons the little girl had spilled. She would not let herself be trapped by pity. She was sorry for the boy, but she had worked hard these last years to build a separate life for herself. She could not throw everything away in a moment of weakness.

Next week when she came back to the hospital, this boy would be gone; but the nurses and other Candystripers would know her secret. They were older and would not tease her openly. But they would treat her as though she were different.

"Oh, Bina!" Nancy looked as though she were about to cry. "If only I understood. If only I could help him. Could anything be worse than to be cut off from everyone like this?"

Why did she have to keep it up? "What about his family," Bina snapped crossly at Nancy, "the ones who have to hear the teasing and jeers because he's different?"

Nancy looked at her with a shocked expression, but the clatter of food trays interrupted whatever she was about to say. The Candy-stripers were busy then, helping the younger children with their food. They wiped up spilled milk and rescued tipped bowls. Through the noisy babble of children's voices, Bina sensed the lonely silence of the mute boy. It was like a cold mist closing her in with him in his loneliness. She would not look at him, and yet she was more aware of him than of any of the other children.

She did not weaken. Let someone else answer the frightened plea of the thin fingers. Nancy stopped to speak to Carl on her way out of the ward, but Bina hurried by.

The head nurse smiled at them. "You girls are a great help here with the children," she said. "Some of them have never been away from home before, and they need a great deal of attention."

The girls handed their pink slips to the head nurse. Their work was over now. Bina started toward the elevator with Nancy.

The hospital smells made Bina feel a little sick. Only it wasn't really the smells, it was something inside her. It was the way she felt when she knew she had done something

wrong. When she was small, her mother would punish her, and the sick feeling would go away. Now she was too old to expect others to point out her mistakes. She had to make things right herself. She had passed a little boy by when she could have helped him.

"I have to run back for a moment," she said to Nancy. "I'll see you later."

Nancy looked at her in surprise, but Bina was in a hurry to do what was right before fear stopped her.

Carl had his eyes closed. Tears ran down his cheeks, and the soundless crying hurt Bina more than screams would have. She put her hand over his, and he jumped and opened his eyes. With her hands she carefully spelled out

comforting words. She could feel him relax when she told him that his mother was sleeping nearby, and he would see her soon. The fear faded from his eyes. He smiled.

The head nurse came over to the crib. "You understand him?" she asked. The curiosity was there in her eyes, but there was admiration, too.

"My parents are also mute," Bina said quietly. For the first time, she was able to say the words without bitterness.

"Both of them? They must be very special people."

"Why, yes, they are." Bina had never thought of that before. They never acted sorry for themselves or expected special treatment. They had built a happy, useful life, in spite of their handicaps. It was Bina, with no handicap, who was filled with self-pity. She had shut people out of her life. And she had shut herself into a lonely silence that they did not know.

"I've explained to Carl that his mother is sleeping and that he will see her soon. Is that all right?" The head nurse nodded, and Bina added, "I'll come back tomorrow to see him. I think he will be all right now that he understands."

Bina was impatient as she waited for the elevator. She wanted to catch Nancy before she finished changing and went home. After all, Nancy was the first one she wanted to invite to her birthday party—and to her home. She could hardly wait for Nancy to meet her parents.

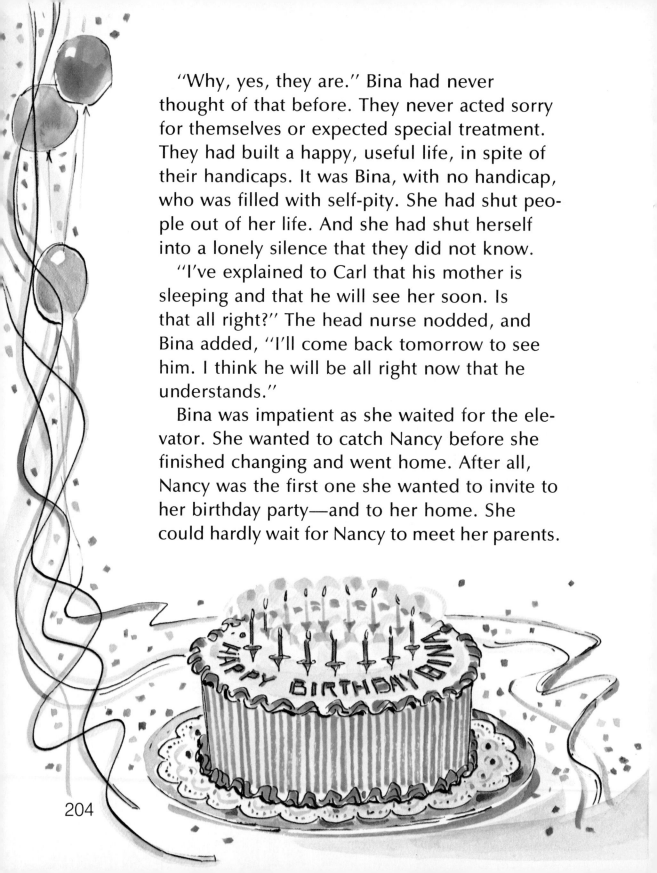

1. How did Bina's parents communicate? Why did they communicate in this way?

2. What was the surprise Bina's mother was planning for her? Why did this upset Bina?

3. Why couldn't any of the nurses talk to the small boy in the hospital? Why wouldn't Bina talk to the child at first?

4. How did the head nurse react when she learned that Bina's parents were deaf-mutes?

5. By the end of the story, how had Bina's feelings about her parents changed?

6. How would you have felt, if you had been Bina? Would you agree with Bina that she suffered more from her parents' disabilities than they did? Why or why not?

Mixed Messages

Susan Stewart and her parents had just arrived in northern France. They unpacked their suitcases quickly and went for a stroll. After walking past a few shops, they decided to go into a clothing store.

Inside Susan found an attractive red beret. The sales clerk smiled as Susan tried it on.

"Isn't it super!" Susan said.

Mrs. Stewart nodded. Mr. Stewart also nodded and then raised his hand and made a circle with his thumb and forefinger.

Suddenly the sales clerk gasped. He strode over to Susan's father indignantly. Muttering angrily in French, he put one hand on his hip and pointed to the door with the other! When the Stewarts didn't move the clerk practically pushed them out of the shop. Susan barely had time to give back the beret.

Once outside, Mr. Stewart protested. "But I said the beret was great. What could have made him so angry?"

Susan and her mother shrugged absently and shook their heads. Then the three turned and continued their stroll.

Mr. Stewart's comment wasn't quite right. He didn't *say* the beret was great. He didn't say anything. His communication was non-verbal. He made a gesture. The gesture meant one thing to him and his family. But it meant something else to the French sales clerk.

Mr. Stewart used a certain hand signal to give a positive reaction. To him and his family, the gesture meant "fine, great, perfect." But in northern France, that same signal means "nothing" or "worthless." The store clerk was angered because he thought Mr. Stewart was insulting his merchandise and, by extension, insulting him.

The hand gesture Mr. Stewart used is also common in Japan. There, it means "money." Had Mr. Stewart been in a Japanese shop when he made the gesture, he might have been told the price of the beret.

The circle-sign is not the only gesture that has more than one meaning. Touching the forehead or temple may mean "clever" or "smart." It may also mean "stupid." Touching the mouth may mean "hunger," "thirst," or "speech." And pointing to the eyes may indicate that sight is very good or very bad.

The meaning of a gesture depends on the situation and the people involved. The

gestures shown below are some of the common signals people use to express an idea or feeling. See how many of them you recognize. Do any have more than one meaning? Afterwards, think of some other common gestures. Then have a classmate guess their meaning.

1. How did the sales clerk respond to the gesture Mr. Stewart made?

2. What did the gesture mean to Mr. Stewart and his family? What did it mean to the French sales clerk?

3. If Mr. Stewart had made the same gesture in a shop in Japan, what might have happened?

4. Why do the same gestures sometimes have very different meanings?

5. What is "nonverbal" communication?

6. Imagine trying to communicate with someone who cannot speak your language. How would you communicate? What could you do to make yourself understood?

7. What gestures have you used today? What did they mean?

four

The PROPHECY

Perhaps you already have read some of the far-fetched tales of Paul Bunyan, the giant logger. "The Prophecy" is the story of how Paul discovers that he and his ox, Babe, will become part of American folklore.

One day Paul was collecting a bundle of moss for Babe. Suddenly he heard a terrible rumble that grew louder each second. He straightened himself and stood on tiptoe so he could see across the trees. The sight that met his eyes was the strangest he'd ever seen.

A stormy wall of dazzling blue cloud rose along the horizon. As it moved closer, Paul heard the flapping of a great many wings. All the blue ganders in creation seemed to be flying for their lives. They jabbered their fear to one another as they shot along the sky.

The next minute Paul was aware that herds of moose and deer were bumping his shins. A big black bear started up his trouser leg for protection. Paul tucked the bear away in his beaver cap, where the bear at once started to hibernate. Then throwing the bundle of moss on his back, Paul rushed home ahead of the storm.

Babe was threshing around and moaning and bellowing. Paul barely had time to throw her the moss and run to his shed before the storm broke.

It was the strangest storm ever known. Nobody would ever have believed it, if it hadn't been foretold. "Before the coming of the blue moon, there will be the winter of the blue snow," the prophets had said for who knows how long.

The air was suddenly filled with gleaming blue snowflakes. The blue wind romped and roared through the swaying pines. Paul sat at his window and watched the blue snow as it piled and drifted and covered the land.

Paul finally moved away from the window. He threw six pine trees into his fireplace and started his dinner. He pulled six deer from his pocket, mixed a delicious stew, and then quickly ate it all. By this time, it was so dark that Paul stretched his huge body across his shed, covered himself with some loose skins, and went to sleep.

How long Paul slept he never knew. But, judging by the size of his hunger when he awoke, he thought it must have been at least a month. "I believe I could eat up the whole of outdoors, if only it could fit in my mouth," he said to himself.

He sat up stiffly and dreamily rubbed his eyes. This was the first time in his life that he could not remember his dream. Then he lumbered awkwardly to his feet. When he opened the door of his shed, he thought he was opening the door to a new life. For a full half day, he simply leaned against his door. Everywhere he looked, there was a sparkle of blue. The ground, the trees, the sky—everything was shining sapphire.

The air was so sweet and warm that it seemed to caress Paul. He had never before experienced such joy. While he leaned against the door he whistled a spring melody.

Suddenly and without warning, there stood before him a lovely spirit, dressed in shining blue. She was almost as tall as Paul, but she stood so lightly that her toes hardly touched the snow.

"I am the spirit sent from the blue moon." She smiled as the sweet music flowed from her lips. "You are in high favor. I am sent to bring you a message."

Paul felt so shy that he tried to hide his clumsy hands. He blushed a bright red.

The spirit only smiled. "You shall never grow old," she said. "You shall always be young with a big heart. And you shall always be a dreamer.

"My special message is to tell you that with the coming of spring you are to free the forests from their long bondage. You are to carry them away to see the world and become a part of it.

"For the past month, while you slept, the blue moon played across the heavens. It has been long foretold that with the coming of the blue moon, a great hero will also arise. You, Paul Bunyan, are that hero. Take Babe, the blue ox, with you wherever you go. Babe will be your helper and friend. Your name is already written among the stars. You will be forever famous."

With a wave of her hand, the beautiful blue spirit suddenly vanished. Paul stood waving his arms wildly, trying to call her back.

"My Babe is a red ox, not a blue ox," he shouted after her. But the only good that his calling did was to waken the ox. Babe let out such a terrible bellow that Paul rushed to the stable to see what was wrong. The sight that met his eyes would have seemed a dream, but Paul remembered the words of the spirit. For there before him stood a blue ox. Babe's big eyes were shiny blue. Her hair had the glow of blue rabbits playing in the snows under the midnight sun. The blue ox was to Paul a symbol. Babe proved that the spirit had told him the truth.

The spring wind was melting the blue snow on all sides. The world of green was beginning to peep through to see the wonderful sight. Paul got his axes and his skins together. He was ready to move off into the unknown to find his waiting fortune.

1. How did all the animals of the forest react to the advancing storm? How did Paul Bunyan react?

2. What was unusual about this snow storm?

3. How did Paul feel after the storm was over?

4. What did the spirit tell Paul? How did Paul know that the spirit's words were indeed true?

5. How is this tall tale like others you have read? How is this tall tale different?

6. Compare and contrast Paul Bunyan's reaction to the storm with that of Sam Gribley in "My Side of the Mountain." How are the reactions of the characters similar? different?

7. Why do you think people have always enjoyed telling tall tales?

8. Have you ever made up your own tall tale? What was it? Did anyone believe your story?

Amelia and the Bear

Amelia Thompson sat on a log bench and leaned against the cabin. The warm June sunshine felt good on her face. Amelia was peeling potatoes for dinner. She looked up as her parents came out of the cabin.

"Be sure to put the potatoes on to cook," reminded her mother. "You and Eli may have a few for lunch."

"Yes, Mama."

"Oh, Antone, I wish we had gifts for Mr. Jacobs," her mother said to her father. "He has given us so much."

"Philip Jacobs understands," Mr. Thompson replied. "Besides, our corn crop will be ready next month, and we will share it with him. That late

freeze ruined most of his corn." He turned to Amelia. "We will be back before dark."

Amelia watched her parents follow the path into the woods toward the bay. There they would row across to Mr. Jacobs's place. She went back to her peeling. Her thoughts were on a story Mama had told about Norway the night before. Amelia couldn't remember much about Norway. When her family came to America in 1848, Amelia was barely six.

Now, four years later, the Thompsons were settlers in the Wisconsin wilderness. They had cleared land, built the cabin, and planted corn, oats, and potatoes. Papa and Mama had told them that their new life wouldn't be easy, and they were right. If it hadn't been for Philip Jacobs, what would they have done?

She looked at their half-grown pig in his sturdy log pen. Amelia remembered the day Mr. Jacobs had brought the little pig to them. He had told them that, with good care, the pig would provide meat for the winter. Mama had kept the tiny piglet near the fireplace all spring and had fed him potato-peeling soup. Papa always reminded them to be thankful to Philip Jacobs for their bountiful blessing.

Eli whispered to Amelia, "The pig is our *only* blessing, so I guess he is bountiful." And that's how Bountiful was named.

Amelia put another potato in the pot and then looked at Bountiful. The pig pushed its snout between the logs and grunted. "I know you don't like being in that pen," Amelia said. "But we can't turn you out. Bears or wolves might get you. Eli has gone to dig roots for you."

Eli was only eight, but he felt as much at home in the woods as he did in the cabin. "Eli will be back soon," Amelia promised. "I'll get you some potato peelings. You must eat and get fat."

Inside the cabin Amelia added a small log to the coals in the fireplace. Then she pumped the hand bellows until the coals glowed. With a puff, flames danced around the log.

Amelia brushed her long blond braids out of her way as she chose a few potatoes from the barrel. She made a face at the thought of eating potatoes *again.* Potatoes were all they had to eat except when she or Eli or Papa caught a fish in the bay. She thought of the bacon, pork chops, and hot cracklings they would have in a few months.

A strange scratching noise made her stop and listen. Suddenly the air was filled with a shrill squeal. She saw Bountiful pushing against the side of the pen nearest the cabin. His snout was between the logs and his small round eyes were rolled back in terror. Then she saw it! On the far side of the pen, a black bear had forced a paw between the logs and was reaching for the pig with long, sharp claws.

Amelia trembled with fear as she watched the pig run back and forth, dodging the sharp claws. Suddenly her fear changed to anger. "No! You can't have our pig!" she shouted.

She started outside, then stopped and looked around. Papa had taken the rifle, but a long, sharp pointed stick standing near the door caught her eye. The corn planter!

Amelia grabbed the pole and crawled toward the pen on her hands and knees. The bear reared on its hind legs and pawed the air. She lay still and watched. Had it seen her? Her heart pounded.

The bear tried to loosen the top log but soon gave up. Then it began clawing and biting one of the lower logs. Amelia inched forward on her elbows and knees. She kept the pig between herself and the bear, hoping it wouldn't see her or catch her scent.

At last, Amelia reached the pen. She crept closer until the pig's snout was only inches above her. His shrill squeals made her head throb as she peered around the corner. The bear's shaggy black haunches were less than three feet away!

Amelia clutched the pole tighter but couldn't force herself to move. Suddenly chips of broken wood showered down on her. The bear had broken through the pen! Amelia jumped up screaming.

"Pig stealer!" she cried. Then she thrust the pole at the bear with all her strength. The sharp point jabbed into the bear's thick hide.

With a thunderous growl the bear reared up, turned toward the woods, and ran off. Amelia leaned against the pen, sighing with relief.

"Amelia! Amelia! Where are you?" her father called as he came crashing through the woods from the direction of the bay.

"Bear!" she gasped, pointing to where it had disappeared into the dense woods. With the rifle ready, her father ran into the woods after the bear. The next thing Amelia knew, her mother was hugging her, and Eli was saying, "Wow! You really fought off a *bear?*"

For supper that night the family had bear meat with their potatoes. Amelia's father told how he had caught the bear. "It wasn't badly hurt, but you scared it half to death," Mr. Thompson said.

"It's very tough meat," grumbled Eli, but Amelia noticed that he took a second helping.

"It is *fine,* and you be grateful, Eli Thompson," scolded his mother. "Now we will have oil for the lamps and a fine rug by Amelia's bed."

"And now we can surely survive the winter," Papa said. His proud smile made Amelia's heart dance.

Amelia and her family did survive that long, hard winter. The Thompsons were a real family, who came from Norway to settle in Wisconsin. "Amelia and the Bear" is based on the true story of how this pioneer girl's courage helped her family overcome the hardships of life in the wilderness.

THINK ABOUT IT

1. When does this story take place? Where does it take place?

2. Why had Mr. Jacobs given a little pig to the Thompson family? How did the pig receive its name?

3. What kind of animal tried to attack the pig? How did Amelia protect the pig?

4. How did the Thompson family make use of the bear that Mr. Thompson killed?

5. What kind of person was Amelia? Give reasons for your answer.

6. What were some of the hardships that the Thompsons faced? How was their life different from the lives of families today?

7. Tell about a time when your quick thinking solved a serious problem. What were your feelings at the time?

Why Don't You Get a Horse, Sam Adams?

In the early days of America, men wore ruffles on their shirts and buckles on their shoes. They rode horseback and swore allegiance to the King of England. But there lived in Boston one man who cared for none of these things. His name was Samuel Adams. His clothes were shabby and plain. He refused to get on a horse. And he hated the King of England.

Samuel Adams was known as a talker and a walker. Six days of the week he would walk about Boston, talking to anyone who would listen. He talked about England, always about England. What he thought about was independence. But it was a long time before he dared say "independence" out loud. Americans were still loyal to the king, even though they were often angry at the way England treated its colonies. And Samuel Adams made it his business to keep the people angry.

From one end of the town to another Samuel walked. Indeed, how else was he to travel? A man cannot say much from the top of a horse except good morning, good evening, or giddyap.

And Samuel Adams had a great deal more than that to say. Still, he did not travel alone. At his side was Queue, his shaggy Newfoundland dog.

Together they went to the docks. While Samuel Adams talked to merchants about the wrongs of the English government, Queue smelled the good smells of Boston Harbor.

Together Samuel and Queue called on shop-keepers and dropped in at taverns.

Samuel's younger cousin, John Adams, often became impatient with all his walking. "Why don't you learn to ride a horse?" he would ask.

But Samuel would not learn. Winter and sum-mer he walked and he talked. Indeed, he paid so little attention to his private business that he became quite poor. His house fell into disrepair. His clothes became shabbier. His shoes wore thin.

Meanwhile, England was imposing taxes on America. First a stamp tax on printed matter—on marriage licenses, on college diplomas, even on newspapers. This made the people of Boston

angry. They tore down the governor's house. They set fire to the tax office. And they elected Samuel a representative to the Massachusetts legislature.

Being a member of the government, Samuel had a chance to talk to more people. But he still walked. Even when England withdrew the stamp tax, Samuel talked and walked. He warned the merchants and the shopkeepers and the people at the taverns not to trust England. It had taxed America once, he said; it would try it again. And indeed a year later it did. This time Americans had to give England money whenever they bought paint, glass, lead, or tea. This made the people angry, very angry. The king decided to send soldiers to Boston to keep order.

They arrived in Boston on October 1, 1768—two regiments of soldiers in red coats. From the harbor they marched—one thousand strong, their drums beating, fifes playing, flags flying, and bayonets fixed. They marched straight to Boston Common, a park in the center of town where

people were accustomed to take walks, play games, and graze their cows. There the soldiers set up tents and settled down for the winter.

It was a long winter. Every time he turned around, it seemed to Samuel Adams, he saw a redcoat. He woke up hearing redcoats drill. He went to bed hearing their bugles. Redcoats stopped him on his walks to ask his name and business. Samuel Adams longed for America to fight the redcoats then and there. But he knew the country was not ready yet for war or independence.

Meanwhile, he kept on talking and walking.

"Why can't you ride a horse like everyone else?" his cousin John asked.

But Samuel just shook his head.

After the redcoats arrived, fighting often broke out between the people of Boston and the redcoats. Finally in 1775, the colonists decided that they had to do something, so they began to hold meetings. People from each of the Colonies came together to discuss what they could do about the way England treated them.

In September, 1775, Samuel Adams and his cousin John were on their way to a meeting in Philadelphia. John and his servant, Fessenden, were on horses; Samuel and his servant were in a two-wheeled chaise. Under such circumstances, it was hard for John and Samuel to talk. John suggested that Samuel could ride Fessenden's horse and Fessenden could get in the chaise. Samuel suggested that his servant could ride John's horse and John could get in the chaise, but John loved to ride. So John trotted along to Philadelphia, and Samuel rolled along, each with his own thoughts.

It took a week or more to go from Boston to Philadelphia. But there were many stops at inns, where John and Samuel could talk together. While stopping in Grafton, Connecticut, John Adams decided to make one last attempt to get Samuel on a horse.

"Riding would be good for your health," he began.

Samuel was not concerned with his health.

Riding was sociable, John suggested. Samuel said walking was sociable and riding in a chaise could be sociable, too.

Well, riding was a more convenient way to get about, John went on. As a leader of the Revolution, Samuel was a busy man and needed to get about easily.

Samuel was not interested in convenience.

Riding was the fastest way to travel, John observed. In time of war, it was sometimes important to move fast.

Still, Samuel was not convinced.

Then John Adams sat back in his chair and took a deep breath. He had one more argument. "You should ride a horse for the good of your country," he declared. America would surely be declaring its independence soon, he pointed out; if all went well, they themselves would be signing such a declaration in Philadelphia. Then they would be not just leaders of a revolution; they would be the heads of a new nation.

John leaned toward his cousin. "A proud new nation," he said. "A great nation. A republic as Rome had been in ancient times. And whoever heard of a great nation with leaders who could not ride horseback?" John listed the heroes of Roman history. He reviewed the names of Roman senators. They all rode horses, he said. And he would not want Americans to be inferior in the least way.

For the first time Samuel looked thoughtful. How could he refuse to get on a horse if the honor of his country were at stake? How could he put a stain on American history—indeed right on the opening chapter?

Samuel closed his eyes and tried to imagine the new nation that John described. Yes, it seemed to him that he could see it—people multiplying, buildings springing up, roads unrolling. And stone statues popping up across the landscape. They were statues of the new nation's first leaders. And they were all on horseback. There was John Adams in stone on a horse. And John Hancock. There were dozens of George Washingtons on dozens of horses. But try as he might, Samuel could not find a statue of himself. If he did not ride a horse, he asked himself, would he not even be granted a pedestal?

When they were ready to continue the journey, Samuel walked over to Fessenden's horse. He eyed it suspiciously.

"She is a very gentle creature," John assured him.

Samuel said nothing, but he allowed the two servants to boost him onto the horse. He listened to John's instructions. He did as he was told. Then the servants rolled along to Philadelphia in the chaise, and Samuel and John rode together.

Everyone agreed that Samuel did remarkably well in the saddle. There was only one trouble. At the end of the day it was discovered that at the place where Samuel Adams and the saddle met Samuel was sore. And everyone agreed that this was no way for a future leader to feel. So at Woodstock, Connecticut, where they spent the night, John bought two yards of flannel. He found a tailor and ordered a pair of padded under-clothes, or "drawers," for Samuel.

The next morning John gave Samuel his final lesson in horseback riding. A future leader of a new nation, he explained, should not have to be hoisted and heaved into the saddle by two servants. He should be able to mount himself. John told Samuel what to do and Samuel did it.

So mounted, in his padded clothing, Samuel rode triumphantly to Philadelphia. The very picture of a noble leader.

And when independence was finally declared one hot July day ten months later, Samuel Adams was ready for history.

THINK ABOUT IT

1. How was Samuel Adams different from most other men of his time?
2. Why did Samuel Adams prefer walking to riding a horse?
3. What was England doing that so angered the American colonists? Why did the King of England decide to send soldiers to Boston?
4. What argument did John Adams use to finally convince his cousin Samuel to ride a horse?
5. Why do you think that Samuel Adams is sometimes called "the father of independence"?
6. Do you think that the American colonists were right to be angry with the King of England? If you had been living in the American colonies at this time in history, how would you have felt about the taxes? What would you have done?

ANANSE and the GLOBE of LIGHT

CHARACTERS

Ananse	Younger Daughter
Older Daughter	Younger Son
Older Son	Narrator

PROP LIST

These things may be real or imaginary.

Hand Props

*white balloon that stands
  for a crystal ball
pitcher of water
scythe made from cardboard
yellow inflated balloon
  for globe of light*

Stage Props

*stool placed at stage right
two low platforms placed
  at stage right and
  stage left that stand for
  wooded bluffs*

SOUND EFFECTS

*water splashing
rustling of leaves
  underfoot*

*popping sound
creaky hinges
drum rhythms*

(**Narrator** *enters stage right and sits down on stool.*)

Narrator: Good afternoon. Hello. Good day. You're about to see a one-act play. It's set in a jungle far away from any place where you might stray. The story will unfold for you a fact that's known to be true. So settle back and listen well to the tale that I'm about to tell. First the characters one by one. Then the tale until it's done . . . . Our story, soon to come alive, is about a family of five! (**Ananse** *enters from stage right, crosses to stage left, as the* **Narrator** *speaks, and then freezes. He walks in a stylized way that depicts a spider. Music may be played offstage to accompany the walk of each character with a different drum rhythm.*)

There is a father named Ananse, and four children. There is an older daughter. (**Older Daughter** *enters balancing a crystal ball on her fingertips. She moves stage left, looking into the ball from all possible angles. When she reaches* **Ananse,** *she freezes.*) and a younger daughter. (**Younger Daughter,** *a very muscular person, enters and strides confidently to stage left. She stops two or three times to flex her muscles for the audience.*) There is an older son (**Older Son** *enters with a scythe. He moves across the stage pretending to clear a path in front of him.*) and a younger son. (**Younger Son** *enters carrying a large pitcher filled to the brim with water. He walks carefully across the stage so as not to spill a drop. At center stage he lifts the pitcher to his lips and drinks from it. Then he joins others at stage left.*)

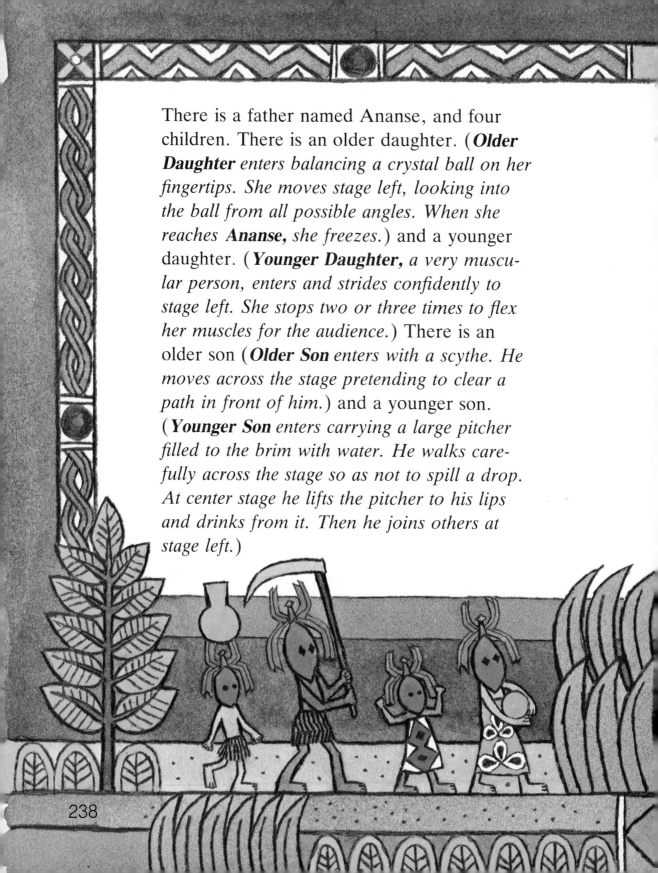

Our story begins at the beginning, of course. And the beginning begins one very dark night in a Ghanian jungle. It is so dark at night that there isn't a star in the sky to be seen. A flickering candle gives off the only light. (*Stage lights dim.*)

Ananse (*Gathers a few objects together and places them in a satchel*): Well, it's time for me to go.

Older Son (*Looks up at* **Ananse,** *surprised*): Father, it's late. Where are you going?

Ananse: I must leave to meet Sky Wonder.

Younger Daughter: Do you know where to meet him?

Ananse: No, but I know I shall find him. I always do.

Older Daughter: But why must you go at night always? It is so dark tonight and there are so many unknown paths in the jungle.

Younger Son: Yes, why must you leave before dawn?

Ananse: Sky Wonder has asked me to come *tonight,* so I must leave now. Do not worry, my children. I shall find my way, and perhaps I will be back before sunrise. Goodnight now.

(**Ananse** *kisses each child, waves and leaves the house.*)

Older Son: Goodnight, Father.

Younger Daughter: We will wait for you.

Others: Goodnight!

(**Ananse** *walks toward stage right as if picking his way through the jungle. He exits and then reappears as the* **Narrator** *begins speaking. There is a rustling of leaves underfoot.*)

Narrator: Ananse must travel far tonight, to an unknown part of the jungle. He walks and turns, turns and walks in the darkness. His journey seems to go on and on and on. Suddenly Ananse discovers that he has lost his way. And because he is lost, Ananse does not know that he is coming to a bluff.

(**Ananse** *climbs onto the platform at stage right. As if unable to see the edge, he turns and falls off.*)

Ananse (*From behind the platform*): Ah - a - a - a - a - a.

(*There is sound of water splashing.*)

Narrator: Meanwhile, Older Daughter has seen something in her crystal ball.

Older Daughter (*Looking into the crystal ball, she becomes frightened.*): Brothers! Sisters! Come quickly! Someone is in trouble. Something has happened. I see it here in the crystal.

(*Older Son, Younger Daughter, and Younger Son rush to her side.*)

Older Son: What is it? What has happened?

Younger Daughter: Tell us, quickly.

Younger Son: Yes, tell us. Who is in trouble?

Older Daughter: Be patient. I'm beginning to see a face. (*She gasps and holds her chest, then she slumps over dramatically.*) It's Father!

Older Son: What? Father?

Older Daughter (*Weeping*): Yes. He lost his way in the jungle and fell over a bluff. Now he's in a lake somewhere!

Younger Son: A lake?

Younger Daughter: But where? Which lake? There are hundreds of ponds in the jungle.

Older Daughter: I don't know. All I see is a lake somewhere, somewhere in all the jungle.

Younger Son: We've got to do something! But what?

Younger Daughter: But how?

Older Son: We'll find him. Come on, follow me!

(*All follow **Older Son** out of the house, whispering worriedly among themselves. Outside, **Older Son** stands frozen to the ground. He concentrates listening to the sounds of the jungle.*)

Older Son: Shhhhhhhhhh! You three. Let me hear the night. Then I will know where our father is. (*He finally points.*) This way. Hurry! We must travel a straight line to the bluff. It will be fastest if we cut our own path through the jungle.

(**Older Son** *pretends to clear a path with his scythe. There is the sound of rustling leaves underfoot. The others grunt and groan as they help him.* **All** *exit at stage left. They enter again and work their way across the stage, climbing the platform at stage right.*)

Narrator: And so, with the help of his brother and sisters, Older Son cuts a trail through the dense jungle. He finds his way directly to the bluff from which Ananse fell.

(**All** *stand in a line looking over the edge of the platform.*)

Older Son (*Proudly*): Well, there's the lake.

Younger Son (*Paying no attention to the others, he steps off the bluff and out of sight. The others are looking intently toward the lake and do not notice that he is gone.*): The water is so clear and clean that it makes me thirsty. Yes, I am very thirsty.

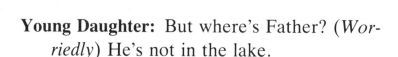

Young Daughter: But where's Father? (*Worriedly*) He's not in the lake.

Older Son: Impossible. Of course, he's in the lake. You just don't see him.

Older Daughter: But can't you see that he's not there? This must be the wrong lake.

Older Son (*Insulted*): Impossible!

Younger Daughter (*She sees **Younger Son** near the water and calls out.*): Brother, what are you doing? Come back here. This is no time to quench your thirst. Stop this minute. You're drinking up the whole lake. It's disappearing right before our eyes!

Older Daughter: Sister, hush. Let him drink. (*Pointing*) Look! Look where I am pointing. As the water goes down I see a fish.

Older Son: Yes, an enormous fish . . . *with our father inside it*! (*Pointing excitedly*) There, between the gills, I see his satchel. He's been eaten by the fish!

Older Daughter: It's too late. We're too late to save him.

Younger Daughter: Oh, no we're not. (*She leaps off the platform and runs offstage. The others look after her.*)

Older Daughter: Where's she going?

Older Son: To the fish, of course. She will find a way to persuade our fish to seek another dinner. Don't underestimate the strength of our younger sister. (*There are grunts and groans of hard work offstage.*)

Younger Daughter (*Offstage*): Open up, you fish. I know you've swallowed my father. Let him out from inside you and I'll let you go.

Younger Son (*Offstage*): Hurry, sister. Pull harder on the fish's jaws. We must get to Father.

(*There is the creaking sound of poorly oiled hinges offstage.*)

Younger Daughter: There you go, fish. Open up, just a little wider.

(*There is a loud pop offstage.*)

Younger Daughter *and* **Younger Son:** Father!
Ananse: Daughter! Son!

245

(**Older Daughter** and **Older Son** cheer and hug on the platform. They watch excitedly as **Ananse** walks on stage, arm in arm with **Younger Daughter** and **Younger Son.** They rush to greet him.)

Ananse (Hugging them all at once): Children! Oh, wonderful children. I truly thought I would not see you again, ever. Oh, children, my children. Come. Let us go home now, together arm in arm, hand in hand on this darkest of all nights.

(**Ananse** and **Children** walk happily around the stage one and a half times as **Narrator** speaks.)

Narrator: And so Ananse and his children begin their journey home. Rejoicing in their togetherness, they walk quickly. The distance of their journey seems short, and soon they are within sight of their home. But something catches Ananse's eye. He stops to look.

Ananse (*Turning to look offstage*): What . . . what is this that I see behind the great fern? A light? A glowing ball? Let me look more closely. Children, wait here while I see what this strange thing is, so close to our home. (*He walks offstage and returns with a lighted globe. He speaks to the globe with respect and reverence.*) Oh, beautiful, mysterious globe of light. You are a most treasured prize to illuminate the night. What shall I do with you? How can I honor you? (*He thinks for a moment.*) I know. I shall give you to one of my children. Yes. To the child that saved me. (*He scratches his head questioningly.*) But who? Which child deserves such a prize?

(*All* but **Ananse** *leave the stage quietly.* **Ananse** *paces back and forth, holding the globe carefully, muttering to himself. Then he stops and smiles as if he has come to a decision.*)

Of course! Why didn't I realize it before? It is my younger daughter who shall receive the prize. For it was she who opened the fish's mouth. Without her help, I would still be inside the creature. (*Confidently*) Yes! I shall give this enchanted globe to my younger daughter.

(**Ananse** *begins to walk briskly toward the house and then stops short and turns around slowly.*)

But . . . how did she know that I was inside the fish? It must have been my younger son and his unquenchable thirst. He drank the water in the lake so that she could find me and the fish. Then it is he, of course, who deserves the light. For without the help of my younger son, I would still be inside the creature. But without the help of my older son and his scythe, no one would have found the lake. And without my older daughter and her crystal ball, no one would have known that I was in trouble! Oh me.

(**Ananse,** *visibly upset, puts down the globe. He holds his chin in his hand and begins to rock back and forth.*)

What *am* I to do? Oh, what should I do? It's all so complicated, much too complicated for a simple soul like myself. (*Looks up, calls*) Sky Wonder, Sky Wonder, will you help me? You have seen how I lost my way in search of you on this dark night. Will you come to meet me now? Will you take this prize and hold it until I can decide what to do?

(*There is the rhythmic sound of a powerful drum.* **Ananse** *shakes his head as if in response to the drums.*)

Yes. Yes. Of course, Sky Wonder. (*He climbs up the platform at stage right and throws the ball up and offstage.*) Yes, take it, Sky Wonder. Take it. (**Ananse** *climbs down and walks offstage muttering and holding head.*) This has been too long a night for me. Too long. Too long.

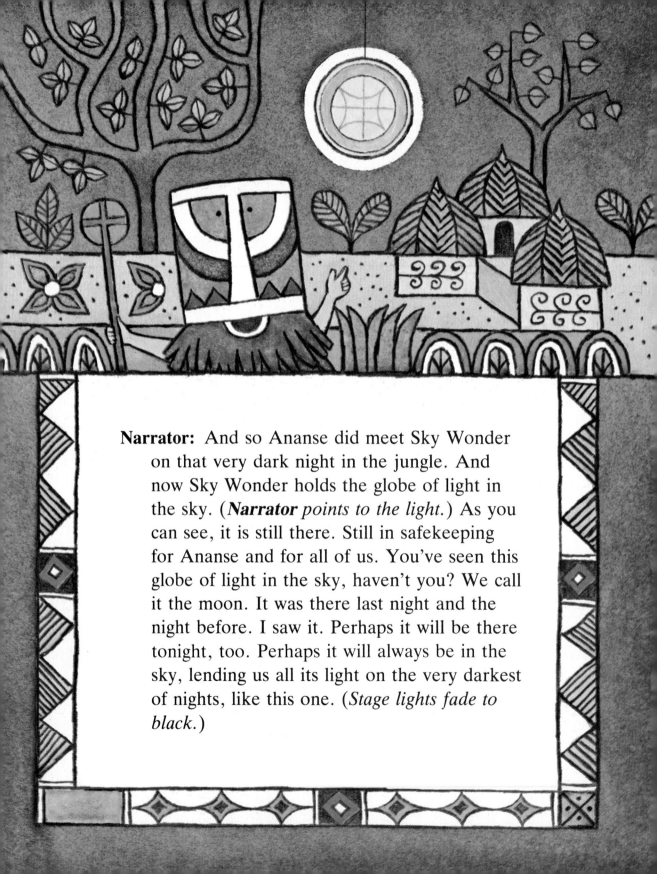

Narrator: And so Ananse did meet Sky Wonder on that very dark night in the jungle. And now Sky Wonder holds the globe of light in the sky. (*Narrator points to the light.*) As you can see, it is still there. Still in safekeeping for Ananse and for all of us. You've seen this globe of light in the sky, haven't you? We call it the moon. It was there last night and the night before. I saw it. Perhaps it will be there tonight, too. Perhaps it will always be in the sky, lending us all its light on the very darkest of nights, like this one. (*Stage lights fade to black.*)

1. What is the setting of this play? How do you know? Who are the characters?

2. Whom was Ananse going to meet?

3. How did each of Ananse's children help to save his life?

4. Why couldn't Ananse decide which of his children deserved the globe of light? According to the story, who now holds the globe of light?

5. What is the globe of light?

6. This play is adapted from an old African folk tale. What purpose did folk tales serve long ago? Why do you think people still like to tell folk tales?

7. Do you know of any tales similar to "Ananse and the Globe of Light"? What do these other folk tales attempt to explain?

8. Have you ever read any other stories about Ananse the spider? Where might you find such stories?

YOU'RE ON STAGE!

When you watch a play on television or on stage, other people perform for you. However, when you read a play, *you* must do all the work. You have to play all the parts. You also have to picture all the scenery in your mind. When you read a play, it's almost as if you are on stage. You become the actor, the director, and the set designer. Although reading a play is harder than just watching one, plays do have clues that help the reader.

Here is the first scene in the first act of a play. Read it and look for type clues that help your reading.

SETTING: *The planet Zig near Star X317. Gray hills are in the distance and gray rocks are all around. A black sun shines in the sky.* **Zog** *and* **Wag** *enter from left. They are dressed in gray.*

Zog: Isn't this where we're supposed to look?
Wag: This is where our lookout saw a giant
 bubble. *(There is a loud noise offstage.)*

Zog and **Wag** (*Grabbing each other*): What's that?

(**Balthar,** *a being from another planet, enters from right. He is dressed in bright colors.*)

Wag (*Turning to go*): Let's get out of here! Run!

Balthar: Don't go. (*He moves closer.*) I come in peace to bring color and fun to Zig.

Zog: Color. Phooey! Who needs it? You're under arrest.

Now answer these questions about the play:

1. Where does this scene take place? How did you find out?
2. The play tells you something about how the characters move around so you can picture the action. What kind of type is this information printed in?
3. Is Balthar on stage when Zog and Wag appear? What tells you this?
4. How do you imagine the scenery and costumes for this play?

253

Arthur the Author

Arthur Wright had a most serious problem. He was twelve years old and hadn't written his first book . . . yet. When Arthur became eleven he said that he would write a book by the time he became twelve. "After all," Arthur told himself, "I want to become an author, so why wait?"

But then there was that problem of getting started! The start was causing Arthur the most trouble. He had a million story ideas, but not one beginning.

"All the beginnings have been written," Arthur thought as he tried to write a beginning to one of his stories. It was a story about a moth who had guilty feelings about eating people's wool clothes. It tried to become a silk worm so it could mend its ways.

This is how Arthur's story looked as he tried to get it started:

Once upon a time there was a moth
There was once a moth
Once there was this moth see
In the olden days there was a moth

"Every beginning is like every other beginning," Arthur said unhappily. "Every story sounds the same." Arthur was definitely troubled.

Mr. Wright, Arthur's father, was a verse writer for the largest greeting card company in the world. He thought there was nothing wrong in starting every verse with "Roses are red, violets are blue . . ." so long as the rest of the poem rhymed and made people feel good.

"Why don't you study how other writers start their stories?" Mr. Wright asked Arthur, reaching for his rhyming dictionary. "Why don't you read something like *Grimm's Fairy Tales*?"

"A lot of good that will do," Arthur said. "I've looked through that book. All the stories begin the same way. Like: There was once upon a time a forester. . .there was once upon a time a soldier. . . there was once a cat. . .there was once upon a time a poor peasant. . .once upon a time there was a funny mouse. . .a frightened deer. . .a sick king. . . a happy princess. You know, Dad, ONCE UPON A TIME THERE WAS A STUCK WRITER AND HIS NAME WAS ARTHUR!"

Mr. Wright could not understand Arthur's problem. Neither could his English teacher, who was no help whatsoever. "Practice, practice, practice. You're a bright boy and it'll come to you yet," she would say.

His reading and writing teacher was no help either. "I agree with your father. Once upon a time is as good a way as any to start a story," he always said.

Nobody could help. Nobody really understood. "Once upon a time doesn't mean anything to me," Arthur said to himself. "If people are going to be writers, they must do it right. They can't imitate anybody else."

Then Arthur got his Great Idea!

If his father couldn't help, maybe talking to other writers would! They might understand and get him started. And what better place to talk to a lot of understanding writers than at a newspaper office? Newspapers are filled with writers! Society writers. Sports writers. News writers. Financial writers. Travel writers.

"And," Arthur thought, "they don't say once upon a time when they write their stories."

Arthur told his father about his idea. He asked Mr. Wright to take him to their local newspaper, the *Tribune-Journal-Globe-Post-Independent-Times.*

"Newspapers are read, violets are blue, we'll get some help, just for you," Mr. Wright answered.

The next afternoon Arthur and his father got off the elevator at the second floor of the *Tribune-Journal-Globe-Post-Independent-Times.* They saw a door with this sign: EDITOR. Mr. Wright talked with a secretary who sat in front of the door. Then she opened the door and disappeared into the office.

Soon a red-faced woman with a yellow pencil behind each ear opened the door. She walked toward Arthur.

"My secretary says you have a writing problem, young man. I'm the EDITOR," she said. "Tell me what it is. Be quick. State it. Who? What? Why?"

Arthur was startled by her fast way of talking.

"I want to be a writer, but I don't want to start my stories the way every other writer does. You know, like once upon a time," Arthur answered.

"Excellent idea. How can I help? Newspapers are for helping."

"Can you tell me how to start my story?"

"How's this?" she exploded. "Extra! Extra! Read all about it! Boy writes story!"

"It's a little loud," Arthur said.

"Doesn't have a classic sound," Mr. Wright said.

"But it will sell and that's what writing is all about. Get their attention. Then they'll read," the EDITOR said.

Arthur felt confused. "But one of my stories is about a moth. I can't say: Extra! Extra! Read all about it! Moth bites coat! That won't do at all. It just doesn't sound right. And if it doesn't sound right, I won't write it."

"Humpfffff," the EDITOR said, "we'll solve this problem yet. I'll call a conference."

In a few moments the EDITOR's office was filled with people whose ears balanced yellow pencils.

"This is Arthur," the EDITOR told the writers. "He has a problem. A writing problem. He needs help getting a start for his story about a moth. Once upon a time isn't what he wants. It's old-fashioned. You people are experienced writers. I want help for Arthur."

The room became quiet as each writer thought about Arthur's problem.

"I have it," the sports writer yelled, jumping up from his chair.

"Let's hear it," the EDITOR said.

"On your book marks, get set, go!" the sports writer said. "How's about that for an original beginning?"

They all turned toward Arthur. But Arthur shook his head.

"Wrong mood," he said.

"Then try this," the financial writer said soberly. "The New York stock market opened strong today, and so does our story."

The room became quiet as the writers turned toward Arthur.

"Nope," Arthur said. "What's a moth got to do with the stock market?"

"Then try this," a reporter yelled. "Who did what, when, where, why, and how?"

"Too questionable," Arthur said.

"I think I have the solution," the gossip columnist whispered. "Start it this way: What well-known moth about town was seen in a strange closet last night?"

"Not bad," Arthur said. "But it doesn't sound at all like me."

All of the writers sighed and returned to thinking hard about the problem.

"Say, Arthur," Arthur's father said. "Why not try this: Roses are red, violets are blue, once upon a time isn't for you!" Arthur just shook his head.

"That gives me an idea," the EDITOR said. "This has got to be it, Arthur. Let's pull all of our ideas together. Your story will start like this:

"Extra! Extra! On your bookmarks, the story begins with who did what to whom when and how as you picture this well-known moth sneaking into a strange closet."

"That's too confusing," Arthur said. "Maybe we'd better go home, Dad. Maybe I shouldn't become a writer after all."

And they left the room with the EDITOR and her writers still thinking about how they could help.

That night Arthur lay in his bed thinking about his problem and how the writers at the newspaper had tried to help him. He thought, too, about the old fairy tale writers and how they always started with once upon a time. It seemed that every writer who ever wrote had a special way of starting a story.

Except Arthur.

Then he thought about how *his* story-starting problem had *started* so many other things happening that day. And then the idea came. Arthur found his start in his problem.

He turned on the light next to his bed. Then he wrote the following in pencil on the pad of paper on the night table:

Montgomery Moth had
a most serious problem...

Arthur studied the sentence. His problem had
become his beginning. Then Arthur knew that
finally he had found a start. Tomorrow he would
finish writing his story.

1. What idea was Arthur trying to develop into a story? What was Arthur's writing problem?

2. How did Arthur's father suggest he solve the problem?

3. With whom did Arthur finally decide to discuss his problem? Why?

4. How did each of the newspaper editors suggest that Arthur start his story? Why did Arthur reject their ideas?

5. How did Arthur solve his problem?

6. Do you think that the beginning Arthur chose was a good one? Why or why not?

7. Do you think the author's purpose in writing this story was only to entertain his readers, or do you think he had another purpose in mind? If so, what do you think it was?

8. Have you ever had a problem like Arthur's? How did you solve your problem?

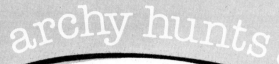

hi
i am a pet cockroach named archy
i like to type letters to my boss
you may wonder how a cockroach can type
well i jump up and down on the keys
thats how
you can see that i dont use any capital
letters or punctuation marks
can you guess why
here is something i wrote for my boss

well boss i went up
to the circus
the other day
and tried to hire
out what do you
want they asked me a
job as an animal
or a job as an artist

265

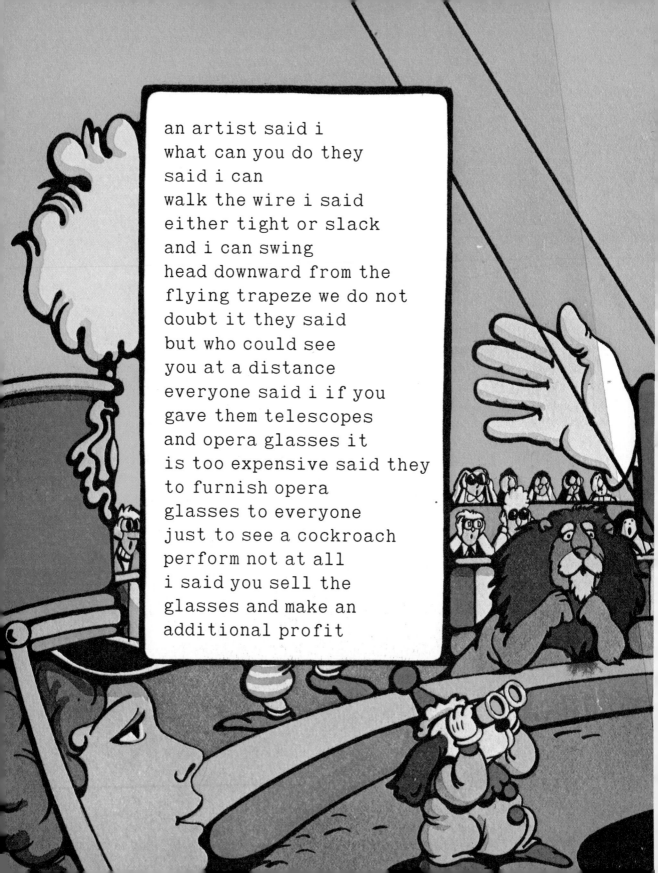

you go out and hire
yourself out to a
trained flea outfit
said they we cannot use
you i consider it
an insult i replied to
be classed with
fleas you should consider
it a compliment said they
another word from you
i said and i
will die in a barrel
of your lemonade and
queer your show
and with this threat
the interview closed
                    archy

Don Marquis

267

The Flowering Peach Tree

The old monk leaned on his rake and looked proudly around the temple garden. Never had it looked more beautiful. Every flower bed was a mass of bloom. Every blossom was perfect. Not a weed, not a beetle, spoiled the picture. Even the gravel in the path had been raked into patterns of long, sweeping curves.

The old monk picked up a twig that had just fallen. He thought what a perfect day it was for the Flower Festival. Soon all the villagers and strangers from far away would be strolling through this garden. They would enjoy its beauty and reflect on

the wonders of nature. Tu Thuc,[1] the mandarin's son, would also be in the garden soon. But now he was in the temple attending the early morning service.

From the pagoda came the chanting of the monks and the smell of sweet incense. Soon the big bronze bell would sound and the morning service would be over. The old monk gave one last sweep with his rake. He picked up one blossom that had fallen from the flowering peach tree. Then he hurried away to his cottage behind the garden wall.

[1]**Tu Thuc** (tü′tük′)

As the bells rang out, the doors of the pagoda were thrown open. The villagers came down the steps and into the garden. First came Tu Thuc, the mandarin's son. Tu Thuc looked handsome in a scarlet silk coat heavy with gold embroidery. His face beamed with pleasure and his eyes sparkled with anticipation. He loved all growing things. He often neglected his duties at court to roam the fields and watch the harvest. Here, in the temple garden, he could feast his eyes on beauty. His great pleasure could be seen in the way he lingered over each beautiful blossom.

Following him came the villagers, dressed in their best. This was a day they loved. In all the province of Tien Du[2] there was no garden equal to this one. Today the villagers could wander through the garden for as long as they wished.

Unnoticed by the villagers, a beautiful girl in a strange robe stood on the steps of the pagoda. She looked amazed by the masses of flowers. Slowly she walked to the first flower bed and gently touched a blossom. She stared curiously at every petal and leaf and leaned over to catch the fragrance. She acted as if she never before had seen a flower. The young girl walked excitedly up one path and down another until she came to the flowering peach tree. Suddenly, she broke off

[2]**Tien Du** (tē en'dü)

a small branch and started to run out of the garden.

At that moment the old monk returned and, seeing what she had done, called out, "Stop her! Stop her! She has broken a branch of the flowering peach tree!"

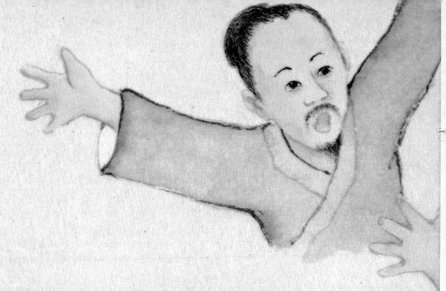

The villagers were stunned. How could anyone destroy a single flower in this beautiful garden? Who would dare to break off a branch from the flowering peach tree? Quickly they surrounded the strange girl until the monk could reach her.

At the far end of the garden, Tu Thuc heard the angry cries and hurried to the pagoda to see what was the matter. He arrived in time to see the old monk lead the girl up the steps of the pagoda and through the open doors. Tu Thuc followed them. Once inside the temple, he watched quietly as she was questioned by the monks. He wondered where she was from.

The young girl was certainly not from his father's court, nor from the villages nearby. She was not wearing the wide pants and long overdress of Tien Du. Instead she wore a long blue robe covered with a design of white clouds. She was dressed as a lady of quality. However, when the monks demanded payment for the broken branch, she claimed she had no money at all.

Far from being proud or angry, she seemed
completely confused. When Tu Thuc saw the troubled look in her black eyes and the droop in her
slender shoulders, he pitied her. He offered to give
his own mandarin's coat to the monks if they
would let the girl go free.

This they agreed to do and immediately helped
him off with his splendid coat. Then he turned to
speak to the girl and was amazed to find she had
disappeared. No one in the temple or the garden
had seen her leave. Tu Thuc ran out to the busy
street, but still there was no sign of her.

For days the villagers talked of nothing but the stranger who had broken the branch from the peach tree and had then disappeared. Where had she come from? Why had she done it? Where had she gone?

At the court of the mandarin, Tu Thuc found his thoughts continually straying to the beautiful girl in the strange blue robe. Each time he opened a book her sad, bewildered eyes stared back at him. Each time he went to the village he hoped to see her in the crowds.

At last he decided to leave his father's court and spend all his time looking for her. He gave up his title, packed a few things to take, and set out on his journey.

For months, Tu Thuc walked from village to village, hoping to find the girl. But no one had seen her.

Finally, at the end of a particularly hot, dusty trip, he came to the seaside town of Than Phu.[3] The road ran past a cove where emerald green waves washed up on a sandy beach. The water looked cool and inviting, so Tu Thuc decided to refresh himself with a swim. He plunged in, swimming vigorously for awhile. Then he rolled over on his back to float lazily in the cool water.

[3]**Than Phu** (tän′fü′)

Overhead, white birds circled against the deep blue sky. Billowy white clouds drifted by. Far out to sea, the waves broke in a tumble of froth and foam on a reef. On one side of the cove, tall cliffs rose high above the sea. Tu Thuc scanned them carefully, looking for birds' nests. As he did so, he noticed high on one ledge the opening to a cave.

Being a curious person, Tu Thuc swam to shore and started to climb the steep cliff. When he finally reached the ledge, he found the cave opening was big enough to walk into.

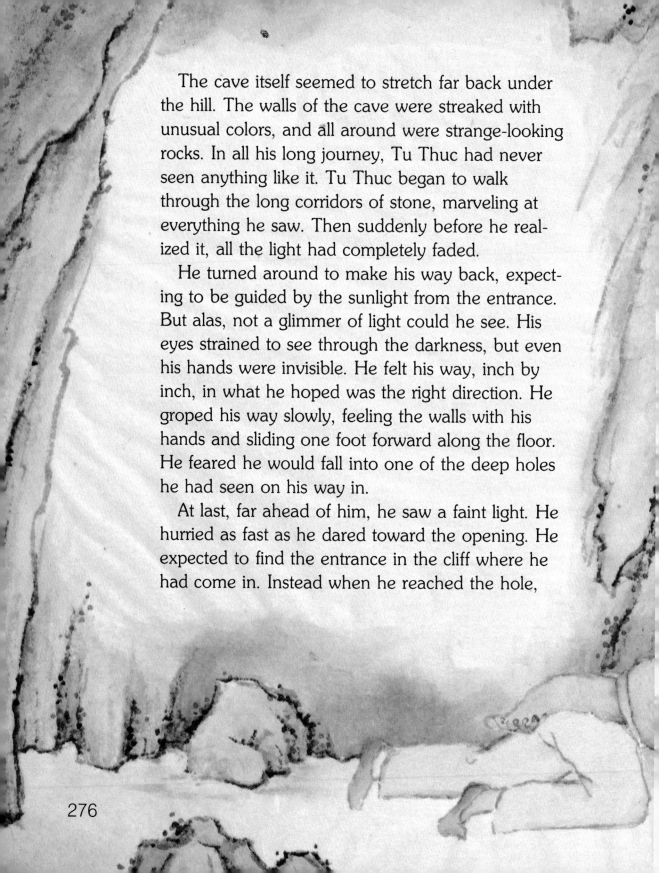

The cave itself seemed to stretch far back under the hill. The walls of the cave were streaked with unusual colors, and all around were strange-looking rocks. In all his long journey, Tu Thuc had never seen anything like it. Tu Thuc began to walk through the long corridors of stone, marveling at everything he saw. Then suddenly before he realized it, all the light had completely faded.

He turned around to make his way back, expecting to be guided by the sunlight from the entrance. But alas, not a glimmer of light could he see. His eyes strained to see through the darkness, but even his hands were invisible. He felt his way, inch by inch, in what he hoped was the right direction. He groped his way slowly, feeling the walls with his hands and sliding one foot forward along the floor. He feared he would fall into one of the deep holes he had seen on his way in.

At last, far ahead of him, he saw a faint light. He hurried as fast as he dared toward the opening. He expected to find the entrance in the cliff where he had come in. Instead when he reached the hole,

he found it was just barely big enough to crawl through. And outside, rather than looking down on the green waters of the cove, he saw nothing but a mass of clouds. As far as he could see, the clouds stretched like a snowy countryside of rolling hills and valleys. Here and there, he saw a high billowy tower.

A strange light tinted the clouds rose and gold and shaded the valleys with purple. In the middle of the field of clouds rose the highest mountain Tu Thuc had ever seen. Its steep sides looked purple in the strange light. Beautiful castles stood on the lower peaks. The castles were pale green or white and gleamed softly, like precious jade.

Tu Thuc was speechless with wonder. He could do nothing but stare at the scene before him. Then he heard two soft voices. Turning his head, he saw two girls walking toward him across the white clouds.

When they got near him, they bowed and said, "We are sorry that we are late. The Lady is waiting for you. Please come with us." Taking him by the hand, they led him across the clouds toward one of the jade castles.

At first he stumbled and staggered as he tried to walk on the soft clouds. Soon he felt lighter and found that his footsteps were getting longer, as though he were almost flying. In no time at all they reached the castle. The two young girls led him into a large room whose walls of jade were carved with designs of flowers and birds. At one end of the room was a raised platform and on it there was a couch made of mother-of-pearl. Reclining on the couch was a beautiful woman.

Motioning for him to sit on a silvery cushion near her couch, the woman spoke. "Tu Thuc, you have been traveling for many months. Do you know where you are?"

Tu Thuc shook his head. "No, I do not," he said. "I have seen many strange places, but never have I seen so beautiful a place as this. Would you mind telling me where this is?"

"It is not surprising that you don't know where you are," said the woman, smiling at him. "You have come through one of the thirty-six caves in the mountain called Phu-Lai.[4] You have walked across the Path of the Clouds to the mountain you are now on, Mount Nam-Nhu.[5] Far beneath you, under clouds, lies the ocean. The foothills of our mountain float over the sea. I am the Lady of Mount Nam-Nhu."

[4]**Phu-Lai** (fü′lī)   [5]**Nam-Nhu** (näm′nü)

Then the lady motioned for the two girls to open a hidden door in the jade walls. Out stepped a beautiful young girl with downcast eyes. Shyly she came forward and stood before the platform. One look at her face told Tu Thuc that she was the girl for whom he had been searching. He started to speak to her, but the Lady of Mount Nam-Nhu motioned him to be silent.

"This is my daughter, Giang Huong,"[6] said the lady. "She once broke a branch of a flowering peach tree in the garden on the pagoda at Tien Du. Here we do not have flowering peach trees. Giang Huong wished us to see the beautiful blossoms. She meant no harm, but she should not have touched them. It was no wonder the monks were angry. I have not forgotten how you saved her. In return, I would like to invite you to be our guest and live here at the castle as long as you wish."

[6]**Giang Huong** (zhong'hüng')

"I accept, happily," said Tu Thuc, "if only Giang Huong will consent to be my bride."

"Yes, that is my wish as well," said Giang Huong softly.

The marriage was celebrated that very day. Everyone came to wish the young couple well. The Lady of Mount Nam-Nhu rejoiced in her daughter's happiness.

Time passed pleasantly for Tu Thuc. With his beloved bride at his side, he explored every ridge and valley of Phu-Lai. Each day brought new pleasure. Life for Tu Thuc would have continued as an endless delight if he had not once caught sight of the ocean. Through a break in the clouds, he had seen the dark blue of the deep water.

From then on, Tu Thuc longed to return to his own land. He remembered the sights and sounds on his family farm and the smells of the village market place. He remembered how grieved his parents had been when he gave up his title and left his home. The more Tu Thuc thought about these things the more he wished to see his own land and people once more. He could not stop thinking about home and became silent and withdrawn.

When Giang Huong discovered his sadness, she said, "For a year we have lived happily together. I cannot believe that you are still thinking of your own world. Why would you want to return to Earth where life is so short? However, you must do as

you wish. Only remember that we may never see each other again if you go."

Much as he loved Giang Huong, the desire to see his parents and his own country grew stronger and stronger. Sadly, he told Giang Huong that he wished to leave.

Tu Thuc was led back to the cave where his adventures had started a year before. He went down to the little cove and the beach. The shrubs

and trees seemed so much taller than he remembered them. He wondered if it was really the same cove.

It took him some time to make his way back to his own village. Many new roads had been built, and he had to stop frequently to ask his way. Even the farms had changed, with new buildings and new dikes around the rice fields. The small marketplace in the village was now three times its size. Busy streets led from it in all directions. The pagoda with its gardens was completely surrounded with buildings. There was nothing left of the flowering peach tree except a gnarled stump.

Try as he might, Tu Thuc could not even find his own home. When he asked the way, people shook their heads and hurried on. Some even looked at him as if he were mad.

Finally an old gray-bearded man tapped him on the shoulder and said, "When I was a child my grandfather told me about a mandarin's son with the same name as yours. He left home years and years ago and met with a great misfortune. He was buried in a cave in the cliffs of Than Phu."

With this, Tu Thuc realized that a year on Mount Nam-Nhu was equal to one hundred years on earth. He also knew his long journey back was fruitless. He thought longingly of his beautiful wife. With an aching heart, he started back on the road to Than Phu.

A fisherman claims he saw Tu Thuc climb up the face of the cliff and walk through the entrance of the cave. He says that he then heard the sound of soft voices as Tu Thuc disappeared from sight. And from that day on no one ever saw him again. Some think someone was waiting to guide him through the cave so that he could return to Giang Huong and be with her forever.

THINK ABOUT IT

1. What was the Flower Festival? Why was the temple garden such a special place?

2. What did the strange young girl do to anger the monks?

3. Why did Tu Thuc take pity on the girl? What did he do to assure her freedom?

4. How did Tu Thuc go about finding the girl once again?

5. Why did Tu Thuc return to his homeland? What did he discover upon his return?

6. Do you think that Tu Thuc could have found happiness if he had remained on Mount Nam-Nhu and not sought his own home?

7. Tell about a time when you had to choose between two things you wanted very much. How did you feel? What choice did you make? Do you think it was a wise choice?

five

Except for a pack of wild dogs, twelve-year-old Karana[1] is completely alone on the Island of the Blue Dolphins.

At one time Karana, her family, and her whole village lived on the island. But many months ago, following the advice of their chiefs Kimki[2] and Matasaip,[3] the villagers sailed on a great ship in search of a better homeland. Karana boarded the ship along with all the rest of her people. But she jumped and swam ashore when she discovered that her younger brother had been left behind mistakenly.

Soon after Karana and her brother watched the ship sail out of sight, the wild dogs took his life. Karana has been alone since then. As this chapter of *Island of the Blue Dolphins* begins, Karana tells of her attempt to leave the deserted island.

Island of the Blue Dolphins

Summer is the best time on the Island of the Blue Dolphins. The sun is warm then and the winds blow milder out of the west, sometimes out of the south.

It was during these days that the ship might return and now I spent most of my time on the rock, looking out from the high headland into the east, toward the country where my people had gone, across the sea that was never-ending.

[1]**Karana** (kä rä′nä)   [2]**Kimki** (kim′kē)   [3]**Matasaip** (mä tä sep′)

Once while I watched I saw a small object which I took to be the ship, but a stream of water rose from it and I knew that it was a whale spouting. During those summer days I saw nothing else.

The first storm of winter ended my hopes. If the white men's ship were coming for me it would have come during the time of good weather. Now I would have to wait until winter was gone, maybe longer.

The thought of being alone on the island while so many suns rose from the sea and went slowly back into the sea filled my heart with loneliness. I had not felt so lonely before because I was sure that the ship would return as Matasaip had said it would. Now my hopes were dead. Now I was really alone. I could not eat much, nor could I sleep without dreaming terrible dreams.

The storm blew out of the north, sending big waves against the island and winds so strong that I was unable to stay on the rock. I moved my bed to the foot of the rock and for protection I kept a fire going throughout the night. I slept there five times. The first night the dogs came and stood outside the ring made by the fire. I killed three of them with arrows, but not the leader, and they did not come again.

On the sixth day, when the storm ended, I went to the place where the canoes had been hidden and let myself down over the cliff. This part of the shore was sheltered from the wind and I found the canoes just as they had been left. The dried food was still good, but the water was stale, so I went back to the spring and filled a fresh basket.

I had decided during the days of the storm, when I had given up hope of seeing the ship, that I would take one of the canoes and go to the country that lay toward the east. I remembered how Kimki, before he had gone, had asked the advice of his ancestors who had lived many ages in the past and who had come to the island from that country. Likewise, he had asked the advice of Zuma, the medicine man who held power over the wind and the seas. But these things I could not do, for Zuma had been killed by the Aleuts, and in all my life I had never been able to speak with the dead, though many times I tried.

Yet I cannot say that I was really afraid as I stood there on the shore. I knew that my ancestors had crossed the sea in their canoes, coming from that place which lay beyond. Kimki, too had crossed the sea. I was not nearly so skilled with a canoe as these men, but I must say that whatever might befall me on the endless waters did not trouble me. It meant far less than the thought of staying on the island alone, without a home or

companions, pursued by wild dogs, where everything reminded me of those who were dead and
those who had gone away.

Of the four canoes stored there against the cliff,
I chose the smallest, which was still very heavy
because it could carry six people. The task that
faced me was to push it down the rocky shore and
into the water, a distance four or five times its
length.

This I did by first removing all the large rocks
in front of the canoe. I then filled in all these
holes with pebbles and along this path laid down
long strips of kelp, making a slippery bed. The
shore was steep and once I got the canoe to move
with its own weight, it slid down the path and into
the water.

The sun was in the west when I left the shore.
The sea was calm behind the high cliffs. Using
the two-bladed paddle, I quickly skirted the south
part of the island. As I reached the sandspit, the
wind struck. I was paddling from the back of the
canoe because you can go faster there, but I could
not handle it in the wind.

Kneeling in the middle of the canoe, I paddled
hard and did not pause until I had gone through
the tides that run fast around the sandspit. There
were many small waves and I was soon wet, but
as I came out from behind the spit the spray
lessened and the waves grew long and rolling.

Though it would have been easier to go the way they slanted, this would have taken me in the wrong direction. I therefore kept them on my left hand, as well as the island, which grew smaller and smaller, behind me.

At dusk I looked back. The Island of the Blue Dolphins had disappeared. This was the first time that I felt afraid.

There were only hills and valleys of water around me now. When I was in a valley I could see nothing and when the canoe rose up out of it, only the ocean stretching away and away.

Night fell and I drank from the basket. The water cooled my throat.

The sea was black and there was no difference between it and the sky. The waves made no sound among themselves, only faint noises as they went under the canoe or struck against it. Sometimes the noises seemed angry and at other times like people laughing. I was not hungry because of my fear.

The first star made me feel less afraid. It came out low in the sky and it was in front of me, toward the east. Other stars began to appear all around, but it was this one I kept my gaze upon. It was in the figure that we call a serpent, a star which shone green and which I knew. Now and then it was hidden by mist, yet it always came out brightly again.

Without this star I would have been lost, for the waves never changed. They came always from the same direction and in a manner that kept pushing me away from the place I wanted to reach. For this reason the canoe made a path in the black water like a snake. But somehow I kept moving toward the star which shone in the east.

This star rose high, and then I kept the North Star on my left hand, the one we call "the star that does not move." The wind grew quiet. Since it always died down when the night was half over, I knew how long I had been traveling and how far away the dawn was.

About this time I found that the canoe was leaking. Before dark I had emptied one of the baskets in which food was stored and used it to dip out the water that came over the sides. The water that now moved around my knees was not from the waves.

I stopped paddling and worked with the basket until the bottom of the canoe was almost dry. Then I searched around, feeling in the dark along the smooth planks, and found the place near the bow where the water was seeping through a crack as long as my hand and the width of a finger. Most of the time it was out of the sea, but it leaked whenever the canoe dipped forward in the waves.

The places between the planks were filled with black pitch which we gathered along the shore.

Lacking this, I tore a piece of fiber from my skirt and pressed it into the crack, which held back the water.

Dawn broke in a clear sky and as the sun came out of the waves I saw that it was far off on my left. During the night I had drifted south of the place I wished to go, so I now changed my direction and paddled along the path made by the rising sun.

There was no wind on this morning and the long waves went quietly under the canoe. I therefore moved faster than during the night.

I was very tired, but more hopeful than I had been since I left the island. If the good weather did not change I would cover many leagues before dark. Another night and another day might bring me within sight of the shore toward which I was going.

Not long after dawn, while I was thinking of this strange place and what it would be like, the canoe began to leak again. This crack was between the same planks, but was a larger one and close to where I was kneeling.

The fiber I tore from my skirt and pushed into the crack held back most of the water which seeped in whenever the canoe rose and fell with the waves. Yet I could see that the planks were weak from one end to the other, probably from the canoe being stored so long in the sun, and that they might open along their whole length if the waves grew rougher.

It was suddenly clear to me that it was dangerous to go on. The voyage would take two more days, perhaps longer. By turning back to the island I would not have nearly so far to travel.

Still I could not make up my mind to do so. The sea was calm and I had come far. The thought of turning back after all this labor was more than I could bear. Even greater was the thought of the deserted island I would return to, of living there alone and forgotten. For how many suns and how many moons?

The canoe drifted idly on the calm sea while these thoughts went over and over in my mind, but when I saw the water seeping through the crack again, I picked up the paddle. There was no choice except to turn back toward the island.

I knew that only by the best of fortune would I ever reach it.

The wind did not blow until the sun was overhead. Before that time I covered a good distance, pausing only when it was necessary to dip water from the canoe. With the wind I went more slowly and had to stop often because of the water spilling over the sides, but the leak did not grow worse.

This was my first good fortune. The next was when a swarm of dolphins appeared. They came

swimming out of the west, but as they saw the canoe they turned around in a great circle and began to follow me. They swam up slowly and so close that I could see their eyes, which are large and the color of the ocean. Then they swam on ahead of the canoe, crossing back and forth in front of it, diving in and out, as if they were weaving a piece of cloth with their broad snouts.

Dolphins are animals of good omen. It made me happy to have them swimming around the canoe, and though my hands had begun to bleed from the chafing of the paddle, just watching them made me forget the pain. I was very lonely before they appeared, but now I felt that I had friends with me and did not feel the same.

The blue dolphins left me shortly before dusk. They left as quickly as they had come, going on into the west, but for a long time I could see the last of the sun shining on them. After night fell I could still see them in my thoughts and it was because of this that I kept on paddling when I wanted to lie down and sleep.

More than anything, it was the blue dolphins that took me back home.

Fog came with the night, yet from time to time I could see the star that stands high in the west, the red star called Magat which is part of the fig-ure that looks like a crawfish and is known by that name. The crack in the planks grew wider, so

I had to stop often to fill it with fiber and dip out the water.

The night was very long, longer than the night before. Twice I dozed kneeling there in the canoe, though I was more afraid than I had ever been. But the morning broke clear and in front of me lay the dim line of the island like a great fish sunning itself on the sea.

I reached it before the sun was high, the sandspit and its tides that bore me into the shore. My legs were stiff from kneeling and as the canoe struck the sand I fell when I rose to climb out. I crawled through the shallow water and up the beach. There I lay for a long time, hugging the sand in happiness.

I was too tired to think of the wild dogs. Soon I fell asleep.

I was awakened by the waves dragging at my feet. Night had come, but being too tired to leave the sandspit, I crawled to a higher place where I would be safe from the tide, and again went to sleep.

In the morning I found the canoe a short distance away. I took the baskets, my spear, and the bow and arrows, and turned the canoe over so that the tides could not take it out to sea. I then climbed to the headland where I had lived before.

I felt as if I had been gone a long time as I stood there looking down from the high rock. I was happy to be home. Everything that I saw— the otter playing in the kelp, the rings of foam around the rocks that guarded the harbor, the gulls flying, the tides moving past the sandspit— filled me with happiness.

I was surprised that I felt this way, for it was only a short time ago that I had stood on this same rock and felt that I could not bear to live here another day.

I looked out at the blue water stretching away and all the fear I had felt during the time of the voyage came back to me. On the morning I first sighted the island and it had seemed like a great fish sunning itself, I thought that someday I would make the canoe over and go out once more to look for the country that lay beyond the ocean. Now I knew that I would never go again.

The story of Karana is based on fact. The island's real name is San Nicolas. It is located off the California coast about eight miles southwest of Los Angeles. The year was 1835 when Karana made her first attempt to leave San Nicolas. Over the years, Karana became well-known as the Lost Woman of San Nicolas. The book *Island of the Blue Dolphins* tells the story of her island life.

THINK ABOUT IT

1. Why was Karana living all alone on the Island of the Blue Dolphins?

2. How did Karana plan to leave the island? Why didn't she feel afraid?

3. When did Karana first begin to be afraid?

4. What caused Karana to turn back to the island? How did the dolphins offer encouragement?

5. Compare Karana's feelings about the island before and after her attempt to escape. Why did she abandon all thoughts of ever leaving?

6. In what way was Karana like Sam Gribley in "My Side of the Mountain"?

7. If you had been Karana, do you think you would have made the same decision she did? Why or why not?

VISION WITHOUT SIGHT

It was dark and stormy that morning in 1871 when the schooner *Brindle* approached the French Pass off the coast of New Zealand. The ship was bound for Sydney, Australia. The schooner's captain had decided to take a short cut. He would steer his ship through, rather than around, the D'Urville Islands. The sailors knew that this route was a risky one, filled with dangerous currents and hidden rocks. But they had been willing to take the risk to save time. No one had counted on a storm at sea to double the danger.

Suddenly a dolphin was seen leaping out of the water. Some of the sailors wanted to kill it, but luckily, they were stopped. The dolphin seemed to be showing a safe route through the channel. With little besides luck to guide his ship safely to its destination, the captain decided to follow the mammal. Days later, the *Brindle* docked in Sydney, thanks to a willing captain and a lone dolphin.

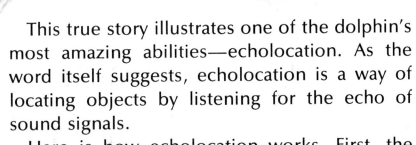

This true story illustrates one of the dolphin's most amazing abilities—echolocation. As the word itself suggests, echolocation is a way of locating objects by listening for the echo of sound signals.

Here is how echolocation works. First, the dolphin sends out a series of sound waves ahead of it. If the sound waves hit an object such as a rock or a fish, they bounce back to the dolphin. Otherwise, the sound waves keep moving through the water. When the sound waves bounce back, the dolphin hears them and knows that something is ahead. If they don't bounce back, the dolphin knows that its path is clear.

Arthur McBride was the first to recognize that dolphins use echolocation. He made his discovery in 1947 with the help of some fishing nets. McBride had been trying to capture dolphins off the coast of Florida. As curator of the nearby Marine Studio, now called Marineland, he wanted to exhibit them to the public.

McBride had already spent several days trying to lure the dolphins into his fine mesh nets. He worked during the daytime. He worked at night. He even worked in murky waters where the dolphins couldn't possibly see his nets. No matter where or when he worked and no matter how he arranged his nets, McBride couldn't catch a single dolphin. Finally he switched to nets that had wider mesh. Only then did he succeed.

Later he asked himself why one kind of net worked well, while another kind didn't work at all. Then the answer came to him. The dolphins weren't relying on their sight to avoid his nets.

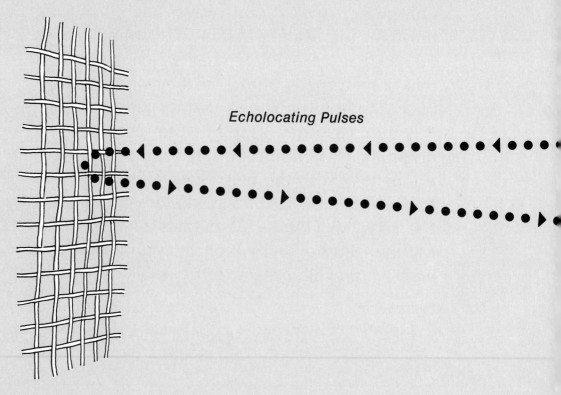

Echolocating Pulses

They were relying on *echolocation,* sonar. McBride reasoned that most sound waves would bounce back from the fine-meshed nets. These echoes would then warn the dolphins away. The wide-meshed nets would have just the opposite effect. Most sound waves would pass through the large holes in these nets. Thus the dolphins would hear few, if any, echoes, so they would not be warned away.

Since 1947, scientists have learned more about dolphins. It seems these sea mammals are always making sounds. Their sounds may be low and grating. Or they may be so high that people cannot hear them.

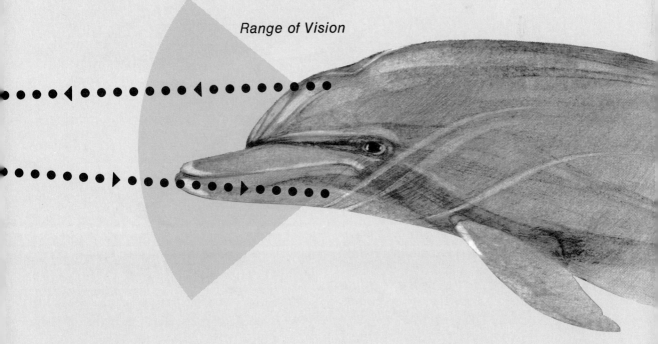

Range of Vision

Dolphins have a larynx or voice box just like other mammals. But their voice box does not contain vocal cords. Instead, it has pockets of air in it. Dolphins probably make sounds by manipulating or vibrating these air pockets.

These sounds are controlled by an organ on the dolphin's forehead. This organ is called a "melon." It works with sound in much the same way as the lens in a camera works with light. The melon focuses the sound into beams or waves. It then sends these waves out into the water in front of the animal. When the dolphin moves its head right and left or up and down, the sound

waves also move. By changing position in this way a dolphin can figure out the exact size of an object—even if the object is almost a kilometer away.

Dolphins seem to enjoy performing for the public. And they and other sea mammals do so at marine shows each year. People are continually amazed to see a dolphin recover a tiny marble from the bottom of a huge tank. People also constantly marvel at how dolphins can find their way blindfolded through a maze of upright poles. Some dolphins have even been known to rescue lost divers. A super sonar system helps them accomplish all these feats.

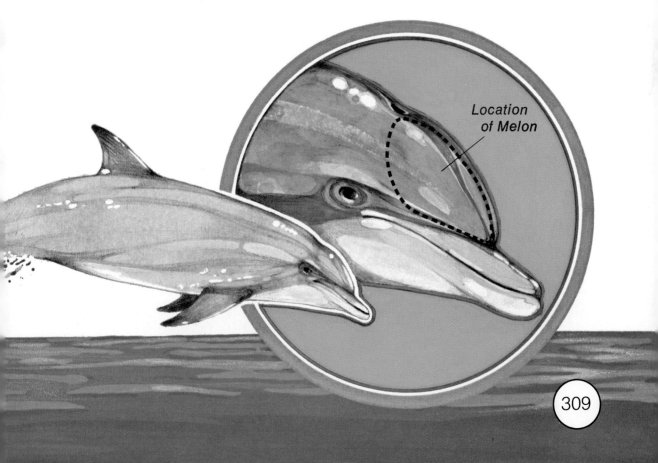

Location of Melon

Dolphins are also patient animals. This makes it easy for scientists to study them. Knowledge gained from these studies is being used in many ways. For one thing, sonar devices for sightless people are now being tested. These devices are based on echolocation. If dolphins can navigate by using sound instead of sight, researchers ask, why can't people? Instruments that give off sound waves can warn users of objects in their path. In the future these devices may be built into canes or eyeglasses.

As their research continues, the scientists who study dolphins and other sea mammals are likely to uncover more interesting facts. Perhaps some of the findings will prove helpful to people. Whatever is found, it's already clear that there is a lot more to a dolphin than meets the eye . . . or the ear.

1. What is *echolocation*? How do dolphins use echolocation?

2. How did Arthur McBride first recognize the dolphin's ability to use echolocation?

3. How is the dolphin's voice box different from that of other mammals? How do dolphins make sounds? What function does the melon serve?

4. How are scientists making use of the knowledge they have gained from their study of dolphins?

5. Think about what you have learned about dolphins from this selection. How do you think dolphins could be trained to help people?

6. Besides dolphins, do you know of any other animals that use echolocation? Where could you find such information?

Bo of the Island

Bo was a gangly young dog when the Carson family brought him along on their two-week vacation on Isle Royale.[1] Buddy Carson wouldn't hear of leaving her dog behind. So Bo traveled with the rest of the family aboard the steamer that stopped at the island.

Bo was a dog of mixed ancestry. A German shepherd ancestor had given him pointed ears, coarse hair, and a shrewd intelligence. An Alaskan malamute[2] had given him his wolfish gray-brown color and a heavy ruff of fur around his neck. And some distant trace of spaniel had given him soft, brown eyes and a heart filled with love for humans.

From the moment he bounded off the steamer, Bo loved the wilderness island. There were wonderful smells he had never smelled before— rabbit, weasel, and chipmunk. As Bo became familiar with the island, he wandered farther and farther from the camp where the Carsons were staying. When the Carsons went fishing for lake trout, Bo would see them off at the dock. When they were gone, he would set off, sniffing as he trotted along.

[1]Isle Royale (īl′ roi′əl)   [2]malamute (mal′ə myüt′)

It got to be a game with Bo to see how far he could wander and still get back before the family returned. Then Buddy would jump onto the dock and say, "Poor Bo! You've had a long wait, haven't you?" Bo would thump his tail with glee.

The last full day of the family's vacation was bright with sunshine following a night of soft rainfall. Bo sensed that this would be his last day on the island. He watched the Carsons carefully as they set out for their last day of fishing.

"Good-bye, Bo!" Buddy called, from the boat.

Bo padded along, his nose close to the damp earth. In his excitement he ran faster and faster. Before he knew it, he was on the other side of the steep hill that separated the campground from the far side of the island.

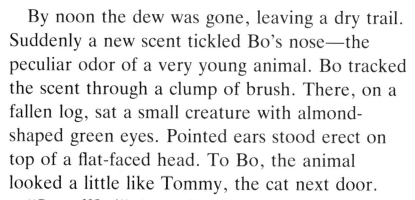

By noon the dew was gone, leaving a dry trail. Suddenly a new scent tickled Bo's nose—the peculiar odor of a very young animal. Bo tracked the scent through a clump of brush. There, on a fallen log, sat a small creature with almond-shaped green eyes. Pointed ears stood erect on top of a flat-faced head. To Bo, the animal looked a little like Tommy, the cat next door.

"Sspp-fffitt!" A small paw slapped angrily at Bo's face. Bo pulled back. In that instant the bundle of fur dropped from the log and scurried into the brush.

Bo bounded into the bushes after it and found the animal curled up against some branches. Gently Bo rolled it over with his nose. A sharp claw ripped at Bo's nose as the animal's paw lashed out in self-defense.

Then Bo heard an ear-splitting cry. "Whroow-fffitts!" The high-pitched howl ended in a spit that froze Bo in his tracks. In a flash the mother lynx was on him, her white fangs bared. The long, sharp claws ripped at Bo's throat.

Bo staggered back, and the lynx was on him again. This time her curved claws caught on his collar with its brass nameplate. Taking advantage of that split second, Bo wriggled free. Bleeding and howling with pain, he fled. Behind him, he could hear the angry screams of the mother lynx.

After a while, waves of dizziness slowed him down. He was on the home side of the hill now about a mile from the Carson camp, but he couldn't make it. Staggering, he fell into a hollow in the earth. Then darkness closed out the world around him.

The rest of that day and all through the night, Bo lay in the hollow. Toward morning he returned to consciousness, but he was still too weak to move.

Several times he could hear the Carsons calling his name. The echo of their call sounded across the island.

Later, he heard footsteps. Surely they would find him now! He tried to bark, but no sound came.

Then he heard voices coming from only a few feet away.

"We'll have to leave when the steamer comes," Mr. Carson was saying. "You know I wouldn't if I thought there was a chance—" His voice trailed off. Bo made one more attempt, but the bark choked in his throat. He went limp. The fight had gone out of him.

Much later, he heard the deep-throated blast of the steamer leaving the island—the last one of the season. Then he slept. For two days Bo slept. His wounds healed with the healing power of a young, healthy dog. Consciousness crept back in mists, bringing with it memories of when he was a puppy at his mother's soft, warm side.

He opened his eyes. Inches away, two eyes glowed like neon lights. A shadowy figure moved about. Was it his brother, Max? No. Max was lost somewhere in the dim past of his puppy days.

The shadowy figure became clearer. It was a thin and rangy animal. Strange sounds—half whine, half growl—rumbled in its throat.

It was young, like Bo. It inched forward, sniffing, until its sharp nose was buried in Bo's heavy hair. Bo lay perfectly still, not moving a muscle.

Satisfied, the young wolf sat down, and the two animals silently faced each other.

Later, the wolf got up and loped away. With the darkness it returned, carrying the half-chewed remains of a rabbit.

As Bo began to eat, he regained strength. By morning he was able to hobble along behind the wolf, who in Bo's mind had become his brother, Max. Once on the trail, Bo's instincts drew him back to the campsite and the Carsons.

As they neared the clearing, Max fell behind, while Bo walked slowly to where the tent had stood. It was gone.

Bo dropped to his stomach with a howl of grief. Then Max crept forward and nudged him back toward the forest.

The sun was setting when they came to a cave-like undercut in the rocks. Max stopped. Before the entrance to the den sat a gray wolf.

The older wolf got to its feet and growled angrily at the young pup who had dared to bring a stranger to their den. Bo hung back.

The young wolf had a mind of its own. In the next minute there was a tangle of fur and fangs as the two wolves fought.

When the fight was over, the gray wolf crawled inside. Bo heard it drop to the floor of the den. He preferred to remain outside.

Bo slept restlessly through the night, dreaming of humans—of their touch and their voices. When he awoke in the cold dawn, his heart felt empty.

Max was there with a lump of meat which he shared with Bo. The gray wolf still licked its wounds inside the den.

By September Bo was stronger and able to go with Max to get food. Everywhere along the trails were signs of winter. Black-capped chickadees whistled their winter song. Snowshoe rabbits already sported white backs.

Then one day, it began to snow. Bo had to sleep inside the den with Max and the old gray wolf.

When the snow deepened, moose and deer bogged down in the deep drifts. Hunting was good for the wolf pack. The wolves slept during the day and hunted all night.

Bo tried to take part in the hunt, but the other wolves would have no part of him. He had to learn to fend for himself. Yet he and Max remained companions.

The bitter winter finally blew itself out. One soft March morning, Bo found the old wolf cold and stiff in the den. Max howled a song of sorrow for one night. Then, true to his wolf's nature, he became restless.

Bo and Max left the den, never to return. From now on they would live wherever the hunt took them. Soon Max would have a den of his own in which there would be no place for Bo.

One day the hunt brought Max and Bo to the old camping ground. Suddenly the stillness of the island was shattered by a terrifying noise overhead. Above them a large silver monster whirred nearer and nearer. As they watched from the brush, the plane landed, and then two men stepped out.

Bo fought back an impulse to bound out of hiding, wagging a welcome. Six months on the island with the wolves had taught him to be cautious.

In the days that followed, Bo watched from cover as the men went about their strange business. They counted the moose and wrote their findings in small notebooks. They set cage traps, baiting them with fresh meat and sprinkling the surrounding area with a powder to take away the scent of humans.

After the men came to the island, the hunting grew meager for the wolf pack. Bo satisfied himself on a diet of mice, but Max's stomach gnawed with hunger, driving away caution. Late one afternoon, Bo and Max were loping through the wet snow in search of food. Suddenly the strong odor of fresh meat came to them.

They spotted the meat, lying fresh and red inside a metal cage. Like a flash, Max leaped toward the meat. In that instant Bo's keen mind warned him of a trap. All of his instincts told him to protect Max. He owed the wolf something for his months of friendship.

As he lunged, Bo's shoulder hit Max, sending him sprawling in the snow. At the same time Bo knew he was caught. The door of the cage sprang shut, trapping Bo inside.

Max let out a mournful howl, as he sniffed the ground around the cage. Then sensing danger, he turned and ran into the woods. Two men were approaching. They had come to check the trap. "That's no wolf," one man shouted as he peered into the cage. "That's a dog!"

"You must be kidding!" said the other man. "Well, what do you know? I'll bet he's as wild as any wolf."

A sniff of the men's scent reached Bo, and
his big tail began to thump against the side of
the cage.

"He's wagging his tail." One of the men came
forward and cautiously opened the cage door.
"Easy, boy, easy," he said over and over.

The man's voice was soothing. When he
touched the ruff of Bo's neck, his hands were
gentle. Bo's heart began thumping with a joy he
hadn't felt for months. His tongue reached out,
and he licked the man's hand.

The man looked Bo over. "He's a little thin, but he seems all right," he told his partner. "He's wearing a nameplate. He belongs to someone named Carson in Duluth.[3] And his name is Bo."

Both men spoke his name again and again. Bo wiggled joyously, hardly able to contain his happiness.

When the men returned to camp, Bo went with them willingly. That night he slept inside the tent flap. His spaniel's heart was filled once more with love for all human beings.

Once during the night he heard Max's long wail. It told him that the young wolf had found other friends and that Bo was already forgotten.

When morning came, the men lifted Bo into the plane, where he settled down. As the plane lifted, Bo saw the entire island—the tall green pines against the snow and the small clearing laced with streams. He saw moving specks that could only be wildlife in search of food. One of those specks might be Max. Unlike the wolf, Bo would always remember his wilderness brother. He would remember even when he was safely back with the Carsons, and Isle Royale was only a passing memory.

[3]**Duluth** (də lüth′)

1. What kind of dog was Bo? To whom did Bo belong?

2. What happened that caused Bo to be left behind when the Carsons departed from Isle Royale?

3. How did Max help Bo survive the long winter on Isle Royale? How did Bo help Max in return?

4. How did Bo signal to the men that he would not harm them? How did the men know to whom Bo belonged?

5. Do you think that Bo would have survived the winter without Max's help? Why or why not?

6. Why would Bo always remember his wilderness friend? Why would the wolf probably not remember Bo?

7. In what ways did Bo seem "almost human"? Have you read any other stories in which animals behave in human ways? Tell about these animals.

Featherwoman

Clay day! The old pickup truck bumps along the dirt road on the Hopi Indian reservation in northern Arizona, heading for the dry wash where deposits of white clay lie. Helen Naha, known as Featherwoman, will use this clay to form the beautiful pots and bowls that have made her famous throughout the southwestern United States.

The truck slides to a stop at the end of the small canyon. As the children pile out and run off to play tag in the manzanita and the spiny, gray-green mesquite, Featherwoman and two men climb down from the pickup's cab. She steps carefully over the rocky ground and around low bushes covered with desert dust. Walking along the walls of the wash, Featherwoman bends down to examine the clay pits. She digs out a bit of the chalky clay and crumbles it between her fingers.

325

After a while she nods to the men and waves her hand toward the deposit. With picks and shovels, they begin digging the white clay from the pit. Then they cram the clay into metal cans that they load into the bed of the pickup truck.

When the digging and loading are finished, blankets are spread on the ground. Everyone enjoys the food brought for the noon meal. It has been a good morning, and there is friendly talking and joking. After the picnic, the pickup truck returns to the village, and everyone helps spread out the clay, which must dry in the sun for two or three days.

After the clay has dried, Featherwoman prepares it for potting. First she crushes it and sifts it, carefully removing rocks, bits of wood, and leaves. Then she soaks the clay in water and mixes it with the *temper*—ground-up pieces of broken pottery that will keep the clay from shrinking and cracking while the finished pot dries. Next, she adds water and kneads her clay as if it were bread dough. There must be no air bubbles in the clay to damage the pot during firing. Featherwoman picks out more tiny twigs and rocks that appear as she kneads. Finally she is satisfied. The clay is now ready to be formed into a pot.

Featherwoman has no drawing to work from. The shape of the pot exists only in her mind. She begins by molding a saucer-shaped base that

looks like a small, curved pancake with a pinched edge. Rolling a lump of clay between her hands, Featherwoman forms a long rope. By coiling, pressing, and pushing the thick rope, she adds the clay to the pinched edge of the base. She turns and molds while she works, adding clay rope after clay rope, until the pot is the size and shape she wants. Then using the simplest of tools—her moistened fingers and a piece of dried gourd—Featherwoman smoothes the sides of her pot. She scrapes and presses until the coils can no longer be seen, and the pot is smooth. She sets it outside to dry in the hot sun. While it is drying, Featherwoman checks it for cracks. If the cracks are small, she mixes a wet paste of clay and smoothes it into the cracks on both the inside and outside of the pot. If the crack is a large one, she will break up the pot and begin again.

327

Although the weather is good and the air warm, many days pass before the pot is finally dry and Featherwoman can begin polishing it. Now she mixes the *slip*—a paint made of thin, watery clay—and rubs it onto the pot with a cloth. Then using her favorite polishing stone—one she found years ago in the nearby river—she rubs her pot, spitting on its surface to keep it moist. She polishes all day, until the pot has a shiny luster.

While Featherwoman is shaping and polishing the pot, ideas for its decoration are slowly forming in her mind. Finally she is ready to begin painting. She makes the paint herself by boiling the juices of the Rocky Mountain bee plant for many hours, until it is reduced to a thick black pigment. For her brush, she cuts a seven-inch length of yucca leaf and chews on one end until the fibrous leaf separates into bristles. Now she begins the difficult task of painting the delicate black design of swirls, zigzags, and fine-line cross-hatching.

She spends many hours painting and takes great care with her design. When it is completed, Featherwoman turns her pot upside down. Using the black pigment, she carefully paints her signature—a large, fluffy feather—on the bottom. The painting is now finished, and the pot must dry overnight. Featherwoman hopes that tomorrow will be a day without rain or wind—a good day for firing her pot.

The next morning, as the sun rises slowly over the sleeping village, Featherwoman steps out onto the bare, fawn-colored earth surrounding the small house. She tests the wind. The air is still and quiet. Even the hawk gliding overhead makes no sound. As the sun spreads its pale orange light, the desert turns red and seems to glow with a light of its own. It is a good day for firing.

A fire built of sheep dung broken into hand-sized chips is soon burning. Featherwoman watches her fire, carefully adding more chips until the coals are smoldering. Poking the coals with a stick, she spreads them out, covering the whole area where she will build her firing oven.

She lays an old piece of asbestos over the coals and arranges pottery shards on top of it. As smoke puffs from the glowing coals, Featherwoman carefully lifts her beautiful pot and places it upside down on the pottery fragments. Then she covers the pot with a layer of shards. Every portion of the pot must be protected from the flames, for should they touch it, the beautiful design would be smudged and spoiled.

Working quickly now, Featherwoman arranges more chips on the fire, building up an oven shaped like a beehive over the pot that is protected by the shards. The sheep chips burn slowly with an intense heat that singes her hair and eyebrows and burns her calloused fingers.

When the oven is complete, she steps back to survey her morning's work. The fire is burning well; there is still no wind to fan the flames and perhaps make the fire hot enough to damage the pot.

For the moment there is nothing more to do. But she cannot remain away long. As the fire burns, she paces from the house to the oven many times. She listens closely for the terrible crack that betrays the breaking of a pot in a fire that burns too hot. She checks the fire often during the five hours it takes to burn down and again reach the temperature of the air.

Finally the ashes can be disturbed. Feather-woman carefully removes her pot from the disintegrated oven and sets it aside to cool. Later she brushes away the ashes and dust with a soft cloth. Then she rubs her pot with a piece of mutton fat to enhance the beauty of the white slip and the black design.

The pot is perfect. Featherwoman's face creases into a smile. Her dark eyes flash her delight. Her strong hands slowly turn the pot around as she examines her work created entirely from materials of the earth. Its beauty will bring pleasure to all who see it.

THINK ABOUT IT

1. Who is Featherwoman? Where does she live? What is the countryside like there?

2. What happens on clay day? Where does Featherwoman find the clay?

3. What is the first step in preparing the clay for potting? When Featherwoman soaks the clay in water, what does she mix with it?

4. What is a slip? How is it used to make a clay pot?

5. After the pot is finished, how does Featherwoman decorate it? How does she make the paint?

6. What does firing a pot involve? Why is it important that the pot be fired on a day when there is no wind?

7. How do you think Featherwoman feels about her finished work? Give reasons for your answers.

8. Describe a time when you've created something from clay. What made the clay difficult to work with?

American Indian Art

No one knows exactly when American Indian art first appeared in North America. Luckily many treasures have survived from the past. These works show that American Indians have expressed themselves on metal, pottery, hides, wood, rock, and sand for many centuries.

The museum pieces pictured on the next few pages show a few of the works created by Indian artists. All except the last painting were done by unknown American Indians of long ago.

As you look at these works of art, decide what is special about each one. Is there something unusual about the colors or design of the work? What does the work tell you about the person who made it and the community that person lived in? In what way, if any, is the work of art useful?

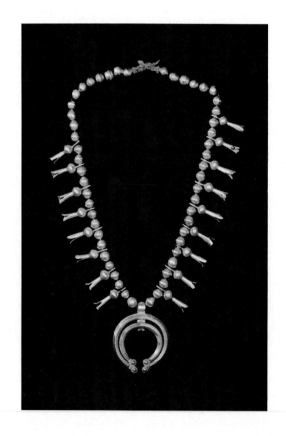

This squash blossom necklace is made of silver. It was worked by a Navajo Indian in New Mexico. The necklace can be seen at the Museum of the American Indian in New York City.

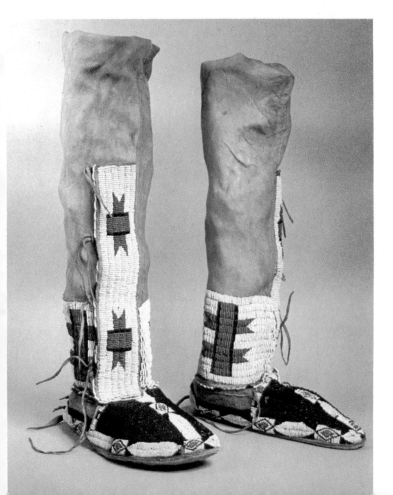

The designs on the quilled birch-bark box and on the beaded legging moccasins are often copied today. The box was created by a Micmac Indian of Nova Scotia. The leggings were made by a Cheyenne Indian living in Wyoming. Both of these works can be seen at the Museum of the American Indian in New York City.

The painting below is a sand painting called *Whirling Logs.* It was created by a Navajo living in Arizona. The painting shows four bars reaching out to the four points of the compass. Father Sky and Mother Earth are also pictured. *Whirling Logs* is also on display at the Museum of the American Indian in New York City.

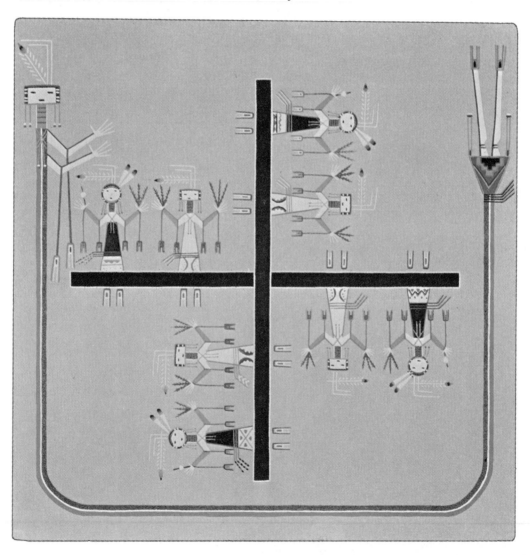

Today, American Indians continue to create works that speak of their past. Allan Houser is one well-known Indian artist. The detail from a watercolor below is by Mr. Houser. The painting is called *Fresh Trail Apache War Party.* It hangs in the Philbrook Art Center in Tulsa, Oklahoma.

Take a Closer Look

In the last two selections, you studied different works of art. You probably found some of the works more beautiful or exciting than others. Perhaps some of the art didn't interest you at all. Whether or not you like a piece of art depends on how you look at it. It also depends on how well you understand what the artist is trying to show or express.

When you look at a work of art, it's important to ask questions. For example, if the work is a painting, decide first what the subject of the painting is. Then look for things that stand out in the painting. What shapes and colors are used? Does the painting show something the way it looks in real life? Is the painting beautiful? Exciting? Sad? How does the painting make you feel?

Look at the paintings of horses on the following page. Then answer the questions.

1. Which painting do you find more exciting? Why?
2. Which painting do you think is more beautiful? Why?

3. Which painting gives you a better sense of a horse's strength?
4. What colors stand out in each painting? How do these colors make you feel?
5. Turn back to the Allan Houser painting on page 337. How are the horses in Houser's painting different from the horses on this page?

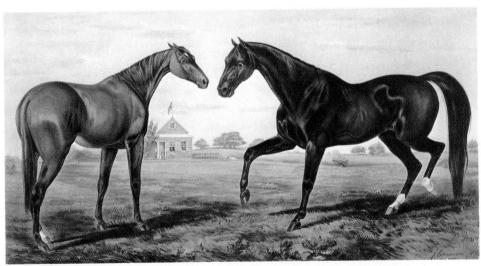

The Golden Apples

"The Golden Apples" is based on a tale first told almost two thousand years ago. The story describes a famous race between Hippomenes[1] and Atalanta[2].

Atalanta is a well-known character in many Greek myths. Before the time of the race, Atalanta had had many exciting adventures. Her father cast her out at birth because he had wanted a son. She was cared for in the forest, first by animals and then by hunters. Later she took part in a famous boar hunt and was the first to wound the animal.

After the hunt, Atalanta found out who her parents were and went to live with them. Her father no longer seemed to mind that she was a daughter and not a son. But he did want her to marry. That is where the story called "The Golden Apples" begins.

[1] **Hippomenes** (hi pom′ə nēz)
[2] **Atalanta** (at′ə lan′tə)

Many men wanted to marry Atalanta because she could hunt and shoot and wrestle as well as they could. Atalanta, however, did not want to marry anyone. As a way of discouraging her suitors, Atalanta said that she would only marry a man who could beat her in a foot race. She knew, of course, that there was no such man.

Atalanta had a wonderful time racing the men who wished to marry her. Young man after young man arrived to race with her. But she always managed to outrun each one of them.

One day a young man arrived who used his head as well as his feet. He knew that he could not run as fast as Atalanta, but he had a plan. This young man, whose name was Hippomenes, had asked the goddess of love for three apples of pure gold. No one could see these apples and not want them. The goddess had gladly given the apples to Hippomenes. Being devoted to love, she wanted Atalanta to marry.

As Atalanta waited for the race to begin, she looked at Hippomenes. He kept his head bent, however, holding fast to the golden apples. Around them everyone spoke of Atalanta's beauty.

The race started. Atalanta flew along the track swift as an arrow released from its bow. A faint flush stained her cheeks. Her golden hair streamed back over her shoulders. She was ahead of Hippomenes when he rolled one of the apples directly in front of her. She paused to pick it up. In that moment he overtook her. They were now running abreast.

Hippomenes threw the second apple, this time a little to Atalanta's left. She had to swerve to reach it, and he raced ahead of her. Almost at once, however, Atalanta was able to overtake him.

The goal was now very near. Hippomenes threw the third apple, and it rolled into the grass beside the track. Atalanta saw the apple gleam through the green of the grass, and she left the track to pick it up. As she reached for the apple, she saw Hippomenes cross the goal.

Atalanta and Hippomenes were married. Her days of freedom had come to an end.

1. Who was Atalanta? Why were so many men eager to marry her?

2. How did Atalanta feel about marriage? How did she try to discourage her suitors? Was she successful?

3. How did Hippomenes win the race against Atalanta?

4. What words would you use to describe Atalanta? How would you describe Hippomenes?

5. Do you think Hippomenes' method of winning the race was fair? Why or why not?

6. What kind of story is "The Golden Apples"? Give reasons for your answer.

7. Describe a time when you wanted something so badly that you used clever tricks to obtain it. What were your feelings at the time?

THE RACE

The following story is another version of Atalanta's famous race. However, this tale was written in the 1970's. As you read "The Race," note how it is like and how it is different from "The Golden Apples."

"What shall I do?" said Atalanta's father, who was a powerful king. "So many young men want to marry you that I don't know how to choose."

"You don't have to choose, Father," Atalanta said. "I will choose. And I'm not sure that I will choose to marry anyone at all."

"Of course you will marry," said the king. "Everybody gets married. It is what people do."

"But, I intend to go out and see the world," Atalanta told him. "When I come home, perhaps I will marry and perhaps I will not."

The king did not like this at all, for he was used to having his own way. "I have decided how to choose the young man you will marry," he told Atalanta. "I will hold a great race. The winner—the swiftest, fleetest runner of all—will win the right to marry you."

Atalanta was a clever girl as well as a swift runner. She saw how she might win both the argument and the race. "Very well," she said. "But you must let me race along with the others. If I am not the winner, I will accept the wishes of the young man who does win."

The king agreed to Atalanta's plan, for he thought he would have his way. He would marry off his daughter and enjoy a fine day of racing as well. He directed his messengers to travel throughout the kingdom announcing the race and its wonderful prize—the chance to marry the bright Atalanta.

As the day of the race drew near, flags were raised in the streets of the town. Banners were hung near the grassy field where the race would be run. Baskets of ripe plums and peaches, wheels of cheese, and loaves of crusty bread were gathered for the crowds.

Meanwhile, Atalanta herself was preparing for the race. Each day at dawn she went to the field in secret and ran across it—slowly at first, then faster and faster. Soon she could run the course more quickly than anyone had ever run it before.

As the day of the race drew nearer, young men began to crowd into the town. Most felt sure they could win the prize. But Young John, who lived in the town, was not so sure. He had seen Atalanta day by day when she came to town to buy nails and wood to build a pigeon house or to find parts for her telescope or just to be with her friends.

Young John had seen the princess only from a distance, but he knew how bright and clever she was. He wanted very much to win the race and to have the chance to talk with her.

"For surely," he said to himself, "it is not right for Atalanta's father to give her away to the winner of a race. Atalanta herself should choose the person she wants to marry. That is, if she wishes to marry at all! Still, if I could only win the race, I would be free to speak to her and to ask for her friendship."

Each evening, after his studies of the stars and the seas, Young John went to the field in secret and practiced running. Night after night, he ran as fast as the wind across the grassy field. Soon, he could cross it more quickly than anyone—that is, anyone except Atalanta.

At last, the day of the race arrived.

Trumpets sounded in the early morning. The young men gathered at the edge of the field alongside Atalanta. The king and his friends sat in soft chairs, and the townspeople stood along the edge of the grassy field.

The king rose to address them all. "Good day," he said to the crowds. "Good luck," he said to the young men. To Atalanta he said, "Good-bye. I must tell you farewell, for tomorrow, you will be married!"

"I am not so sure of that, Father," Atalanta answered. She laughed as she looked up and down the line of young men.

"Not one of them can win the race," she said to herself. "I will run as fast as the wind and leave them all behind."

Then, a bugle sounded, a flag was dropped, and the runners were off!

The crowds cheered as the young men and Atalanta began to race across the field. At first they ran as a group, but Atalanta soon pulled ahead, with three of the young men close behind her. As they neared the halfway point, one young man put on a great burst of speed and seemed to pull ahead for an instant. But then he gasped and fell back, while Atalanta shot on.

Soon another young man, tense with the effort, drew near to Atalanta. Reaching out as though to touch her sleeve, he stumbled and lost speed. Atalanta smiled. "I have almost won," she thought.

But then another young man came near. This was Young John, running as steadily and as swiftly as Atalanta herself. Atalanta felt his closeness, so in a sudden burst of speed she dashed ahead.

Young John might have given up at this, but he never stopped running. "Nothing at all," he thought, "will keep me from winning the chance to speak with Atalanta." On and on he ran, swift as the wind. Soon he was running beside Atalanta toward the golden ribbon that marked the end of the race. Atalanta raced even faster to pull ahead, but Young John was a strong runner and stayed even with her. Smiling with the pleasure of the

race, Atalanta and Young John reached the finish line together. Together they broke through the golden ribbon.

Trumpets blew. The crowd shouted and leaped about. The king rose. "Who is that young man?" he asked.

"It is Young John from the town," the people told him.

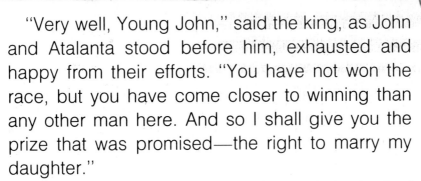

"Very well, Young John," said the king, as John and Atalanta stood before him, exhausted and happy from their efforts. "You have not won the race, but you have come closer to winning than any other man here. And so I shall give you the prize that was promised—the right to marry my daughter."

Young John smiled at Atalanta, and she smiled back. "Thank you, sir," said John to the king, "but I cannot marry your daughter unless she wishes to marry me. I have run this race for the chance to talk with Atalanta. Only if she is willing, am I ready to claim my prize."

Atalanta laughed with pleasure. "And I," she said to John, "cannot marry before I have seen the world. But I would like to spend the afternoon with you."

As the crowds went away, Atalanta and Young John sat and talked on the grassy field. They ate bread and cheese and purple plums. Atalanta told John about her telescopes and her pigeons. John told Atalanta about his globes and his studies of geography. At the end of the day, they were very good friends.

The next day, John sailed off to explore new lands. Atalanta set off to visit the great cities.

Each of them had wonderful adventures and saw marvelous sights. Perhaps they married or perhaps they never did. In any case, they did become friends. And it is certain that they both lived happily ever after.

THINK ABOUT IT

1. According to this version of the story, who decided that a race should be held?

2. Did Atalanta agree to her father's plan? What condition did she set?

3. Why was Young John so eager to win the race? What did he do to prepare for it?

4. How did the race turn out? What happened as a result?

5. How was Young John different from Hippomenes, the winner of the race in the older version of the story?

6. Compare the events of "The Golden Apples" with the events of "The Race." Which events are the same? Which are different? How are the outcomes different?

7. What do you think might have been the author's purpose in writing this modern version of the myth?

8. Which version did you like better? Give reasons for your answer.

9. Have you ever had to do something because someone else wanted you to do it? What happened? How did you feel?

six

Sona Goes Sailing

Every Sunday evening, Sona Baronian's uncles, great-uncles, aunts, and cousins by the dozen gathered for Sunday dinner at Sona's house. They gathered there because that's where Nana, the oldest member of the family, lived.

One day Sona and her friend Tommy O'Brien decided to become sailors. They worked every afternoon helping to make Uncle Jerry O'Brien's boat seaworthy so that they could sail it into San Francisco Bay. When Sona asked Nana for permission to go sailing on Sunday afternoon, this is what Nana said:

"Sunday!" she exclaimed. "Did you say Sunday? I have been thinking about sailing, which is hard enough. And about meeting your Mr. O'Brien. But not about changing our whole family life. No. That is too much."

So Sona ran away to sea. The following story tells what Sona found out about Nana and about herself as a sailor. You can read the whole story in *Sunday for Sona*, the book from which these pages were taken.

"Sona!" Tommy called. "Is that your grandmother walking down the dock?"

"It can't be!" Sona said. She pulled her breath
in. It was.

There was Nana, in her black coat and her little black hat, scarf blowing in the wind. There
walked Nana, her back straight and her step
brisk. But somehow to Sona she looked small
and alone.

"Say," Mr. O'Brien said, "it's good of her to come to see us off. I'll feel better, too, knowing her personally."

"What's she carrying?" Tommy asked.

"That's her satchel," Sona said.

"What's in it?" Tommy asked.

"Sometimes treats," Sona said. "But I don't think she'll have treats today."

"Why not?" Jerry O'Brien said. "It's a special day."

Nana looked carefully at each boat she passed. She came nearer and nearer. It was getting too late for Sona to run.

But suddenly she did run. Straight to her grandmother.

"Oh, Nana," she said as she threw her arms around her, "I'm sorry. I shouldn't have run away!"

Nana looked down at Sona's face and nodded gently. She put her satchel down and gave Sona a hug. For a long moment neither one spoke.

"Never mind," Nana said finally. "I have been wrong, too. I know you have never deceived me before. So I had to think—what has driven you to it this time? I know, I left you with too hard a choice. And we did not talk about it enough. Now, never mind. I have come to see this *North Star* and to meet the sailor, Uncle Jerry O'Brien."

"A pleasure, ma'am," called Jerry O'Brien. "I hope you'll sail with us."

"There is room?" Nana asked.

"Certainly," Jerry O'Brien said. "Sails four easily. Even five."

"Oh, Nana," Sona said, "you don't have to. Not for me. I don't think you'll like it."

Nana looked at her sternly. "I came to this country on a big ship," she said. "I sailed the seas before you were born."

"Good for you," said Jerry O'Brien. "That settles it." He reached out and helped her onto the boat. "Welcome aboard," he said.

Nana opened her satchel and pulled out a brightly wrapped bottle.

"I thought we might have a christening ceremony," she said.

"You mean break the bottle?" said Sona. "On our fresh paint?"

"Maybe splinter the wood?" Tommy said.

"Perhaps we could have a toast instead," said Mr. O'Brien.

"Exactly as I thought," said Nana. She handed each one a small paper cup. "We have grape juice," she said. "Sona's favorite drink."

"Ma'am," said Jerry O'Brien, "my hat's off to you. You've thought of everything. Tommy, get your harmonica. Can't have a celebration without music."

He lifted his cup. "Happy voyages, *North Star*," he said. They stood in place as Tommy played "Anchors Aweigh."

Nana smiled. "Good," she said. "A song of the sea."

Now Tommy started the motor and Mr. O'Brien took charge of the tiller, steering the boat past the row of small boats at the dock.

Nana and Sona sat opposite each other. "Beautiful," Nana nodded as they looked ahead at the opening sight of the bay.

"Wind's perfect," Mr. O'Brien said. "Take the tiller, Tommy, and I'll hoist the sails. Hold her into the wind."

In a moment the white sails rose. First the large mainsail, then the smaller sail, the jib. With the motor turned off now, the boat began to rock with the waves and the wind.

Sona caught her breath. After all this time it was really happening. "We're sailing!" she said. "We're really sailing."

"Look at that," Nana said. "Like wings."

"See, Nana," Sona said. "Over there is the Golden Gate. You go through there and on to the South Seas. Maybe to Tahiti."

"Wind's shifting," Mr. O'Brien said. "I'll take the tiller again. Sona, you're in charge of the jib. Now as I call, let the jib go. Ready about! Hard-a-lee!"

The small sail swung around to the other side of the boat.

"Tighten the jib sheet!" called Mr. O'Brien. "Pull!"

The ropes bit into Sona's hands. She pulled as hard as she could, and finally made them fast to a cleat on the deck.

Nana moved quickly from her seat to the one across. "Balance the weight," she said.

"Mrs. Baronian," said Jerry O'Brien, "you are a natural sailor."

"Certainly," said Nana.

"Coming to a choppy patch of water," said Jerry O'Brien.

"Good," Nana said.

The boat rolled, tipped. It found its balance again.

"Good," she said again. "Now we are matching wits with the sea."

"Right," said Jerry O'Brien, as water came splashing over the rail.

Sona didn't think it was so good at all.

"It was better when it was smoother," she said.

"But this is more exciting," Tommy said.

Sona held on to a rail as the boat tipped and tilted. The waves were getting larger. The boat was leaning, leaning, almost into the water. A strange something inside her seemed to be going round and round in a wavy pattern. The spray on her face was salty. Too salty. She wondered why she had liked the smell of salt water. She didn't like it now. She didn't like being so wet. She didn't like anything.

Her eyes kept trying to close against the bright light. But she had to stay awake. She had to be in charge of the jib.

Now that thing inside of her was floating up and down. Up and down.

Suddenly the boat lurched.

"Tighten that jib!" called Jerry O'Brien. "Tighten it!"

But Sona's eyes felt heavy and her fingers felt mushy.

"Let me!" Nana said. She grasped the rope firmly.

"More!" said Jerry O'Brien. Then, "Good! Good for you, Mrs. Baronian."

"It is nothing," said Nana. "Just sense."

"We're almost out of it," Tommy said as the boat leveled itself. "I wasn't even scared. Were you, Sona?"

Sona didn't answer.

"We can bear off now," said Mr. O'Brien. "We're all right."

"Are we?" Sona said in a small voice. "We're still bobbing up and down."

"This is nothing," Mr. O'Brien said. "It's a beautiful breeze."

Nothing seemed beautiful to Sona. "It smells strange," she said.

"The smell of the seven seas," Nana said.

"Right," said Jerry O'Brien, "and we have a southwest wind. We can sail on this tack all the way to Sausalito."

"Is it far?" Sona asked.

"We'll go as far as we like," Mr. O'Brien said.

Sona thought she had already done that.

Nana dipped into her satchel again. "I brought cheoregs*," she said. "Pastries, but not sweet."

"Lucky you thought of it," Tommy said. "I'm hungry."

"A treat," said Mr. O'Brien.

"Sona," said Nana. "Your *cheoreg?*"

But Sona didn't answer. She closed her eyes and wished the boat would stop rocking. She wondered how they could eat. Maybe she would never eat again.

"Sona!" Nana said again. "Don't you want a *cheoreg?*"

"No," Sona said, her eyes still closed. "Please, no."

"Ah," Nana said. "A feeling from the sea. I remember. Here, I have something better for you." She found a package of soda crackers. "Try."

*__cheoregs__ (chir′ogz)

366

Sona tried two. But it didn't help. Even her face felt stiff. And with each roll of the boat she felt worse.

Nana shook her head. "Too bad," she said.

Mr. O'Brien nodded. "It is too bad," he agreed. "But I'll tell you one thing, this is supposed to be a pleasure trip, and if it's not a pleasure for Sona we'll turn back. No sense in it."

Now Sona felt more miserable, because she was spoiling the sail for everyone else. But mostly she wanted to get home and lie down.

When the boat had been tied up, the first thing they did was to let Sona off. She sat on the dock, and was surprised at how quickly she felt better.

When the sails were down and in the sail bags, Nana shook hands with Mr. O'Brien.

"Thank you for taking me," she said. "It was a wonderful adventure."

"My pleasure," said Mr. O'Brien. "In fact, I appreciated your help, since I lost part of my crew."

Sona's face grew hot.

"I'm sorry, Mr. O'Brien," she said. "I guess I'm not a sailor at all."

"Foolishness!" said Nana. "You will become one. It is in your blood!"

"She's right," said Mr. O'Brien. "Lots of new sailors have trouble at first. You'll come around."

"Maybe," Sona thought. "Maybe."

Nana turned to Mr. O'Brien. "I hope you and Tommy will come home with us," she said. "Our whole family waits to have Sunday dinner."

"We wouldn't want to interfere in a family party," said Jerry O'Brien.

"Friends are family," Nana said. "Come!"

1. Why wouldn't Nana give Sona permission to go sailing on Sunday afternoon? What did Sona do as a result of Nana's refusal?

2. Why did Nana come to the dock? What did she bring with her? Why?

3. What is a jib? What did Mr. O'Brien mean when he asked Sona to "tighten the jib sheet"?

4. What happened to Sona when the boat hit rough water? Who took over Sona's duties?

5. Who turned out to be the better sailor, Nana or Sona? Why?

6. What kind of person do you think Nana was? Give reasons for your answer.

7. How did Nana and Sona feel about each other? How do you know?

8. Have you ever found that it took you longer than you planned to learn something? What were you trying to learn? Why do you think it took longer to learn?

TALL CITY

Here houses rise so straight and tall
That I am not surprised at all
To see them simply walk away
Into the clouds—this misty day.

Susan Nichols Pulsifer

370

On Watching the Construction of a Skyscraper

Nothing sings from these orange trees,
Rindless steel as smooth as sapling skin,
Except a crane's brief wheeze
And all the muffled, clanking din
Of rivets nosing in like bees.

Burton Raffel

In the poem on page 371, a poet describes his feelings on watching the construction of a skyscraper. In the following selection, another writer describes how he feels about the same thing. Joseph Husband has put his thoughts down as prose, not as poetry. As you read "Skyscraper," think about how Mr. Husband uses words and sentences to make you see certain pictures. Then ask yourself if he writes prose as though he were writing poetry.

SKYSCRAPER

The old building had fallen in a cloud of broken brick and plaster. From my window I could look down into a deep hole. Far down in the foundation, sturdy roots for a new skyscraper were being planted.

When the foundations were finished, the first thin steel columns stretched toward the sky. Soon a hundred columns stood like sprouting shoots in a well-planted garden. As the crossbeams fell into place, the great orange skeleton shaped itself. Then, above the noise and vibration of the street, came the angry clatter of the riveters.

I saw the frame pile up with amazing speed. The orange ribs of the skyscraper surged higher and higher. As through prison bars, I saw the distant blue of the harbor. The view from my window was no longer the same.

Like beetles, the steelworkers climbed sure-footed over the skeleton frame. Far out on the end of narrow beams they hung. On the tops of slender columns they clung, waiting to swing the girders into place. Braced against nothing but empty space, they pounded red-hot rivets with their clattering hammers.

I thought also of other workers.

Of the designers of this tall tower.

Of the engineers who planned each bolt to fit perfectly, with only their ideas and their books to guide them.

Of the millworkers who molded each beam in the steel mills of a distant city.

Of the steelworkers who made each girder so carefully that the beams fell softly into place, rivet hole to rivet hole.

When the skyscraper was almost finished, I stood on the top floor of the tower. Above, from the light steel ribs of the dome, a flagpole pointed to the drifting clouds. Standing on its base, a man was arranging the tackle which would lift him up to paint the flagpole. He saw me and leaned down.

"Come up," he shouted.

I climbed the ladder and, with his arm to steady me, crawled out above the dome. There was room for my feet beside his. I heard him laugh beside me.

"Don't break off that pole. I've got to climb it."

I looked down. The curving ribs of the dome ended twenty feet below. Beyond, the roofs of neighboring buildings lay flat and small in the sunlight. The streets of the city reached to the harbor and the hills. Here and there were the open spaces of the city squares; far off, the green sweep of a city park. Above the roofs, wisps of steam and smoke lay softly on the breeze.

Like a series of crooked fingers, the docks caught the edge of the harbor. The water was a quivering green, dotted with two toy boats that crossed and recrossed, leaving a churn of white smoke above.

Straight down, in the street, the cars crawled in two thin lines. Everywhere people swarmed upon the pavement, like moving dots.

Far below, the noises of the street—the living cry of the city—rose like the murmur of a river in a deep canyon. Beside me, the steeplejack leaned easily against the pole, his eyes watching the distant glimmer of the sea. I looked up, and the slowly moving clouds seemed suddenly to stand still. The tower took the motion, and the flagpole seemed to bend to earth.

Down in the street, I joined the crowd that had gathered on the sidewalk. Their necks bent back as they watched the tiny speck at the top of the flagpole.

"Pretty high up," said someone.

"Yes," answered another, "but they're putting in the foundation for a higher one on the corner."

THINK ABOUT IT

1. From where did the writer watch the construction of the skyscraper? What workers did he think about as he watched?

2. What did the world look like when the writer finally stood atop the new building?

3. What did the steeplejack painting the flagpole look like to the people on the street?

4. To what does the writer compare the steel columns that formed the skeleton of the skyscraper? Do you think that this is a good comparison? Why or why not?

5. To what does the writer compare the steelworkers? What other comparison might he have used?

6. Do you think that the writer of this selection might also be a poet? Why or why not?

7. Tell about a building you have watched being built. What impressed you the most? Why?

Alligator on the Escalator

Through the revolving door
Of a department store
There slithered an alligator.

When he came to the escalator,
He stepped upon the track with great
   dexterity;
His tail draped over the railing,
And he clicked his teeth in glee:
  "Yo, I'm off on the escalator,
  Excited as I can be!
  It's a *moving* experience,
  As you can plainly see.
  On the moving stair I go anywhere,
  I rise to the top
  Past outerwear, innerwear,
  Dinnerwear, thinnerwear—
  Then down to the basement with
    bargains galore,
  Then back on the track to the top
    once more!
  Oh, I may ride the escalator
  Until closing time or later,
  So tell the telephone operator
  To call Mrs. Albert Q. Alligator
  And tell her to take a hot mud bath
  And not to wait up for me!"

Eve Merriam

378

379

THE LOST UMBRELLA OF KIM CHU

It was a very special umbrella, given to Kim Chu's father by the "mayor" of Chinatown in New York City for his contribution to the neighborhood's New Year's celebration. It was the only one of its kind, with a bamboo handle that housed a secret scroll. The umbrella was a family treasure. And Kim Chu lost it at the library.

Until she could find the umbrella, Kim was not able to rest. Her search took her to the Staten Island Ferry. There she met her friend Mae Lee. Together they spotted the umbrella in the hands of the "millionaire man."

A wide smile spread over Kim's face when she
saw Mae Lee. Now things would begin to happen. Now the two of them would work together
to get the umbrella back from the millionaire
man. It was not going to be easy, the way he was
hanging on to it. But she and Mae Lee together
would carry it off . . . somehow.

For a few minutes Mae Lee leaned against the
railing. She stretched her elbows out behind her.
She let her eyes fall now and then on the big,
black umbrella. She did it carelessly, as though
she weren't really *looking* at it—as though her
mind were on anything else but it.

Then, with her hands clasped tightly behind her, she strolled across the deck. She walked in front of Kim to the other side of the boat. Before rounding the bend on that side, she looked back at Kim. A slight nod of her head, a hitch of her shoulder, and a long stare that meant, "Follow me!" Then she disappeared around the bend.

Kim stood up and stretched. Then she, too, strolled to that side of the boat. Mae was waiting for her by the railing. No one was sitting nearby, so no one would overhear the conversation or get the idea that something was up.

Still Kim and Mae took special care with the way they spoke to one another. They spoke out of the sides of their mouths—lips opened just a crack at the corners—a way they had often practiced at school. It sounded curious, like another language or a code. This was bound to throw off an eavesdropper, if one came by.

Mae Lee muttered, "You know what happened? This. I left the library the minute they put up the sign about returning your father's umbrella. I wanted to help find it, but I had to hurry to catch the El and make my boat. I was late already, so I tore up the stairs to the El when I heard a train coming . . . and . . . I made it!"

"Train . . . yes . . ." said Kim breathlessly as though she herself had just run up those El stairs.

Mae went on. "Now listen to this, will you? As the door of the train slammed shut behind me, I spotted that man in the wet, dark suit, hanging onto that umbrella with the bamboo handle. That man rushed onto the platform and dropped his nickel in. But he was too late! 'Hold it! Hold it!' he bellowed, seeing that the next door to mine was still open. But that door slammed in his face, too. Was he mad! He shook the umbrella after the train as we got going. If I could have gotten off the train right then I would have. And I would've followed the crook, kept my eyes peeled on him. Because I do think he *is* the crook . . . But the door was closed, I was in, and he was out!"

"O-o-h!" gasped Kim. "He must know the secret of the handle. . . ."

"Exactly what I thought!" said Mae. "It just flashed into my mind that the umbrella he waved at the train was your father's. You couldn't help but see how wet he was. Why would a man who was carrying an umbrella that big get to be so wet? Because he just stole it, I said to myself. So-o-o . . ."

"So-o-o," repeated Kim impatiently.

Mae continued, "At the very next station I got off my train and waited for the next one. I figured that the mad, wet man would be on it and so I'd get on it, too. I had to keep my eyes on him and that umbrella if I could."

"So . . . what happened then?" asked Kim, forgetting to speak code.

"Sh-sh-sh!" said Mae. "Careful how you speak. There may be spies in the cabin. Well, it all happened as I thought. From the platform where I was standing I could see into the cars of the next train when it slowed up. Sure enough! There was that man sitting by the window in the second car. I got on and sat down right opposite him. I looked, without his knowing it, long and fast at the umbrella, wondering how to get it for you."

Kim's eyes were shining at the thought of such kindness.

Mae went on, "That man was probably wondering how the girl . . . me . . . that he'd seen in the window of the train he'd missed was now here on this train, sitting right opposite him. Maybe he thought I had seen him steal the umbrella? Because, as we neared South Ferry Station, he began to clutch the umbrella between his knees the way he is doing now."

"I hope he's scared," said Kim, "seeing you standing right beside him on the ferry. I hope he's trembling. To think we have to catch a thief. And such a big one! A millionaire thief! Wow!"

"Well, we have to, we have to," said Mae with a shrug. "So we must get back to work. I'll go the long way around and stand by the man. You go back to your seat by the laughing woman."

"You've noticed how much she laughs?" said Kim.

"Yes," said Mae. "I notice everything."

"She knows that man. She was talking to him," said Kim.

"She was?" mused Mae. "Maybe they're in cahoots," she said.

Kim sighed. "But she does seem so nice! I hope she's not in cahoots," she said. She began to tremble. "We're surrounded by crooks!" she murmured.

"Don't shake!" said Mae. "This spot will be our meeting place to say what we think we have found out. We report right here!" Mae smacked the railing with her hand.

"Yes," said Kim, "and I'm not trembling now. See?" And she slapped the railing, too.

"All right," said Mae. "We have about fifteen minutes before the ferry reaches Staten Island. We have to work fast. I'm off. Pretend you never laid eyes on me before in your life. We must bamboozle them."

Mae Lee strolled away, hands clasped carelessly behind her. She disappeared around the bend at the front of the ferry.

"What a brave girl," Kim sighed. "She probably never trembles." Then, her hands also clasped carelessly behind her, Kim strolled back to her seat beside the woman, who was shaking with laughter again.

It was hard to think that such a jolly person could be in cahoots with a crook. It just must be that the book she was reading *was* an awfully funny one, thought Kim. She looked at the name of the book—*War and Peace.* It didn't sound funny. The woman had her finger on line five of page forty-nine, not to lose her place while chuckling.

The man was still sitting there, clutching the umbrella and reading his newspaper or pretending to. Then Mae Lee came strolling along. She resumed her watching position at the railing. She rocked back and forth on her feet from heel to toe. And she glanced around sometimes, as though looking at the sights. But she took it in that the man was still on page two of his newspaper. Still, she could understand his not making swifter progress, for the print was very fine.

Then, suddenly, the man began to rock back and forth on *his* feet although he was still sitting down. Both Kim and Mae noticed this. They gave one another the "on guard" stare. Had the man's feet gone to sleep? Was he trying to wake them up for a stroll around the deck? If so, should Kim and Mae follow him? Although they were not yet near shore, perhaps he had decided to go to the rope so he could hop over. Maybe he wanted to be the first one off the ferry. Then he could dash up the hill with his stolen umbrella. Could they catch such a long-legged man?

Mae signaled Kim to meet her at the railing. They both lost no time in getting there.

"He's waking his feet up," said Mae.

"To make a quick getaway," said Kim.

"Yes, I thought the same thing. Listen, Kim," said Mae solemnly, "we're nearing the Staten Island side. We haven't much time left."

When she heard that, Kim wished the ride
could last forever so she would not have to go up
to the millionaire man and say, "Give me back
my father's umbrella." "Maybe it's not my
father's umbrella after all?" she said, losing faith.

"Oh, it's his all right," said Mae reassuringly.

"How am I going to get it away from him?"
asked Kim desperately.

"Good question," said Mae calmly. "But don't
worry. We'll think of something . . . people
always do."

"Maybe I should ask the jolly woman to help
us," said Kim. "But she's reading . . . I don't like
to bother her."

"She's only pretending to read, and he is pretending, too. They stay on the same pages. That
proves it. They're in cahoots. They're watching us
the way we're watching them. That's what tickles

the woman's funny bone. Very funny!" she sneered. "But don't let on in any way that *we* know that *they* know we are watching them."

Kim sighed. Here the umbrella was, so close to her. How to get it? Oh, how to get it?

Mae said, "Have courage, friend. The moment is coming when we will have to know what to do. And he'll know!"

Suddenly Kim grew angry. Her black eyes flashed. "He knows the secret of the handle. He knows that in the whole wide world there is not another one like it. It's one of the seven wonders of the world . . . just about! We will get it back!"

"Yes!" said Mae, equally angry. "And he's in cahoots with a person who thinks its funny! But now we have to get back to our positions. The idea must come to us before we reach that buoy ahead there!"

Kim looked at the buoy. "O-ooooh!" she said, for it wasn't far away. And she turned to go back to her seat.

Around the bend now . . . well-ll! There, in the seat, the millionaire man was sitting and talking out of the corner of his mouth to the laughing woman. He was still clutching the umbrella tightly between his knees. Both their heads were behind *The Wall Street Journal!*

"In cahoots! They really are in cahoots!" thought Kim aghast. And she tore back after Mae Lee.

Will Kim and Mae Lee be able to get back the prized umbrella? They don't even have a plan of action yet, and the ferry is about to dock at Staten Island. If they don't act quickly, all their efforts will have been for nothing.

Find out who the millionaire man is and how Kim and Mae Lee handle their problem by reading the whole story in *The Lost Umbrella of Kim Chu* by Eleanor Estes.

THINK ABOUT IT

1. What was so special about the umbrella that Kim Chu had left at the library?

2. What did Kim Chu and her friend Mae Lee think had happened to the umbrella?

3. What made Kim and Mae think that the laughing lady and the millionaire man were in cahoots?

4. What evidence is there in the story that the millionaire man may indeed have taken the umbrella?

5. Why would someone who was a millionaire *steal* an umbrella? Do you think that there may be some other explanation for why the man has Kim's father's umbrella? If so, what might the explanation be?

6. If you had been in Kim's place, what would you have done to try to get the umbrella from the millionaire man?

Travel Plans

What if the millionaire man did jump off the ferry and dash away? Kim didn't know Staten Island very well. She could have used a map to help her find her way around. Knowing how to read a map makes it easier to get from place to place in a strange town and in your own town, too.

Here's part of a map of an imaginary city. Pretend that you live there. Find the school on the

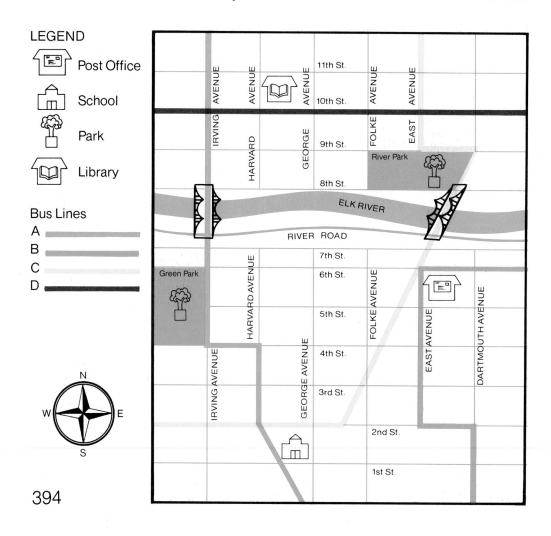

map. Here's a hint—look at the key and see how a school is marked. Then read the map to answer the following questions.

1. What route would you take to go from school to Green Park?
2. Where is the post office? How do you know?
3. If you walk north on George Avenue, can you get across the river? Why or why not?
4. How are the bus lines shown on the map? Which bus line is green? Which bus line runs east and west on 10th Street?
5. Which bus lines go by the school?
6. What bus would you take to go to the library from school? Where would you get off and on?
7. Your dentist's office is on the corner of 6th Street and Dartmouth Avenue. To go there after school you have to take one bus and transfer to another where the bus lines cross. What buses would you take? Where would you transfer?
8. From the dentist's office you want to get to your house on Irving Avenue and 5th Street. What route should you take?

Now find and read another map. Get a bus, subway, or street map. Plan some trips. Pick one place to start from. Then pick a few other points on the map. Write down the routes you would take to get there. List your starting point, the streets and buses you would take, the directions you would travel in, and your destination.

ZEELY

Elizabeth and John Perry (alias Geeder and Toeboy)
are spending the summer on their Uncle Ross's farm.
Hoping to see a falling comet or other spectacular
events, they decide to sleep outside on the front lawn.
They don't, in fact, see a comet. But what they do see on
their first morning in the country draws Geeder into a
summer-long adventure of intrigue and mystery.

Almost any minute now, the people to whom Uncle Ross rented land would come down the road. Uncle Ross had said they came every morning as soon as the sun was well up in the sky. It was just about time, and watching them would be something to do.

"Wake up, Toeboy!" Geeder whispered loudly. "I think I hear them coming!"

Toeboy leaped up before he looked where he was going and hit his head against a branch. He was still half asleep when Geeder yanked him to the ground before they could be seen.

They knelt low by the hedge. Trying not to move or blink an eye, they watched Mr. Tayber and his daughter come into view along Lead-back Road. What they saw was no ordinary sight. They watched, spellbound. Nothing in the world could have prepared them for the sight of Miss Zeely Tayber.

Zeely Tayber was more than six and a half feet tall, thin and deeply dark as a pole of Ceylon ebony. She wore a long smock that reached to her ankles. Her arms, hands, and feet were bare, and her thin, oblong head didn't seem to fit quite right on her shoulders.

She had very high cheekbones, and her eyes seemed to turn inward on themselves. Geeder couldn't say what expression she saw on Zeely's face. She knew only that it was calm, that it had pride in it, and that the face was the most beautiful she had ever seen.

Zeely's long fingers looked exactly like bean pods left a long time in the sun.

Geeder wanted to make sure Toeboy noticed Zeely's hands, but the Taybers were too close, and she was afraid they would hear her.

Mr. Tayber and Zeely carried feed pails, which made a grating sound. It was the only sound on the road besides that of Mr. Tayber's heavy footsteps. Zeely made no sound at all.

You would think she would, thought Geeder, she was so long and tall.

Geeder and Toeboy stayed quiet as the Taybers passed, and the Taybers gave no sign that they saw them hiding there. Uncle Ross had said that they were not known to speak much, even to one another.

Geeder and Toeboy watched the Taybers until they went out of sight. It was then that Toeboy said, "Let's go watch them in the field."

"No," said Geeder quietly, "no, Toeboy." She could not possibly have made him understand how stunned she had been at seeing Miss Zeely Tayber for the first time. Never in her life

had she seen anyone quite like her.

"They sure are different from any people I've ever seen. I wonder what kind of person Zeely is." Geeder's voice was full of the awe she felt for her. "But you know what I think? I think we've found a new people that nobody's ever heard of!"

All that morning, Geeder talked to Toeboy about Zeely. When they sat down for lunch with Uncle Ross, Geeder asked, "How long have those Tayber people been around this town?"

"Oh, it's been about a year and a half now," Uncle Ross said.

"That's a long time," Geeder said. "I guess you've gotten to know Mr. Tayber and the girl real well in all that time."

Uncle Ross smiled. "No," he said, "I wouldn't say that. The Taybers aren't easy to know. They stay aloof from the whole town." He paused. "One day, the town had no thought of them. The next day, there they were, hammering and putting storm windows in that old house."

"Just like that?" Geeder said, snapping her fingers.

"No, not exactly like that," Uncle Ross said.

"It's just that the first time we saw them, they were taking care to fix up that house. Strangers. And they stayed on, still strangers."

"Strangers," Geeder said. But that was all she said. She asked no more questions.

But by nightfall, Geeder was ready to talk about Zeely Tayber once more. As she and Toeboy lay in their beds on the lawn, she began.

"You would think Zeely would have all kinds of friends," Geeder said. "But there she goes with just Mr. Tayber. She hardly even talks to *him*."

"He doesn't talk much to her, either," Toeboy said.

"That's because both Zeely and Mr. Tayber are different," Geeder said, "with ways about them none of us can understand."

As the weeks passed, fine and sluggish, Geeder and Toeboy fell into a lazy routine. Each morning, they arose early to watch the Taybers come down Leadback Road. Each night, they talked of Zeely Tayber under the stars. Yet, try as she might, Geeder couldn't learn anything new about Miss Zeely.

One day, Geeder and Toeboy headed for the shed. Uncle Ross had told them what he wanted them to do there. They were to stack magazines and catalogs in neat bundles and tie them so they could be carted away.

Geeder had an odd feeling whenever she entered the shed. It was cool and shadowy, always. Both she and Toeboy were barefoot and the earthen floor of the shed felt clean and fresh. The whole place made whispering seem quite natural. The roof was boards, and long stripes of sunlight slanted to the floor. The sun got tangled in dust and cobwebs and glowed in dark corners. All was still. What little noise Geeder and Toeboy made was muffled, fading quickly. They took a good look around before settling down to work.

They sat close together. Toeboy stacked the catalogs, and Geeder had the magazines.

"I love going through old pictures," Geeder said. "It's the best fun of anything."

"It's not fair," Toeboy said. "You could let me have some of the magazines."

"Well, you can't have any," Geeder said. "Just do what you're supposed to and be quiet about it."

Toeboy was angry, but he contented himself with the catalogs anyway. He had two bundles of fifty stacked and tied before Geeder had stacked any magazines.

"You're not supposed to read them," he told her. "That's not fair at all."

"I'm just looking at the pictures before I stack them," she said.

"You'd better not let Uncle Ross catch you."

"You worry so much about nothing!" Geeder said.

"I believe I'll just go tell Uncle Ross," Toeboy said. He got up, heading for the door. Geeder smiled after him and continued turning the glossy pages of a magazine.

Toeboy stood at the corner of the shed. He waited for Geeder to come after him but she didn't. He stood, fidgeting and trying hard to be quiet. Finally, he came back inside. He knew instantly that something was wrong.

Geeder bent low over a magazine. On her lap were two more magazines that slowly slid to the floor. She pressed her hand against the page, as if to hold on to what she saw there. Then, she sat very still and her breath came in a long, low sigh.

"Geeder?" Toeboy whispered. "I'm not going to tell. I was only teasing you."

She didn't hear him. He crept up beside her and tried taking the magazine from her, but she wouldn't let go. He looked over her shoulder.

What he saw caused him to leap away, as though he had seen a ghost.

"I knew it all the time! I knew it!" Geeder said to him.

Geeder had found something extraordinary, a photograph of an African woman of royal birth. She was a Mututsi. She belonged to the Batutsi tribe. The magazine Geeder held said that the Batutsis were so tall they were almost giants.

They were known all over the world as Watutsis, the word for them in the Swahili language. Except for the tribal gown the girl wore and the royal headband wound tightly around her head, she could have been Zeely Tayber standing tall and serene in Uncle Ross's west field.

Toeboy carefully read what was written under the photograph of the African girl. "Maybe Zeely is a queen," he said at last.

Geeder stared at Toeboy. It took her a few seconds to calm herself enough to say, "Well, of course, Toeboy—what do you think? I never doubted for a minute that Miss Zeely Tayber was anything else!"

She was quiet a long while then, staring at the photograph. It was as if her mind had left her. She simply sat with her mouth open, holding the picture; not one whisper passed her lips.

Uncle Ross happened by the shed. He didn't see Geeder and Toeboy at first, they sat so still in the shadows. But soon, his eyes grew accustomed to the darkness. He smiled and entered. Geeder aroused herself, getting up to meet Uncle Ross. She handed him the magazine without a word. Uncle Ross carried it to the doorway. There, in the light, he stood gazing at the photograph, his face puzzled.

"The same nose," he muttered, "those black eyes, black as night." He looked from the photograph to Geeder, then to Toeboy and back to Geeder again. "So you believe Zeely Tayber to be some kind of royalty," he said, finally.

"There isn't any doubt that Zeely's a queen," Geeder said. Her voice was calm. "The picture is proof."

"You may have discovered the people Zeely

406

is descended from," Uncle Ross said, "but I can't see that that's going to make her a queen." He was about to say more when he noticed Geeder's stubborn expression. He knew then that anything he might say would make no difference. He left the shed without saying anything else, and when he had gone, Geeder danced around with the photograph clutched in her arms.

After seeing the magazine pictures, Geeder's curiosity about Zeely will not be satisfied until she uncovers the true origins of her Uncle Ross's exotic neighbor. Is Zeely of royal Mututsi birth, or merely an extraordinary woman? To follow Geeder's search for the answer to this question, read Zeely.

1. Where did Geeder and Toeboy spend their summer?

2. What did Zeely Tayber look like? What was so mysterious about Zeely and her father?

3. What did Geeder discover as she and Toeboy were working in the shed? Who did Geeder think Zeely Tayber really was? Did Uncle Ross share this opinion?

4. How did Geeder feel about her discovery?

5. What kind of person is Geeder? Give reasons for your answer.

6. Do you think that Zeely Tayber really is an African queen or do you think Geeder is letting her imagination run wild? Why?

7. Has anyone ever impressed you the way Zeely Tayber impressed Geeder? Who was that person? What special qualities did he or she have?

seven

MEET THE AUTHOR

Barbara Corcoran

Barbara Corcoran calls herself "a new Englander by birth . . . and a Westerner in spirit." Born in Hamilton, Massachusetts, in 1911, she now lives in Missoula, Montana. Although she has lived and worked in several states, she calls Montana "the state I love best." Many of her books are set in the Far West; they show her love for this rugged wilderness country.

All her life, Barbara Corcoran wanted to be a writer. From college days on, she wrote plays, stories, and radio scripts. But she has also been a typist, a stage manager, a story clerk, a copywriter, and an English teacher. Then, in 1966, she began *Sam,* her first book for young people. Since then, she has written over sixteen books. Wanting to devote more time to writing, she stopped teaching in 1969.

Ms. Corcoran most enjoys writing for young adults because they are "at an age when everything happens." A disciplined writer, she is at the typewriter from 9:30 a.m. until noon. After lunch, she either revises her manuscript or does research for the book she is writing. Ideas for her books

come from the memory of her own experiences, from her friends, and from news stories.

Some of Ms. Corcoran's characters are based on people she has known. For example, there is a girl who was a student in one of her classes. Ms. Corcoran wondered how this student would get along if she suddenly found herself in the wilderness. She answered that question for herself by writing *Sasha, My Friend*, part of which you are about to read.

Among the many awards and citations Ms. Corcoran has received for her writing is the William Allen White Children's Book Award of 1972 for *Sasha, My Friend*. The recipient of this award is decided upon by Kansas school children in grades 4 through 8. They are given a list of books from which to choose.

The author would most like her readers to remember the wolf in *Sasha* because wolves are nearly extinct in Montana. As you read the following excerpt, try to think about how you would get along in the wild. Then you might try to honor the author's wish and remember the wolf.

Sasha, My Friend

Not long ago Hallie's mother and father were in a
car accident. Her mother had died in the accident,
and her father had been badly injured. Hallie and her
father move from Los Angeles, California, to a
Christmas-tree farm in Montana in the hope that a
more peaceful setting would help him to recover.
Having grown up in a city, Hallie finds it difficult to
adjust to her new life in the wilderness. She misses

*her friends back home, especially Em, and she also
misses going to school. Now she gets her lessons in
the mail.*

*One person who helps Hallie adjust to her new
surroundings is Black Thunder, an Indian. While
walking through the woods with him one day, Hallie
discovers a white wolf pup whose own mother had
been killed in a trap. She decides to make the wolf
pup her pet, and she brings him back to her trailer.
The following excerpt from* Sasha, My Friend *shows
how Hallie learns to care for her pet whom she has
named Sasha.*

Hallie had to feed Sasha by dipping her fingers in milk and putting them in his mouth. The wolf seemed to be very hungry, and it took a long time to feed him. Her father made a box for him lined with gunnysacks. Sasha immediately clawed his way to the top of the box and fell out with a thump on the barn floor, so Hallie and her father covered the box with chicken wire.

When night came, Hallie begged permission to take him into her room. "Something might get at him out in the barn," she said.

"I never thought I'd share quarters with a wolf," her father said. "All right. Just remember he's not housebroken."

"I'll put newspapers on the floor," Hallie said. "It's no different than when we had Champ."

"It's slightly different," her father said. "At least it will be in time."

When Hallie went to bed, Sasha snuggled up on the floor beside her and promptly went to sleep. She was awake for a long time planning all the things that she and Sasha would do. She didn't want to think about the time when he would be too big to stay with her. Maybe her father would change his mind about that. He would get fond of Sasha too. She reached down and rubbed the soft fur on Sasha's sleeping head. "You've got to be very good," she murmured. He stirred and stretched his legs.

In the middle of the night she was awakened by a mournful howl. She sat up in bed to see Sasha on the floor in a circle of moonlight. Again he lifted his nose and howled. It was a wild unearthly sound. Sasha didn't remind Hallie of a dog anymore. He was a wolf all right.

She swung her feet to the cold floor and picked him up. He nuzzled her as she took him under the blankets and went to sleep again.

In the morning her father said, "Judging from the howls, his majesty was missing his mama."

"Poor Sasha," she said. "It's a strange sound."

"It's beautiful when you hear a pack of wolves off in the forest. It's almost like music. I don't know that I find it quite so entrancing when it's practically in my ear." But he patted Sasha. "We'll go into town and see the vet today. He'll soon be wanting more than milk."

She played with him all morning and after lunch her father turned the truck around and they drove into town. Sasha rode in Hallie's lap. It was Hallie's first trip to town except for the time she had slept through it on the way up. She was curious. And she didn't mind going to town, not now that she had Sasha.

It was smaller than she had imagined. There was one general store and post office, a feed store, a barbershop and a blacksmith shop. The sidewalk was a high wooden one, rickety in places. Most of the buildings were built on stilts. That was to avoid getting snowed in all the time, her father said. There weren't many people on the streets, and most of those that

were there were on horseback. The street
looked like the set for a western movie.

Her father stopped the truck in front of the
general store. "You stay here," he said. "I'll
find out where the vet is. Keep the wolf out of
sight."

"Why?"

"I don't imagine the ranchers in this town are
crazy about wolves." He jumped down and
went into the store. When he came back, some
time later, he had an armful of mail and some
packages.

"Sorry to be so long," he said. "Folks around
here like to talk. You have some mail." He
tossed it into the back.

"What's in the package?"

"Books and stuff I ordered."

"I suppose my mail is lessons." She stretched her neck to see.

"Yes, and a letter from Los Angeles."

She recognized Em's round handwriting. She wished she could read it right then, but she had Sasha to hold onto. "Did you find out where the vet is?"

"He's out in the country a mile or so." He drove down the narrow street.

"How does such a little town support a vet?"

"Ranchers. He's a big-animal vet."

"Will he know about Sasha? Sasha's so little."

He laughed. "He isn't going to stay little. I don't know how much he'll know about raising a wolf, but he'll know more than we do."

The vet lived in a small white frame house that needed painting. He had a big barn and several outbuildings. A small faded sign said, "J. L. Meyers, D.V.M."[1]

"You wait here a minute," her father said. He went up to the door and rang the bell. Hallie saw the door opened by a big man in shirt-sleeves. He didn't look like her idea of a vet, but of course she didn't know any big-animal vets. Her father talked to Dr. Meyers for a moment, and then he motioned Hallie to come in. Holding Sasha securely in one hand, she

[1] **D.V.M.**—Doctor of Veterinary Medicine

jumped down out of the truck and went to the house.

"This is my daughter Hallie," her father said, "and this is her wolf."

Dr. Meyers smiled. He had a big pleasant ruddy face. "Come on in," he said. "First wolf patient I ever had." He led them into a small office, where he sat down in a swivel chair and peered at them. Then he reached for Sasha, His hands were huge, but he held the little wolf gently. "A white one," he said. "That's very unusual."

"He's beautiful, isn't he?" Hallie said.

"He's a pretty little fellow." The vet turned Sasha around in his hands. Sasha grabbed his finger and chewed. Dr. Meyers laughed. "Glad he hasn't got his teeth yet." He looked at Hallie. "What do you plan to do with this little creature?"

"I want to keep him alive," Hallie said. "His mother was killed in a trap and he would have died."

"Hmm." The doctor continued to study Sasha. "Most of my clients would think I was crazy, doctoring a wolf. They don't like wolves much in these parts. I think a lot of it is superstition. Given normal circumstances most wolves will stay away from the livestock on ranches. They feed off other wild animals. They don't like to mess around where there are people either. Wolves are smart."

"That's what Black Thunder said," Hallie said.

Dr. Meyers grinned. "That's what Black Thunder said, did he? Sometimes I think he's planning on becoming a vet."

"Oh," Hallie said quickly, "he said you were a wonderful doctor."

Dr. Meyers put Sasha back in Hallie's hands. "Now you want to know what to feed this wolf, right?"

"Yes, please," Hallie said.

He got up and went into another room. It was quite a while before he finally came back with a feed sack. "I mixed up some stuff. Like I said, I never took care of a wolf before and I could be wrong. But try this out. Mix it with a little warm milk. If he doesn't like it, let me know." He looked at Hallie over the top of his glasses.

"Thank you very much," she said.

Her father took the sack and then paid
Dr. Meyers.

"I really shouldn't take any money for it,"
Dr. Meyers said. "It's like you might say a scientific experiment." He put the money in his
pocket. "Let me know how the little guy makes
out."

"We will," Hallie said.

The doctor took them to the door and shook
hands with them. "Good luck," he said.

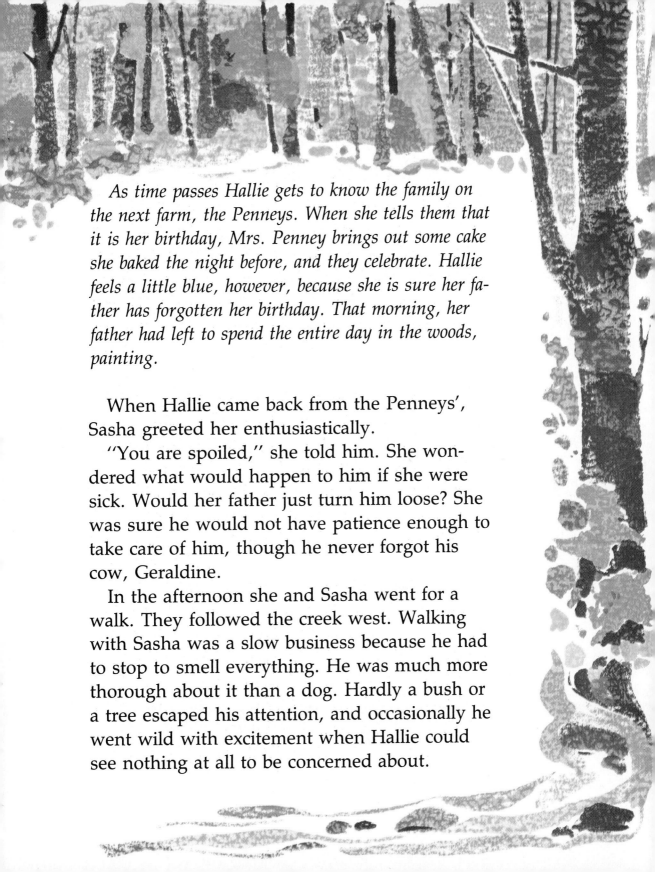

As time passes Hallie gets to know the family on the next farm, the Penneys. When she tells them that it is her birthday, Mrs. Penney brings out some cake she baked the night before, and they celebrate. Hallie feels a little blue, however, because she is sure her father has forgotten her birthday. That morning, her father had left to spend the entire day in the woods, painting.

When Hallie came back from the Penneys', Sasha greeted her enthusiastically.

"You are spoiled," she told him. She wondered what would happen to him if she were sick. Would her father just turn him loose? She was sure he would not have patience enough to take care of him, though he never forgot his cow, Geraldine.

In the afternoon she and Sasha went for a walk. They followed the creek west. Walking with Sasha was a slow business because he had to stop to smell everything. He was much more thorough about it than a dog. Hardly a bush or a tree escaped his attention, and occasionally he went wild with excitement when Hallie could see nothing at all to be concerned about.

Once he stopped, his nose quivering and every muscle tensed. Hallie looked around. Then she saw what his nose had discovered. A fawn stood in some brush, his protective coloration making him almost invisible. He was very young, all legs and ears. Enchanted Hallie stood and watched him. She picked up Sasha so he couldn't go close. He was making growling sounds in his throat and quivering all over.

As Hallie watched, the doe appeared out of the woods and crashed into the area where the fawn stood. Pushing the fawn with her nose, she got him started. They disappeared in a moment, but Hallie could still hear them. She sat down on the bank of the creek, hoping they might come back. When they didn't, she released Sasha and he loped over to the place where the deer had been, sniffing furiously.

Most of the ice was gone from the creek, and the water rushed over the stones with a merry sound. The day was warm, but when Hallie put her hand in the water it was icy. Near her a large hawthorne bush was in flower. She reached for one of the white petals that were faintly tinged with pink. A long thorn scratched her hand. Later, as she knew from Black Thunder, there would be tiny thorn apples that were delicious to eat. She held the petal in her hand studying its delicate structure. The bush smelled good.

Sasha came back and sat beside her, his
tongue lolling out. He was getting bigger every
day. His ears stood up large and attentive on
his well-shaped head, but he still had his baby
fur, soft and white as the lamb's. She wondered
if his mature coat would be white.

"You're not a baby anymore," she told him.

He took her wrist in his teeth and held it,
looking at her with his big eyes. She laughed
and took him in her lap. At once he wanted to
play. He rolled out of her lap and ran away,
dashing back again and pawing her with his big
front paws, like a young dog.

When she was tired of wrestling with him,
she got up and they walked on a little further.

Eventually they came to a beaver dam and stopped to inspect it. It was an intricate cone-shaped house made of sticks and mud. Nearby were the gnawed stumps of young trees that the beavers had cut down. The stumps stood about a foot above the ground.

Sasha sniffed out the whole area very carefully and then came back and sat at Hallie's feet.

She turned back and walked slowly downstream to the trailer. The forest seemed alive with small animals and birds. An Oregon junco with pink side feathers chirped at her from a yellow pine, and a mountain jay followed them for a way, his blue and black plumage bright against the green of the trees.

When she got home, her father had still not returned, although it was getting late. There were trout to cook for dinner, but they wouldn't take long. She decided she could wait a little while before she started dinner.

She picked up her copy of Keats and a letter that had come the day before from Em, and went to lie in the haymow. Sasha, tired from his walk, stretched out at her feet and fell asleep.

She re-read the letter slowly, trying to recreate in her imagination all the things that Em talked about. Several of her friends had gone to the dog show in Pasadena, and Em had shown her miniature schnauzer in the puppy class. He had won a ribbon. That night they had gone to Brown's for hot fudge sundaes to celebrate and then to a movie at Grauman's Chinese. She didn't say what the movie was.

Hallie lay on her back in the sweet-smelling hay and tried to remember exactly the taste of Brown's hot fudge sundaes. She tried to remember the faces of her old friends, but she could not remember all of them with clarity. Her whole past life seemed to blur and fade like a TV camera shot.

She opened the volume of Keats at random and read for a while, lying on her back with the sunlight slanting in through the opening in the wall. She grew sleepy, put down the book and half dozed. ". . . charm'd magic casements on perilous seas forlorn . . ." Was that how it went? The words kept running through her mind. In her imagination she saw the sea pounding over a jetty, throwing the white spray high into the air. Perilous seas forlorn. She fell asleep.

The barn was nearly dark when she awoke. She sat up, startled. It was long past time to start dinner.

When she went into the trailer, her father had already lighted the stove and rolled the fish in corn meal.

"I'm sorry I'm late," she said. "I fell asleep in the haymow." She reached for the frying pan.

"You sit down," he said.

She looked at him, puzzled. He never cooked anymore.

"People shouldn't have to cook on their birthdays."

"I thought you'd forgotten," she said.

"Of course not." Expertly he flipped the fish into the frying pan. "Sit down and enjoy your leisure."

She sat in the dinette and told him about the fawn and the beaver and the hawthorne bush, and the cake at the Penneys'.

"I had a good day too," he said. "By the way, I have something for you." He got up and came back with a big cardboard carton. He cut the string and pushed the package toward her. "Happy birthday."

She could not imagine what it was. It seemed to take forever to get the carton open. Whatever it was, it was heavy. She reached in and lifted it out. "A radio!" she said. "Oh, that's wonderful."

"Now you can listen to music from all over the world."

She turned it on, and the sound of a flamenco filled the little room. Her father tapped his heels merrily on the floor. "Olé,"[2] he said.

---

[2] **Olé** (ō'lā')

432

Music had been one of the things she had missed the most. She listened eagerly. When the number was over, an announcer said something in Spanish.

"We'll have to brush up on our foreign languages," her father said. He was watching her with a pleased expression. She turned the dial and they heard a man speaking French. Charmed, she kept turning the dial, pausing to listen to the different stations.

"Thank you so much," she said. "It's a wonderful present."

"I have one other little thing." He went into the living room and came back holding a small canvas, faced toward him.

"A picture for me?" She had some of his finished paintings, scenes in the forest that she thought were very good.

He turned it toward her. It was a painting of Sasha. The wolf was standing in the doorway of the barn, his head up, his two ears pricked to attention.

"Dad!" For a moment she couldn't speak. It was a fine likeness of Sasha, and she was touched that her father had done it for her. She set the painting on a chair and put her arms around him in a quick hug.

He laughed. "You and that wolf," he said.

Does Sasha continue to live with Hallie or does he return to the wilderness? Does Hallie want to stay on the farm, or does she yearn for the kind of life she used to know? Read Sasha, My Friend, and find out the answers to these questions.

THINK ABOUT IT

1. Why was Hallie afraid to keep Sasha in the barn at night?

2. What happened that made Hallie realize for the first time that Sasha was different from a dog?

3. Why were most of the buildings in town built on stilts?

4. When did Hallie first realize that her father had not forgotten her birthday?

5. Compare the way Hallie and her father felt about Sasha. How were their feelings the same? How were they different?

6. How did Hallie feel when she learned she had gotten some mail? How do you know?

7. If you went to live in the wilderness, what are some of the things that you would miss? What are some of the things that you would like about your new way of life?

AN INTRODUCTION TO
VETERINARY MEDICINE

"Doctor, we have an emergency!" The doctor flings open the doors to the operating room. "Quick," she says. "In here."

A man and woman watch anxiously as the cart is wheeled into the operating room under the huge light. The room is filled with complicated equipment. Feverishly, the doctor checks the patient's pulse. Strapping little wires to the patient's head, the doctor tells the orderly, "Hook this up through the phone to the lab in the city. We have to have an EEG immediately." The doctor prepares for emergency surgery without delay.

Outside the room, the man and woman comfort each other. "We shouldn't worry," the man says to his wife. "Fifi is in good hands. She'll be barking again in no time."

Barking? Yes, that's right. Fifi, the patient in this drama, is a dog, not a person. The hospital serves animals, not people. And the doctor is a veterinarian, or D.V.M., not an M.D.

Today's modern veterinary hospitals aren't too different from hospitals for people. And the role of today's veterinarian isn't too different from the role of a human doctor.

However, animal medicine was not always so similar to

436

human medicine. Veterinary medicine, as a serious science, began in India thousands of years ago. The ancient Indians had a great respect for animals. Because of this, the government paid for numerous well-equipped animal hospitals. The Indians were not only remarkable for their hospitals, however. They learned a lot about the treatment of animals by watching them. In this way, the Indians learned that animals often have the ability to heal themselves. By noting that sick elephants usually licked salty ground, for example, the Indians discovered that salt is a good cure for elephant colic.

There are written records that show the Chinese, the Egyptians, the Greeks, and the Babylonians also cared for animals. But none of these ancient cultures was as advanced as that of India in the field of veterinary medicine.

One of the greatest early veterinarians was a Roman farmer by the name of Varro. Varro discovered that the cause of a disease could be found through its signs or symptoms. Varro also may have understood the danger of infection through tiny germs. He wrote, ". . . as they dry, swamps breed certain animalculae which cannot be seen with the eyes and which we breathe . . . into the body where they cause grave maladies."[1]

Varro was the last scientific veterinarian of ancient times. After him, interest in animal medicine declined. Instead of veterinarians, barbers and other unqualified individuals performed remedies on animals that usually did more harm than good. Also, chants and weird medicines replaced the careful

---

[1]J. F. Smithcors, *Evolution of the Veterinary Art,* p. 66.

observation and study of animals. Eventually, the livestock of Europe began dying faster than people could bury them. By the mid-1700's, 200 million cattle had died in a 50-year period.

At last, in the year 1761, the first veterinary college was founded in France. Modern animal medicine had gotten its first foothold in old Europe.

But what about the New World, the American colonies? Actually, veterinary medicine began here about 100 years behind the times. The first public veterinary hospital was not founded until 1879. Until then, the colonies had been a natural paradise for animal life. The countryside was pest-free, and the animals suffered no contagious diseases.

Eventually, of course, diseases did come—mostly from Europe. The number of animal victims began to bring back memories of the European plagues. Finally, Iowa State College opened the first public veterinary college, and American veterinary medicine had caught up with modern times. Some early veterinarians, in fact, followed up their veterinary studies with degrees in human medicine.

Today, veterinarians have too much to learn about their own field to get degrees in human medicine. Today's vets have much to consider, too. For example, they have to decide whether to concentrate on research or actually take care of animals. They also have to decide whether to open a private practice, join someone else in partnership, or work in a hospital.

But the most important decision vets have to make concerns the kind of animals they wish to treat. Most vets

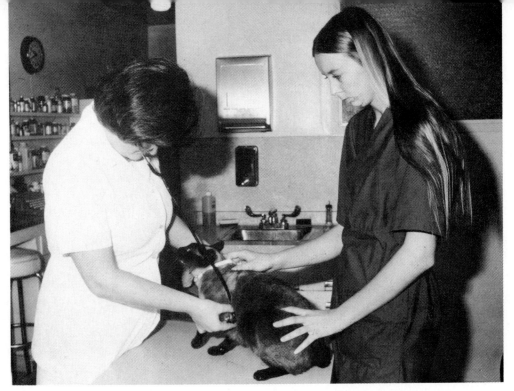
A small-animal vet is examining a Siamese cat on the examination table.

think of animal practice as divided into small and large animals. A small-animal practice is usually one in which the vet cares for household pets. Cats and dogs fall in this category. A large-animal practice is usually one in which a vet cares for large, valuable animals raised for riding or for food. Horses, cows, and other farm animals fall in this category.

There is another choice, of course. A veterinarian might choose to work for a zoo, treating both small and large animals. The life of a zoo veterinarian is probably the most exciting of all. In a single day, this veterinarian may operate on an orangutan, rub a rattlesnake's rash, and x-ray an alligator. Like all veterinary work, the work of a zoo vet requires quick thinking and good judgement. It also requires a deep love of the animal patients. Dr. Dolensek, the Chief Veterinarian of

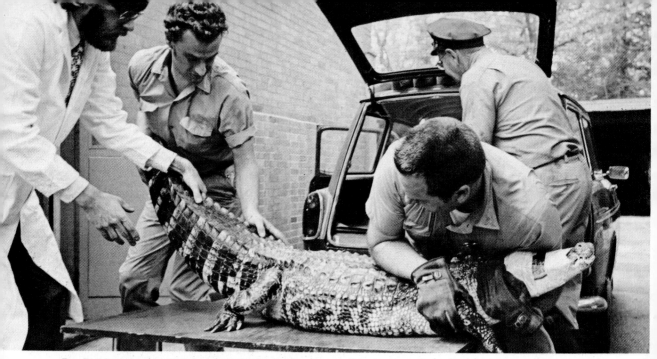

Dr. Dolensek, the Chief Veterinarian at the Bronx Zoo in New York City, and two zoo-keepers are strapping down an alligator to a table so that the alligator can be brought to the x-ray room to have its picture taken.

the Bronx Zoo, once said this about his job: "The hardest thing is the responsibility. Every time I handle an animal I'm causing him distress— discomfort, fright, pain, perhaps even death. I always hope I'm right to do it, but sometimes I'm wrong."[2]

For a small-animal vet, dealing with the pet owner is the most difficult part of the work. One vet has found a way to deal with this problem. He says, "In my experience, the more a client knows, the better he or she can cooperate for the sake of the animal. Your chief responsibility is to the animal. Between you and the animal stands the owner. . . . Your best bet is to make the owner an ally. . . . No matter what pressure you're under, you have to learn to do this if you're going to be a successful veterinarian."[3]

Do you like animals? Do you think you would like vet-

[2]Bruce Buchenholz, *Doctor in the Zoo*, p. 6.   [3]Patricia Curtis, *Animal Doctors*, p. 44.

erinary work? If so, there is one warning veterinarians repeat over and over. That is, make sure your love of animals is deep enough to withstand the disappointments and hard work. Although most people love animals, vets warn that only a few are willing to devote their lives to animal care.

To become a vet, you should begin your training in high school. Take as many science and math courses as possible. You should also spend some time caring for animals. You might join an organization dedicated to this purpose. Or you might ask a local veterinarian if you can work as an assistant over the summer.

The minimum amount of college required to get into a graduate veterinary program is two years. However, most veterinary students have completed four years of col-

lege. The veterinary program itself lasts four years. The first half includes courses in the basic medical sciences. In these courses, you learn about the anatomy or bodily structure of animals and the chemical changes that occur inside their bodies. You also learn about the tiny plant cells called *bacteria* that can cause disease. In the remaining time, student vets begin to work with animals, learning how to diagnose and treat illnesses. They also learn surgical techniques.

The course work for a vet is much like that for a medical doctor. In one sense, though, the vet may have a more difficult task. A doctor needs to learn only about human beings. A vet has to learn about many kinds of animals, from apes to zebras.

Before you decide to become a veterinarian, you should realize that getting

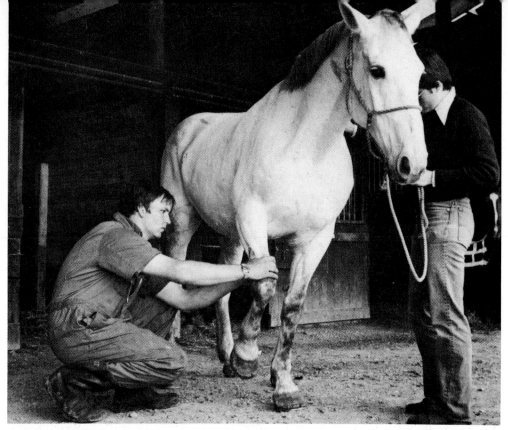

A big-animal vet is examining a horse to determine where the animal is feeling pain. The vet presses different parts of the horse's leg in an attempt to accentuate the pain and get a response from the horse. This procedure is necessary when the patient cannot tell the doctor where it hurts.

into veterinary school is not easy. There are only 22 of them in the United States, and the average first-year class size in each school is 88 students. In addition, the cost of a veterinary education is high.

There are other things to consider as well. One thing to ask yourself is how physically strong and healthy you are. Working with large animals often requires brute strength. You must also not mind long hours, the sight of blood, or endless questions from anxious owners. And, since the animals cannot actually tell you where they hurt, you must be especially observant.

If none of these facts discourages you, you can expect a rewarding career in veterinary medicine. You will probably live comfortably and enjoy the respect of your community. But perhaps your highest reward will come as you live out that part of the Veterinarian's Oath that states, "I solemnly dedicate myself and the knowledge I possess . . . to the relief of suffering animals."

THINK ABOUT IT

1. Why were the veterinarians of ancient India so special?
2. What did the Roman farmer, Varro, discover about infection?
3. What is a small-animal practice? a large-animal practice?
4. Why did it take so long for the first public veterinary hospital to be founded in the United States?
5. Imagine that you are already in high school and think that you would like to become a vet. Why is it a good idea to spend some time caring for animals?
6. Describe the kind of person who is most likely to succeed as a Doctor of Veterinary Medicine.
7. If you were going to become a veterinarian, would you prefer to work with small or large animals, or both? Why?

THE OLD and THE NEW

The following three poems are examples of haiku, a Japanese form of poetry which first appeared in the thirteenth century. Haiku are special because they say so much in just three short lines. They usually express an emotion or tell something about nature.

Read the first poem and imagine the colors of spring that the poet saw. Read the next two poems. How did the poet feel when the edelweiss bloomed? How did she feel about the arrangement of the trees in the forest?

Spring color swatches:
black tilled earth, barley green fields,
golden winter wheat.

The mountain was lost
in that first wondrous moment
the edelweiss bloomed!

A giant redwood
abreast the pigmy forest . . .
lopsided nature—

Helen Stiles Chenoweth

444

Concrete poetry is a more modern form of poetry which became popular in the early 1950's. In concrete poetry, the shape or visual structure of the poem helps to give it its meaning. Look at the following example of a concrete poem. Where does the poem begin? What do you like about it?

WITH THEM

COULD FLY OFF

I WISHED THAT I

INTO THE SKY

FLY OFF

SOME CROWS

ONCE I SAW

SKY DAY DREAM   *Robert Froman*

445

Do Bananas Chew Gum?

Sam Mott could add up the digits in a telephone number within seconds and rattle off facts about dinosaurs with ease. He had a keen imagination and a good sense of humor. But when it came to reading, writing, and spelling, Sam Mott had problems.

Every time Sam's father got a new job, the family had to move. Altogether, Sam had lived in five different states. Wherever he went to school his classmates soon discovered that Sam was not as good as they were in reading, writing, and spelling. When he moved to California the school there

gave him special tests to help identify his problems. The tests showed that Sam had a *learning disability.* This meant that Sam was not doing as well as he could in some areas of his schoolwork. His teachers felt that with professional help and a lot of hard work, he would be able to improve.

When Sam's father's job brought the family to a suburb of Chicago, Sam looked forward to sixth grade in a new school. If he was careful, he could hide his learning problems from his classmates. In the following excerpt Sam begins a job babysitting for Alex and Chuck Glass. The excerpt begins with Sam overhearing his parents discussing him.

"Look, Reba, the kid's not going to die of it."
Dad's low voice carried under my bedroom door.

"I just want to know how he's going to live with
it," Mom shouted back.

It was Tuesday, May 10, my first day baby-sitting
for Alex and Chuck Glass. I was still in bed, but I
was awake. My folks think I'm out like a light until
they wake me up at seven. But early in the morning is when I hear them talk about me.

"Well, Sam may not go to college . . ." my dad
said, trying to make her laugh, I guess.

"College? Ernie, get serious. At this rate the child
won't ever hold down a decent job. I hope he
even makes it as a baby-sitter."

"Sweetheart, he's only twelve. It takes some kids
longer to learn. You know that. I don't see why

they need to draw attention to him by giving him more tests."

"Look, how do we know those California tests were correct? Personally, I'm glad they're going to test him again. I'm glad I signed the permission slip. And I don't know why you have to be so bull-headed. *Something* is clearly wrong with him." She turned the water on in the bathroom and shouted over the noise. "The teacher just said they wanted to find out how they could help him. So a few kids find out he's not Einstein.* They'll find that out soon enough anyway."

My dad exploded. "I had a terrible time in school, and I made it. The kid's just like me."

"Well, that's no reason for you to do his home-work. It's not your grade. It's not your head."

"But it's harder stuff this year, Reba. That chapter on the Vikings isn't kid stuff. Besides, he likes it when I help him."

"You're not helping. You've got to let him work it out himself."

I closed my ears with the pillow. Through the feathers their voices sounded like a TV tuned low in the distance *(dum-dum-dum-dum)*. They hadn't told me I was going to have to take tests again. I hated those tests. All those questions I couldn't an-swer. To keep from thinking about it I opened my eyes. The first thing I saw was the shelves across from my bed, full of books neatly stacked because I'd never read them. "Someday you'll *want* to read

*Einstein (īn′stīn) 1879-1955, a brilliant American scientist

them, Sam," my mom always said. But I wanted to read those books about as much as I wanted to sleep with a tarantula.

In a pile of orange crates next to the bookcase I had stashed all the treasures I'd found in the five states where we'd lived. My mom says I find stuff because I slouch and keep my eyes down. I don't know, but I find good stuff. Not just dimes in sidewalk cracks, either, but a ring with a red stone, amber bottles, a railroad spike, old license plates, one watch that runs and one that doesn't, and stuff like that. My mom says it's junk, but it's my junk and I like it. It drives her up the wall.

She was always saying, "Why don't you *organize* it, Sam? Straighten it up. Make lists so you'll know what you've got." What she was trying to do was get me to practice writing, which I liked about as much as I liked to read.

I closed my eyes tight and found a suitcase of gold bricks that a hijacker had dropped from an airplane onto a beach, breaking open an oyster that hid thirteen perfect pearls. Then Mom opened the door and called, "Sam, it's seven. Rise and shine."

The rest of the day I didn't find so good. No lucky dime, no lucky day. Mom told me Dad wouldn't help me with my homework anymore because it spoiled me. ("I rot," I told her, but she didn't laugh.) Then Mrs. Bird gave a spelling test I did so bad on I felt like tearing it up.

After school I met Alex and Chuck by the kin-
dergarten door, and we galloped to their house like
we were horses . . . .

I was sitting in the Glasses' kitchen trying to read
this long, dumb typewritten note full of hard words
from Mrs. Glass when Alex screamed, "Help, Sam,
murder!" I grabbed my Social Studies book from
the kitchen table, figuring to smash the rattlesnake
that was swallowing him whole, and dashed into
his room.

The room was a mess. A crumpled bedspread
hung off the top of the bunk bed where Chuck was
trying to break Alex's arm.

"Get him off me," Alex yelled. I strolled over
and tickled Chuck's bare feet to break his hold. He
shrieked and tumbled off his brother, giggling.

But they were at it again like bear cubs as I
cruised for a good place to sit. The walls and ceiling were covered with green vine wallpaper to
make it look as big as all outdoors, but it was a little room. Most of the dresser drawers were open,
which made it even smaller. There was this red
wicker toy box without a lid, and, thumbtacked to
the ceiling, a green, dinosaur-shaped piñata with
pop eyes. Pajamas, used towels, and dirty socks
covered the floor, so there wasn't a whole lot of
sitting space.

I decided on the rocket-print chair in the corner where Al the tiger cat was curled up, sleeping. I nudged him out and flopped down sideways. My head rested on one pillowed arm and my feet dangled over the other. The chair didn't have any slats holding up the seat, so I sank deeper and deeper.

I shuffled through the dumb Social Studies book until finally I came to a drawing of a dead Viking. "You two just keep playing, OK?" I told them. "I've got a test tomorrow." They stopped wrestling and peered down at me.

"What grade are you in, Sam?" Alex demanded. "You're big."

"Sixth, and it's a pain," I told him. I am big. I'm five foot six, bigger than any other sixth grader, which makes me the tallest kid in school. My ears are big, my black eyebrows are bushy big, and my feet are size eleven.

"Do you wrestle?" he went on.

"Only if I have to," I said. "Now keep quiet so I can study."

Chuck flipped himself off the bed as fast as spaghetti sliding off a plate, grabbed one of my untied gym shoes, tossed it into an open dresser drawer, pulled himself up on a chinning bar in the closet doorway, and hung by his knees. Chuck said he wanted to be Spiderman when he grew up. I think he'll make it. His long yellow-white bangs dangled and his brown eyes gazed at me sharply.

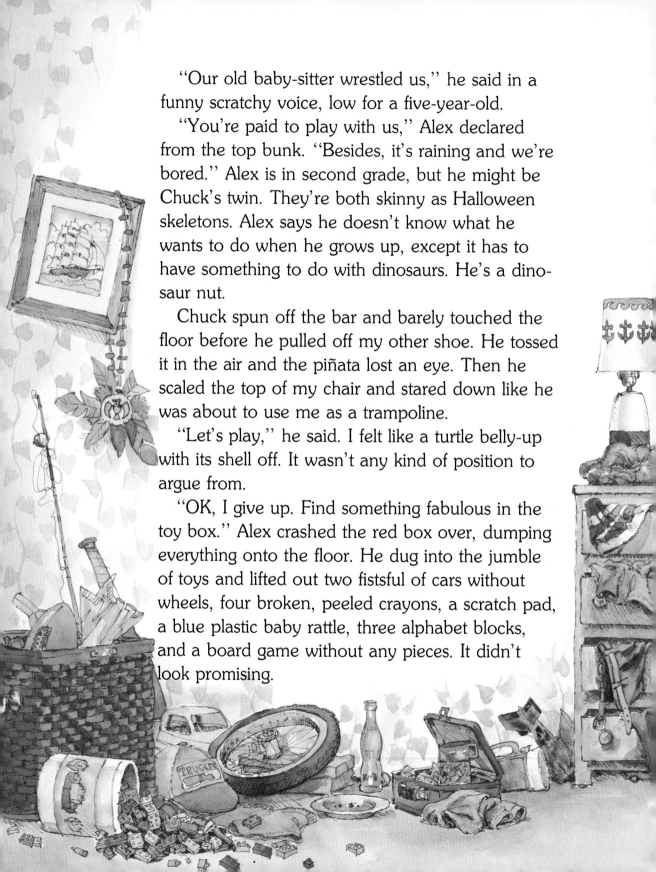

"Our old baby-sitter wrestled us," he said in a funny scratchy voice, low for a five-year-old.

"You're paid to play with us," Alex declared from the top bunk. "Besides, it's raining and we're bored." Alex is in second grade, but he might be Chuck's twin. They're both skinny as Halloween skeletons. Alex says he doesn't know what he wants to do when he grows up, except it has to have something to do with dinosaurs. He's a dinosaur nut.

Chuck spun off the bar and barely touched the floor before he pulled off my other shoe. He tossed it in the air and the piñata lost an eye. Then he scaled the top of my chair and stared down like he was about to use me as a trampoline.

"Let's play," he said. I felt like a turtle belly-up with its shell off. It wasn't any kind of position to argue from.

"OK, I give up. Find something fabulous in the toy box." Alex crashed the red box over, dumping everything onto the floor. He dug into the jumble of toys and lifted out two fistsful of cars without wheels, four broken, peeled crayons, a scratch pad, a blue plastic baby rattle, three alphabet blocks, and a board game without any pieces. It didn't look promising.

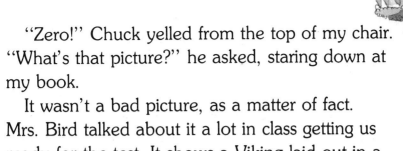

"Zero!" Chuck yelled from the top of my chair. "What's that picture?" he asked, staring down at my book.

It wasn't a bad picture, as a matter of fact. Mrs. Bird talked about it a lot in class getting us ready for the test. It shows a Viking laid out in a grave with one shield at his head and another at his feet. Two stirrups are spread over his legs, a really fancy engraved dagger and a two-edged sword lay by his side, and in another part of the grave are the bones of two horses. Underneath this Viking they'd found a gold coin. It would have been fabulous to find all that.

"It's a Viking," I told him. I thought I'd better make it brief. I didn't know how long he could balance.

"A Minnesota Viking?" Chuck asked, amazed. "Where are his shoulder pads?" He squatted down, teetering on the chair top.

I laughed. "This guy was meaner than a million football players. He fought people with his sword and took their gold."

"Gee," Chuck breathed. "What's he laying *there* for?"

"He's dead," I shrugged. "It's just a picture. My dad said he was found by archeologists—you know, those guys who go around digging up treasures."

Chuck brightened. "Hey, Sam," he said. "Make us a treasure hunt." And he tilted forward.

I reached up, pushed his toes off the chair, and watched him land on his feet like an inflated punching clown.

Alex shuffled through the toy heap and handed me the scratch pad with a stubby green crayon. "You hide something and then draw a map showing us how to find it."

Well, look, I'm no artist. I've got to admit it. At school I'd cut out pieces of paper and pasted them down so Mr. Kemper had said they were "interesting," but I have this very hard time making things look just right. Still, I didn't want to get fired for not playing with the kids. Mrs. Glass had said she'd give me eight dollars for four days a week and I already knew how I'd spend the money.

I rolled out of the slatless chair and wandered into the kitchen looking for something to hide.

"No peeking," I yelled, because that's what they were doing.

The phone rang. "Glasses' house. This is the baby-sitter," I said, like I was some kind of recorded message.

"Oh, Sam," Mrs. Glass laughed over the phone. "You sound so official. That's great. Listen, what I called about was not really to check up on you but

to find out if the dog was dead and if Chuckie took
his medicine without any trouble."

Some questions just don't have answers. I
couldn't think of anything to say at all.

"Sam?"

"What dog?" I asked.

"Rooster," she said. "Rooster. I locked him in
the basement all day. I never did that before, but
after what he did to my rug yesterday . . . . Sam,
didn't you let him up yet?"

"No, I . . ."

"Didn't you read my note? I typed it out special
because my handwriting's so bad."

"I started to, but . . ." I glanced down at the
note on the table. No way, though, could I talk and
read at the same time.

"So the dog is still cooped up in the basement."
She sighed, annoyed. "Isn't he barking?"

"No, I . . ."

"And good grief, that means Chuckie hasn't
taken his pill."

"I guess not, I . . ."

"The nurse at school gave him one at eleven-
thirty. He's supposed to have another at three-
thirty. It's after four. Look, do I have to come
home?" She was very mad.

"No, no. I'll give it to him right now. Where is
it?"

"It *says* in the note I typed out. It's all there.
Can't you *read*?"

"Sure. Sure. I'm sorry. We just got to playing
and stuff. I'll do everything right now. We'll see
you around five-fifteen." I hung up, looked again
at the jumble of words on the note, and felt sick.

"Alex," I yelled. "Let the dog up from the
basement."

The boys barreled down the hall, opened the
door to the basement, and called, "Rooster. Here,
boy. Come on, Rooster." I heard scratchy paws on
the steps and then this fat old brown and white
cocker spaniel started running around and around
my legs, yelping. At least Rooster wasn't dead.

"Chuck," I said. "Where are your pills?"

"I don't like pills," he told me, and crawled under the kitchen table.

"They're on the top shelf up there," Alex pointed, "where we're not supposed to go."

"How many do you take?" I asked Chuck as I climbed on a chair and took down a bottle from where Alex had pointed me.

"I don't take pills," he shouted at me from under the table.

"One every four hours," Alex said. "They're because last week he had an infected toe."

"Is this it?" I asked Alex. I didn't want to feed the kid poison.

"Sure, that's what is says on it, doesn't it? Chuck Glass."

I looked hard at the label. It seemed filled with print. But I think that's what it said. *Chuck Glass. One every four hours.* I was almost sure. I took

one out, put the lid back on, and put it on the shelf next to the bag of marshmallows.

"As soon as you take this, I'll hide a treasure," I said.

"OK," he said. He took the cup of water I had filled for him and gulped the lump down.

"Scoot," I told them. "I'll come in when it's ready." As soon as they left I climbed back up and took down the marshmallow bag. There were four marshmallows in it. They must have been left over from winter hot chocolate because they were stale and hard as marbles. I took them into the living room and stuck them under the pillows of the long brown velvet sofa.

Then came the hard part. I took the green crayon and drew a picture of the sofa and the coffee table in front of it. I put an X on the sofa. It was an awful picture. Even I couldn't tell what it was supposed to be. You couldn't tell which side was up.

"If you don't come, I'm going to jump off the ship and drown," Chuck yelled. So I quickly printed TOP at the top.

When I got back to their room the boys were standing on the upside-down toy box waiting for me. I knew it was a pirate's ship because Chuck was wearing a black paper pirate's hat with a skull and crossbones on it. It was the kind that you get at birthday parties when you're a little kid, along with a bag of chocolate coins wrapped in gold paper.

"What ho, matey?" Alex asked with a serious salute. "Have you found the buried treasure?"

"Aye, aye, sir. I got the pirate's map," I told him, "just before I made him walk the plank and the sharks ate him, toes first."

Chuck giggled. "Gimmie," he said, grabbing the paper and hopping off the box. "Splash," he said.

I took my book out to the living room to wait while they hunted around. I could hear them arguing and whispering. Then they shot off into the kitchen, smashing around in cabinets and shuffling through the pans.

"What are you guys doing?" I yelled at them finally. "You're not hot out there in the kitchen. You're not even warm. You're cold as ice."

"Mom keeps all her pots in the kitchen," Alex yelled back.

"Why are you looking for pots?" I called.

The two boys marched into the living room, Rooster waddling behind. Alex shoved the pad at me and pointed at my word on it.

"P-O-T spells pot," Chuck said, beaming because he could read. I looked at Alex.

"Well, that's what it says, doesn't it?" he demanded.

I looked at the pad. He was right. I'd written the dumb word backward. I used to do that a lot. It was really crazy. Then I started to laugh. Actually I didn't feel much like laughing. It wasn't funny at

all, but I put on the old clown act and ha-ha-ed
until the kids started laughing, too.

"Will you look at that," I said. "I must have
been thinking backward or something." I forced
another big ha. "That was really a dumb mistake.
What I meant was *top,* not *pot.* See, this is the top
of the page."

Gee, I hadn't done anything that stupid in a long
time. I thought I must be getting worse.

"It's not a very good picture," Alex said.

"I didn't want to make it too easy," I told him. "But I will tell you that right now you are very, very hot." I flung myself down on the sofa pillow that hid the marshmallows.

They looked at my map, looked at me, looked at the map again, tossed it on the floor, and started to search any old place. I sat and watched, thinking about how dumb I was.

After about five minutes of crawling around on his belly, searching under lamps and plants and stuff, Chuck thought about bouncing me and lifting the cushions.

"I found it, I think," Chuck yelled. "I think I found it."

Alex ran over and they both looked at the four scruffy marshmallows. Rooster, tail wagging low, sniffed them and walked away. "Is this supposed to be it?" Alex asked, sneering. "The treasure?"

"Well," I said, picking one up very, very carefully like it was made of thin glass. "You've got to understand that this is fabulous treasure. These are petrified dinosaur eggs." I held it up high over their heads. "They're worth a million dollars each. The reason you don't see them very often is they're sweet, see, and little kids, sometimes by mistake, eat them—petrified shell and all."

Chuck began to take one, but Alex batted his hand. "What kind of dinosaur?" he asked me, testing.

"Brontosaurus," I told him. My dad used to read me books about prehistoric stuff when he was on a dinosaur kick. We even went to a museum once to see dinosaur skeletons. I bet I knew almost as much as Alex did. "Brontosaurus," I told him, "the guy with the long spiked tail."

Alex liked this game. It was his kind of game. He gave me a big wink and glanced over at Chuck. "Will they hatch?" he asked.

"Hatch? Maybe. But they're petrified, see. And at least one of them has a petrified baby dinosaur inside."

Chuck grabbed one and stuck it in his mouth, whole.

"*Give* it to me!" Alex yelled, furious, poking him in both cheeks. "You can't eat dinosaur eggs."

Keeping his mouth clamped shut, Chuck's bottom lip jutted out and he began to cry.

"Give me the egg. *Give* me it," Alex was yelling when the front door swung open and Mrs. Glass walked in.

"Mom, make Chuckie give me the dinosaur egg," Alex wailed. Chuck stood there, mouth shut, huge tears rolling down his marshmallow-fat cheeks. His pirate hat sagged over his ear.

Mrs. Glass sat down on the living room rug and pulled the boys down with her. "Now tell me the whole story," she said to them, frowning at me like it was all my fault. She hugged Chuck, who started crunching away again on the petrified marshmallow, though you could still see the tear streaks on his cheeks. "Did you take your pill?" she asked him. He wrinkled his nose and nodded his head.

Alex gave Chuck a punch and told her about the treasure hunt.

"But that sounds like fun. Honestly, sweetie pie," she said to Alex, "it's just a game."

"He was cheating," Alex grumbled. "You don't *eat* games."

"But there are still three marshmallows left," she said, clearly irritated.

"The one he's eating," Alex said, looking Chuck straight in the eye, "is the one with the baby dinosaur in it."

Chuck stopped chewing and started crying again.

I smiled at her very big like "Aren't they cute little rascals?" She stared at my teeth. "Do you like your orthodontist, Sam?" she asked me.

I stopped smiling. "I guess," I told her, shrugging my shoulders. "Dr. Reynolds is all right. But I think Alex and Chuck are a little young. I mean, they don't usually give you braces until you're much older—like me."

"I was thinking of much, much older—like me." She laughed. "I want to do something about my front teeth," she said. "Do you think that's silly? My husband thinks it's silly." She smiled and I could see that her front teeth were crooked.

"It looks to me like you've got a severe malocclusion of the upper mandibular palate," I told her.

"No kidding?" she said, frowning.

"You want your teeth to look like *Sam's*?" Alex asked, astonished, forgetting all about the missing egg.

"Oh, I don't know," she said. She looked closer at my braces. "They don't look exactly gorgeous, do they? I wonder how long I'd have to wear them. Well, I want to talk to an orthodontist anyway." She ran her tongue across her teeth. "Severe malo— Look, write his name down for me, will you, sweetie? My hands are covered with marshmallow from weepy Chuckie." She gave him another hug.

"It's Dr. *Reynolds*," I told her, trying to get out of writing it down.

467

"I won't call him right away," she said. "I'll have to think about it. Please write his name down in case I forget it. Use the pad in the kitchen."

"Oh, listen, that reminds me," I told her. "I've got a three o'clock appointment with Dr. Reynolds tomorrow afternoon. I should get here by three-thirty at the very latest. Can the kids walk home from school by themselves? I mean, I could get another kid to come stay until I get here or something."

She bit her lip, thinking. "I don't know. Look," she said, "I'm just not sure you're up to this at all," and her eyes swept the room. The sofa pillows were on the floor. Rooster stood wagging his tail. "I mean you're . . ." She looked down like she didn't want to say it. "I was going to tell you. . . . When you didn't even read my note . . ."

"Please," I begged, stopping her before she finished. "I know I can do it. It was just a mistake. We were busy, and I forgot about the note." I tried to tuck in my shirttail and smooth my hair.

"We're not babies," Alex told her. He thought we were just talking about tomorrow. "We'll get home at three-fifteen. So what's going to happen in fifteen minutes?"

"I could eat a dinosaur egg in fifteen minutes," Chuck said. He grabbed one and disappeared out of the room.

"I'll cancel the appointment," I told her, desperately. "First thing in the morning, I will."

"No. No, it's OK," she said finally. "OK, I guess. For the time being. Now where's the name of that tooth straightener?"

I grabbed my book and then my raincoat from the hall, rescued my shoes from their hiding places in the boys' room, went into the kitchen, and, as slowly and neatly as I could, printed on the pad,

DR RenLDs

I ran into the living room and handed the paper to her, folded.

"Good-bye, you guys," I said, and dashed out into the rain as fast as I could, fast enough that she didn't have time enough to fire me for being stupid.

Does Sam get to keep his job as baby-sitter for Alex and Chuck? Is he able to continue to hide his learning problems from his new friends? To find out what happens to Sam, read Do Bananas Chew Gum? *Then, you will also understand how the book got its name.*

1. Why does Sam's father feel that Sam does not need to take more tests?

2. What two things did Mrs. Glass tell Sam to do in the note she left for him?

3. Why was Sam surprised when Alex and Chuck looked in the kitchen for the buried treasure?

4. Do you think Alex and Chuck enjoyed their first day with Sam as their baby-sitter? Why or why not?

5. Do you think Mrs. Glass was pleased with the way Sam handled his job responsibilities? Why or why not?

6. How do you think Sam feels about having a learning disability? Why do you feel as you do?

7. If you were Sam, would you want to be helped, or would you be content to live with your problems? Why?

The VIKINGS

Adventurers, warriors, raiders, looters, traders, colonizers—these are all terms that have been used to describe the Vikings. Who were these people? How have these words come to describe them? How did the Vikings influence the course of history?

The term *Vikings* refers to the people living in the Scandinavian[1] countries of Norway[2], Sweden[3], and Denmark[4] from the early 790's to about 1100. People were living there for centuries before that, however.

During the Viking Age, Europeans called the Scandinavians *Norsemen*, *Northmen*, or *Danes*; the term *Vikings* was not used until after the Viking Age. It probably came from the Scandinavian word *vic*, meaning *bay* or *inlet*. The Scandinavian coastlines are cut by many bays and inlets. The term *Vikings* meant those

---

[1]**Scandinavian** (skan′də nā′ vē ən)   [2]**Norway** (nôr′ wā)
[3]**Sweden** (swē′ dn)   [4]**Denmark** (den′ märk)

people who roamed the waters, raiding and looting towns along the way.

Because Scandinavia is cut off from the rest of Europe by sea, most of the Vikings knew nothing about European learning. While most could not read or write, they were excellent at crafts. Scandinavia is rich in forests, and so they became skilled lumbermen and carpenters. They built solid houses of logs and clay and decorated their furniture with beautiful carvings. They also became skilled metalworkers, for the northern mountains were rich in iron. From iron they made their own tools, kitchen utensils, and weapons. Much of their jewelry was made of gold and silver. They got these metals by trading with other countries.

Within time, every Viking community had its own district court, or *thing*. At meetings of the *thing*, all the landowners had a say in the affairs of their community. They settled arguments, made laws, and judged criminals.

The few Vikings who could read and write were considered magicians having unusual powers. Their writings were thought to be signs of good luck or charms against evil spirits. Because the Vikings did not yet have the papyrus and parchments of the European countries, they wrote on flat pieces of wood or stone. It was difficult to write on these surfaces. So the characters of their alphabet were made up of straight lines. Their alphabet had twenty-four characters, or *runes*. It was later simplified to sixteen characters. Each rune stood for one or more sounds.

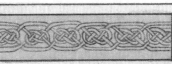

A rune stone

Because most people could not write, stories were passed down by word of mouth. The stories of their heroic adventures were called *sagas*. It was not until the twelfth century that they were written down by European monks and scholars hired by Viking chieftains. Today these stories tell us much about Viking life. They are considered a major contribution to literature.

By the end of the eighth century, the Vikings were growing restless. There were those who yearned for adventure, and there were those who yearned for riches. They had already begun trading with merchants in England, France, Byzantium[5], and Arabia.[6] They had seen the merchants' precious metals, religious ornaments, silks, gems, and spices. Now they craved these things for themselves.

In addition, the population was increasing rapidly, and farmland was growing scarce. The surrounding countries were either poorly defended or their people were fighting among themselves. The time for invading these lands was now perfect.

As master shipbuilders, the Vikings set out to explore and conquer in vessels

[5]**Byzantium** (bi zan′shē əm)
[6]**Arabia** (ə rā′bē ə)

better than those of other countries. Viking ships were light and easy to steer. They were *clinker-built*. This meant that the planks of the hull overlapped one another for extra strength. These ships were long and narrow, which is how they got their name *long boats*. At each end was a high, rising post carved in the shape of a dragon's or snake's head or tail. This was to ward off evil spirits and to frighten away the enemy. They had fifteen to thirty pairs of oars for rowing up river. They also had a woolen sail for sailing at sea.

Much is known about Viking vessels because some have been discovered in Norway beneath mounds of earth and clay. When a Viking chieftain died at war, he often was buried in his ship. He had his weapons and other belongings buried with him.

The Oseberg ship

One warship which has been uncovered is the *Gokstad*,[7] named for the place where it was found. Discovered in 1880, it was built around 900. It is 76 feet long, only 6 feet, 4 inches wide, and 6 feet, 6 inches deep. In 1893, a Norwegian, Magnus Andersen,[8] sailed across the Atlantic from Norway in a ship built just like the *Gokstad*. He reached Newfoundland, Canada, in less than one month. The ship was fast and easy to steer. It also withstood fierce storms.

The *Oseberg*[9] ship, discovered in 1903, was built around 800. Smaller and more richly carved, it is thought to have been the vessel of a Viking queen.

That the Vikings navigated as well as they did is amazing. They did not even have the aid of a compass. Instead, they navigated by looking for landmarks, such as mountains, rocks, sheets of ice, and islands. They also used the raven, a land bird. When the raven was let go at sea, it flew to the nearest land. The ship would then follow it.

By the late 900's, the Vikings were able to determine latitude. They did this by using the North Star, which never moved, and a wooden instrument that they had made. The *husanatra*,[10] as it was called, was probably a stick about a yard long with notches carved in it at equal spaces. At night, the navigator held the stick in front of him as he gazed at the North Star. He noted which notch lined up with

[7]**Gokstad** (gŭk′ städ)   [8]**Magnus Andersen** (mäng′ nəs an′ dər sən)
[9]**Oseberg** (üs′ ə verg)   [10]**husanatra** (hüs′ ən ät′ rä)

the star. If, the next night, a different notch lined up with it, then he knew his ship had been blown off course. Then he steered his ship either north or south to get back on course.

There were three groups of Vikings, named according to their homelands. They were the Norwegian Vikings, the Swedish Vikings, and the Danish Vikings. The Viking invasions began in 793, when the Norwegian Vikings attacked and raided a monastery off the east coast of England. They wanted its treasures. This started a wave of raids against England, Ireland, the Isle of Man,[11] and also Scotland.

In the mid-800's, the Norwegian Vikings went further from their homelands. They burned towns in France, Italy, and Spain. By the late 800's, they dared to cross the rough waters of the North Atlantic, and they began migrating to Iceland. In 982, a Viking chieftain named Eric the Red left his home in Iceland and sailed west. He landed on a continent which he named Greenland for its lush country. Soon, he and other Vikings settled there. Later, in a voyage from Iceland to Greenland, a sea captain named Bjarni Herjulfsson[12] sailed off course. Eventually, he spotted the mainland of North America.

Ten years later, most of the cropland in Greenland had been taken. Then, people became interested in the new land that Herjulfsson had seen. Around 1000, Leif

[11]**Isle of Man** (īl ov man)
[12]**Bjarni Herjulfsson** (byär′ni her′yülf sən)

Ericson,[13] son of Eric the Red, went westward from Greenland to find it. He landed in a place that had many grapevines. So he called it *Vinland*.[14] Historians disagree about its exact location. It might have been Maine, Massachusetts, or even Newfoundland. The Vikings never settled there. About 500 years later, Columbus rediscovered the very same land.

The Swedish Vikings went east, as far as the Black and Caspian seas. They set up many trade centers in what is now western Russia. By the late 800's they set up the first Russian state.

The Danish Vikings went south to Germany, France, England, Spain, and the Mediterranean coast. In 1016, they conquered England and ruled there until 1042.

[13]**Leif Ericson** (lāf er'ik sən)

[14]**Vinland** (vin'lənd)

The Vikings sailed from Scandinavia in three main directions from the A.D. 700's to the 1000's. The Danes went south and raided Germany, France, England, Spain, and the Mediterranean coast. The Norwegians traveled to North America. The Swedes went to eastern Europe.

From *The World Book Encyclopedia* © 1981 World Book-Childcraft International, Inc.

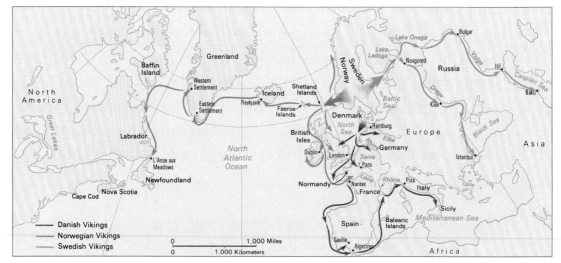

By 1100, the Viking Age had come to a close. The Vikings had set up trade centers and colonized many of the lands they had invaded. They had realized that trading offered a more stable and prosperous life than did raiding and looting. In time, they learned the ways of the people living in the countries they had settled. Today, they are known for having established many of the trade routes still in use. Certainly, without their courageous spirit, seaworthy ships, and unusual ability to navigate, this could not have happened.

THINK ABOUT IT

1. What does the term *Vikings* mean?
2. Why were the runes made up of straight lines?
3. Why did the Vikings make ship posts that were frightening to behold?
4. What are the three main reasons why the Vikings set out to explore and invade other lands?
5. Why do you think it was natural for the Vikings to become skilled carpenters?
6. Why do you think the Vikings looked upon those who could read and write as magicians?
7. How would you feel if you discovered land that you thought no one else knew about?

Inside a Passenger Ship

Ships have changed dramatically since Viking days. As more and more people traveled across the seas, there was a demand for larger ships to accommodate them. Shipping companies competed for business by making larger, faster, and more luxurious ships. From the 1920's through the 1940's, the large passenger liners were considered to be the queens of the sea.

You are looking at the Queen Elizabeth 2, a British-owned ship. Built in 1968, it is the last of

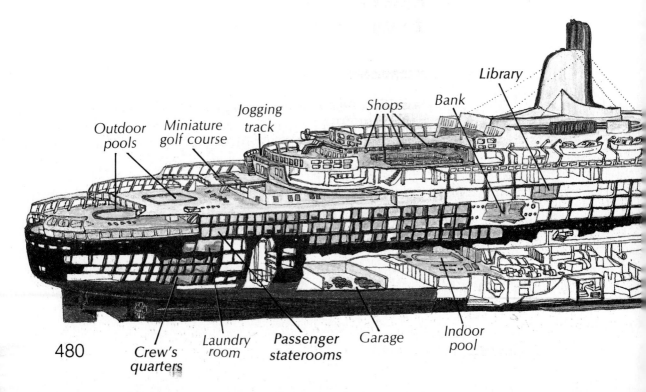

Outdoor pools

Miniature golf course

Jogging track

Shops

Bank

Library

Crew's quarters

Laundry room

Passenger staterooms

Garage

Indoor pool

the large liners. The need for new liners ended as more and more people took to the air for much faster travel at less cost.

Imagine a ship that is 963 feet long and 105 feet wide, a ship that can hold 1740 passengers and 1000 crew members. That's a lot of ship, and that's the Queen Elizabeth 2. Examine the cutaway diagram below to find out what is inside the ship. Then use it to answer the following questions:

1. Can people take their cars on the ship? their pets?
2. Where can people find books to read? enjoy a concert? cash a check? see a doctor?
3. What kinds of recreational facilities are available for both children and adults?

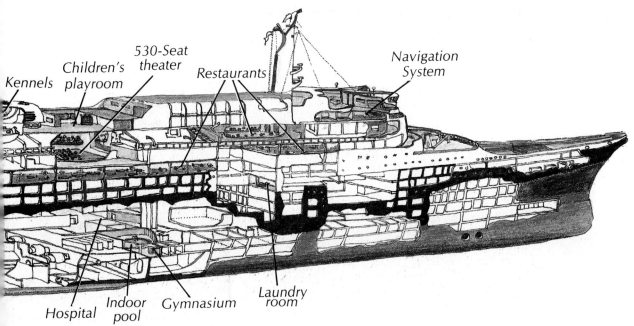

Kennels Children's playroom 530-Seat theater Restaurants Navigation System

Hospital Indoor pool Gymnasium Laundry room

MEET THE AUTHOR
William Pène du Bois

Born in Nutley, New Jersey, in 1916, William Pène du Bois is a famous author and illustrator of children's books. His best-known work is *The 21 Balloons,* for which he won the 1948 Newbery Medal. This award is given for the best children's book of its year.

Since boyhood, William du Bois has had three great interests: France, the circus, and mechanical inventions, especially balloons. On the walls of his room hang pictures of French castles, circus drawings, old colored prints of balloons, and drawings of his own inventions, like the balloon merry-go-round. But how did Du Bois become interested in these things?

Long before he could read, he spent hours pouring over pictures in books. His favorite books were written by Jules Verne. Verne's science fiction stories had fascinating pictures of strange machines that traveled under the sea, over the land, and through the air.

Between the ages of eight and fourteen, Du Bois lived in France where his love for the circus grew. By the time he was eleven, he visited the French circus weekly. He enjoyed, especially, the clowns, and he drew pictures of his favorite ones.

Du Bois says that the two greatest influences on his art were his father, both a painter and art critic, and a math teacher he had in France when he was ten. The teacher would study his students' homework pages as though they were works of art. If a page was neat, he expressed his approval; if it was sloppy, he frowned and tore it into four equal pieces. In this way, Du Bois gained a useful sense of order which he carried to his art work.

Before he begins to work, he collects all the art supplies he will need, lining them up in orderly rows. He draws each line slowly and with precision. He makes only one drawing a day, but it must be the best he can do. As he draws, he develops his ideas. Then, when he is ready to write, he writes quickly.

The characters he creates are always good. You are about to meet two of them in the following selection from *The 21 Balloons*.

THE
21
BALLOONS

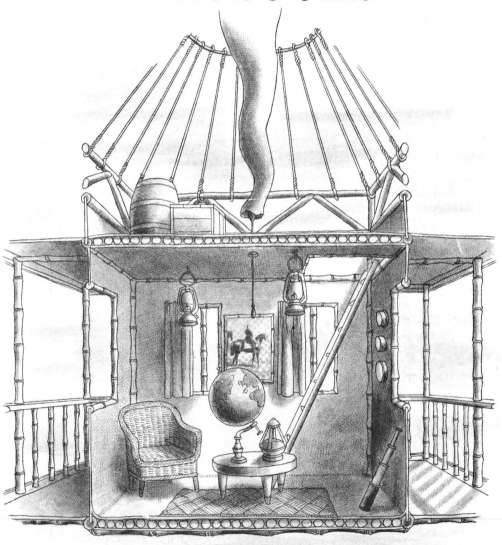

illiam Waterman Sherman, a retired professor who had taught math for forty years, looked forward to a year of rest and relaxation. He thought this could best be done by traveling around the world in a gas balloon specially designed for the yearlong trip.

On August 15, 1883, Professor Sherman boarded the basket house of his balloon craft, the Globe. *It was large enough to provide the professor with the basic comforts of life. A staircase led to the roof of the house where he stored his year's supply of food. A balustrade built around the roof prevented the food from falling off it. He used the small porch built around the basket house as a lookout. A balustrade also enclosed the porch.*

The balloon was filled with gas, and the cords that held it to the ground were cut. Up, up, the balloon rose, and for three weeks Professor Sherman drifted peacefully through the air. Then, suddenly, his trip was shortened by an unexpected event. In the excerpt from the book that follows, Professor Sherman explains his adventure to the Western American Explorers' Club, of which he is a member.

The seventh day, Ladies and Gentlemen, was dreadful.

I shall never forget the seventh day of my voyage for as long as I live. Just about everything went wrong, and my dreams of spending a year in a balloon were shattered. The first thing I noticed on the morning of that fateful day was a small speck in the distance. I figured it had to be land. Land on my seventh day out! I must have flown straight across the Pacific Ocean at a fabulous speed! I had originally hoped that the winds would blow me in different directions and that I would spend at least a month without seeing any land. The small speck in the distance before me was slowly taking on the shape of a little volcanic island. Most of it was mountain, and a column of smoke slowly rose from it into the blue sky.

Then, from out of nowhere, appeared sea gulls. They were the same kind of birds that had seen me off in San Francisco, and now they were welcoming me to an island I hadn't wanted to visit.

At the sight of the gulls, I dumped my garbage overboard. I thought this was a fine idea. I was not

only feeding the gulls but also making my basket
lighter. This way I could rise up high enough to
clear the island and get away from it. However, it
didn't work out quite the way I had hoped. The
gulls plunged into the water after my food. One of
them grabbed what was left of the smoked turkey I
had been living on for most of the week. He took it
onto the very top of my balloon and settled down to
devour it in comfort. The other gulls dived for all of
the smaller pieces of food in the ocean. Then they
flew back up to where I was and noticed their friend
feasting on cold turkey on the top of my balloon.
They started to caw and fight over it. They were out
of my reach and all I could do was pace around my
small porch, hoping that nothing would happen to
my balloon. I leaned over the balustrade, looked

up, and saw one lone sea gull gliding very slowly over the *Globe*. His head hung down with that frightening look of a hawk studying his prey. He circled slowly around the balloon once, then dove. He aimed straight for the turkey. Whether he got it or not, I'll never know. There was loud and confused sea gull action on top of my balloon. They all seemed to fly away at once, and then I heard something terrible. It was the sound of a sea gull beating his wings and cawing for breath in the thin atmosphere inside the silken bag of my balloon.

On this seventh day of my trip, which was supposed to last a year, I found myself with a hole in my balloon the size of a sea gull.

I was heartbroken. It was impossible for me to get at the hole in order to attempt to mend it. The *Globe* had already begun to lose altitude. I had to try to land on the island. I was descending quickly and I knew that I would be in the ocean long before I reached the island. I started throwing things overboard to make my basket house lighter so that I would fly above the water longer. Since I knew nothing about the island I was approaching, I decided to save all of my food in case I needed it to live on when I landed. I threw overboard everything I could not eat. This included chairs, a table, books, a water distiller, water cans, dishes, garbage containers, cups, saucers, charts, globes, coat hangers, clothes, and more. Whatever I could lay my hands on I threw out the windows, through the doors, or off the porch. In this manner I rid myself of anything which weighed anything. The *Globe* continued to descend at a speed which was far too great if I were to make the island. I had to throw away my food. I threw all of the heavier canned goods first. This wasn't good enough. I threw the fruits, vegetables, smoked meats, everything in my house. I looked overboard. I was only a few hundred feet above water and the island was still over a mile off. Then I discovered something new and more frightening. A school of sharks was following

490

me in the water beneath and swallowing the food I threw as soon as it hit the water. This meant that I had to make the island or fall among the sharks. I was desperate.

There was nothing left in the house to throw overboard. I threw most of the clothes I was wearing next, leaving on my right shoe. I walked around the porch and, clinging to the windowsills with my arms, I kicked the balustrade off the porch with my right foot. The balloon still had a half mile to go.

There was only one thing left to do. I climbed up on the roof of my basket house, pulled the ladder up and threw that overboard. Then I cut the four ropes which attached the house to the balloon at each corner and tied them together tightly. I looped my left arm through these ropes. Then I slashed all of the other ropes supporting my house. My basket house fell and splashed among the sharks and the *Globe* gave a small leap upward. I kicked off my right shoe and hoped I would be safe.

A minute or two later, I felt my toes hit the water. I shut my eyes, afraid to see if any sharks were about. But my toes only skipped once or twice on the water's surface when I found myself being dragged across the beach of the island. The giant deflated bag of the *Globe* came to rest on top of a tall palm tree.

I was exhausted, burned by the sand, and too weak to crawl out of the sun into the shade. I must have gone to sleep on this beach.

After having slept for four or five hours, I found myself being gently awakened. I opened my eyes. My body was bright red from sun and sandburn. I looked up at what I thought was a man kneeling over me, shaking my shoulder and speaking to me in perfect English. "Wake up," I thought I heard him say. "You've got to get out of the sun. Wake up, wake up." I thought this must be part of some wild dream. The idea of a man who spoke English on a small volcanic island in the Pacific seemed so odd. I shut my eyes again. But as soon as I did this, I felt my shoulder again being shaken and heard this same voice which kept saying, "Wake up, wake up; you've got to get in the shade!"

I shook my head and opened my eyes again. There was a man kneeling over me. As I sat up he stood up. He was handing me some clothes, and he was dressed in a most unusual manner. This man didn't look like a native, an explorer, or a traveler. He looked like an overdressed aristocrat lost on an empty volcanic island.

He was wearing a carefully tailored white morning suit with pin-striped pants, white tie, and a white hat. The suit he was urging me to put on was just the same as the one he had on, only in my size.

"Where am I?" I asked.

"You are on the Pacific Island of Krakatoa,"* he answered.

494   *Krakatoa (krak ə tō′ ə)

(When Professor Sherman mentioned the word "Krakatoa," a feeling of excitement ran through the audience. Recently there had been news stories telling that half of Krakatoa had blown up in the greatest volcanic eruption of all times.)

"But I always thought that no one lived on Krakatoa," I told the gentleman in the white morning suit. "I always heard that the volcanic mountain made living on the island impossible."

"This is Krakatoa, all right," he said. "And we who live here are pleased that the rest of the world still thinks that no one lives on Krakatoa. Hurry up, put on your clothes."

I had put on the white pin-striped trousers and the shirt as the gentleman handed them to me. The shirt had starched cuffs and a detachable wing collar. I didn't bother putting on the collar, and started rolling up my sleeves. "Let's go. Lead on," I said.

"Come, come," said the gentleman from Krakatoa. "You can't come and visit us like that. Is that the way you would call on polite people in San Francisco, New York, London, or Paris? Roll down those sleeves. Put on this collar, vest, and coat." As he was saying this he was smiling warmly to show that he meant no ill feeling. He was merely setting me straight on Krakatoa style and manners. "I'll admit," he continued, "that on other islands in the Pacific it is all right to give up shaving and haircuts and to wear whatever worn clothes are available.

Here, we prefer a more elegant way of life. You, sir," he said, "are our first visitor. I am certain that you will be impressed with the way we live. I hope you will be impressed anyhow. Since we believe in keeping this place absolutely secret, I believe you will be spending the rest of your life as our guest."

While he was talking, I had rolled down my sleeves. He handed me a pair of cuff links made simply of four diamonds the size of lima beans. He handed me diamond studs with which to button up my shirtfront. I attached my wing collar. He held a small mirror so that I could more easily put on my tie. As I put on my white hat I was filled with many emotions. I thought that this was the silliest situation I had ever been in. I was also giving a lot of thought to his remark about being a guest of the people of Krakatoa for life. It was with deep, mixed feelings that I assured the gentleman that I was already quite impressed.

"Well, come then." he said. "First I'll show you our mountain."

He had led me through a small forest of palm trees. The underbrush was thick and wild, similar to the untouched jungle life found on any Pacific island. My host walked through this in a most peculiar way. He was holding up his pant legs and carefully picking the right spots on which to rest his feet. He did this because he did not want to disturb the

creases in his suit. Since my suit was borrowed, I felt that I had to treat it with equal care. We must have made a funny sight, two gentlemen in white suits and hats tiptoeing through the jungle.

Suddenly a remarkable change took place in our surroundings. As we neared the mountain, the underbrush in the jungle became less and less and then ended altogether. Instead of thick wild roots, giant ferns, banyan trees, and the usual webs of jungle life, I found myself walking on soft green grass. It smelled and looked as though it had just been mowed. It was like a tropical garden in the zoo of some great Capital. I was quite surprised by this and remarked about it to my host. He explained that the underbrush had been cleared everywhere except for a fringe of jungle all the way around the island. This was done so that people in passing ships would think that no one was living there.

When we were about a hundred yards from the foot of the mountain we stopped and sat on a bench. I took the opportunity to introduce myself. "My name is Professor William Waterman Sherman," I said, extending my hand. He shook hands with me and said, "I am Mr. E."

"Mr. E. what?" I asked.

"Simply Mr. E.," he said. "I shall have to explain about that later. The reason I suggested that we sit down on this bench is that we are quite close to the mountain. The mountain has been quiet all morning. This is rare. It is seldom quiet for more than an hour at a time. When the mountain starts rumbling, you will feel the whole island shake beneath you. You will find this frightening and unpleasant at first. We all did. It will take you some time to get what we call 'mountain legs.' 'Mountain legs' are to us what 'sea legs' are to sailors. Before we got our 'mountain legs,' many of us were as sick as a passenger on a rough sea voyage. I am just warning you so that you won't be scared. The land is roughest near the mountain."

It seemed as if this explanation had been a signal for the mountain to perform. We had just left the bench and continued on when we heard a noise like muffled thunder coming from underfoot. This noise became louder and louder, and the surface of the earth started to shake and roll. I ran back to the bench, lay on it, and clung to it with all my might. I looked at Mr. E. He was calmly moving up and down with the surface of the earth like a bottle in rough water. The earth didn't crack or split beneath us at all. I thought that being in Krakatoa was like riding on the back of some giant prehistoric animal. The noise could be compared to great stomach rumblings. The surface of the earth was like some huge bit of animal hide, stretching and buckling over large muscles and bones.

Mr. E. waved to me to come on. He was standing in a very relaxed way, as if he were on firm ground. Except, he was moving up and down. I felt very dizzy. I fell down four times between the bench and Mr. E. To my complete shame and disgust, I became ill while attempting to get to my companion. Grabbing me by the arm with a firm grip, Mr. E. helped me off the ground.

"You can see now why Krakatoa was always considered unfit to live on," said Mr. E.

"I couldn't be more convinced," I groaned.

"That's the peculiar thing about nature," explained Mr. E. "It guards its rarest treasures with greatest care. Every year on other Pacific islands hundreds of natives lose their lives trying to bring up pearls from the floor of the sea. Man pays nature a high price for pearls. This noisy volcano on Krakatoa has frightened people away from the island for centuries. This fickle, dangerous, and fearful mountain has a mine at its feet. I am now leading you to this mine."

We reached the foot of the mountain with great difficulty because I could not walk as easily as Mr. E. We were suddenly standing on a piece of ground which didn't move at all. I can assure you that I was relieved. There was another bench on this still piece of earth and I ran to it and sat down. I looked out over the quivering landscape and listened to the loud rumblings. I found I couldn't stand to look at it for any length of time. Just the sight of this billowing lawn and the bending and bobbing palm trees almost made me ill again. Mr. E. sat beside me for a while and then suggested that we move on. He took me to a wall of the mountain behind this second bench. In the wall was an entrance covered up by an old wooden door from a ship. Mr. E. reached in his pocket and took out two pairs of glasses with dark lenses. "You'll need these," he explained. "Whatever you do, do not remove them while in the mines." I put them on. Mr. E. moved the old door to one side and asked me to follow him. I obeyed.

As soon as I entered the mines I understood why the ground above, where I had just been, didn't move. I understood why the walls about me didn't move and why the ceiling and ground beneath me

didn't budge. I understood why this was a peaceful place in a rumbling, throbbing landscape.

Ladies and gentlemen, the walls, the floor, and the ceiling of this mine were made out of the hardest of all of nature's minerals. It was made out of pure, clear, dazzling diamond. I was up to my ankles in diamond pebbles. The floor was covered with diamond boulders and diamonds as big as cobblestones. Here, even the famous Jonker Diamond would have been as impossible to find as a grain of salt in a bag of sugar. This was diamond in its cleanest state, ready to be cut. It was pure crystallized carbon unmarked by any form of dirt.

I was dumbfounded. I had read about and seen pictures of the famous salt mines of Poland and the crystal caves of Bermuda. Here was a sight a thousand times more blinding and wonderful. This was a sight that would make the greatest fairy tale seem real.

I waded around in the diamonds and picked up great handfuls of the jewels, letting the smaller ones slip through my fingers. I juggled with two heavy diamonds the size of baseballs. I suddenly felt like a small child let loose in a candy shop.

"May I have some of these?" I asked. My voice was trembling.

"Sure," he said, "fill your pockets if you wish. But come outside with me for a moment."

I eagerly stuffed my pockets and followed him

out of the mine. The sunlight outside seemed dark in comparison with the sparkling, blazing brightness inside the mine. Even without our dark glasses it seemed as though the blue sky had suddenly turned gray. It was hard at first to see any color in the tropical landscape. But then our eyes became used to the sunlight and the grass again became green. The sky became blue, and my companion's face took on a healthier glow.

"Sit down," he said, pointing to the bench nearest to mine. "I have quite a bit to tell you. You may think that your landing on this island was all by accident. The only accident is that the wind blew you exactly in the direction of Krakatoa. The fact that a hungry sea gull dove into your balloon, forcing you to land here, might be called an accident. But if that hadn't happened, I would have seen to it that you would have landed here. If you had flown over Krakatoa, you would have been the first outsider ever to do so. You would have seen that there are houses on the island. You would have seen our buildings, parks, and playgrounds. You would have told the rest of the world that there are people on Krakatoa. We wouldn't have liked that at all. You have seen our diamond mines. That is, you have seen one of them. There are many other unexplored plots of ground around the base of the mountain where the earth doesn't ever move. Do you understand now why you will have to remain our guest forever?"

"I do indeed," I assured him.

"Later on, after you have had time to think this over carefully, I know that you won't want to leave Krakatoa. There is fabulous wealth and power attached to owning a share in the mines. You do own a share now because the mines belong to all who know they exist.

"So now that you are here, you are automatically a citizen of Krakatoa. You own a share of the mines. If you could spend all the money you are worth, you would have to spend a billion dollars a day for the rest of your life. But if you took your share of diamonds to another country, you would be making a horrible mistake. Diamonds are worth a lot because they are extremely rare jewels in other countries. Unloading a boatload of diamonds in any other port of the world would cause the diamond market to crash. This means that the price of diamonds would drop to next to nothing. Then your cargo would be worth no more than a shipload of broken glass.

"Every year, the people of Krakatoa take trips to a different foreign country. We buy our supplies for the year and return to Krakatoa. We each take with us one fairly small diamond which we sell to different brokers in different big cities of the country we visit. At first we thought we should promise not to tell anybody about Krakatoa and the secrets of our diamond mines. But this wasn't necessary. You will find that out as soon as you go to a different country. You'll start thinking of the fabulous wealth in diamonds you have back in Krakatoa. Then you will understand the value of diamonds in other countries, and remember that telling of Krakatoa would destroy the diamond market. You will find out that you will not even mention the Pacific Ocean.

"You asked me a short while ago if you might have a few diamonds. Help yourself. It is only natural to want to carry some around your first few days here. We are so used to them that we just leave them in the mines. They are worthless to us here. We each own a fortune about one hundred times as big as the Treasury of the United States. But there is no place here to spend money, so we leave them where they are."

This talk made me feel rather silly. I meekly walked to the mines and tossed back the mere half-million dollars' worth of stones I had picked up. My mind was spinning. The excitement of my crash, the rolling of the ground, and these unbelievable mines had completely exhausted me physically.

The earth had stopped rolling by this time for one of its few brief daily pauses. Mr. E. pointed to an extraordinary group of houses in the distance. "That is our village," he explained. "We are headed that way."

Fearing that the earth would again start to roll, I

ran to the village from bench to bench. I was followed closely by Mr. E., who seemed to enjoy my fear of the earth's volcanic action. When we at last stopped in front of Mr. E.'s house, I was completely worn out.

"Will you lead me directly to my room?" I asked him. "I have had enough excitement for today. After a good night's sleep, I know that I shall be better able to understand this great island."

Mr. E. kindly showed me to a room, gave me some pajamas, brought me a meal, and said, "Good night."

I thanked him, ate the meal in bed, and dropped off into a deep sleep.

What other unusual things does Professor Sherman learn about the island and the people living on it? How is the island governed? How does the professor come to leave the island? To find out the answers to these questions, read The 21 Balloons.

1. How did Professor Sherman feel when he first saw land on the seventh day of his trip? Why?

2. Why did he dump his garbage out of the basket house when he saw the sea gulls?

3. Did the professor think that people lived on Krakatoa?

4. What are "mountain legs"? Can a person get them immediately? How do you know?

5. How do you think the professor felt about the way people dressed on Krakatoa? Why do you feel as you do?

6. How do you think the professor felt when he first saw the diamonds? Why do you feel as you do? How do you think he felt after he learned about the worthlessness of the diamonds on Krakatoa? Explain your answer.

7. Have you ever been somewhere that seemed very different from the place you live? How was it different? How did you feel at first? later?

DIAMONDS

Jacobus Jonker was a diamond miner in South Africa. One day in 1934, on his day off from work, he took a walk in his backyard. It had rained all night long. Jonker looked at the muddy mess that the rain had made of his yard. Then he saw an odd-looking rock that was about the size of an egg. He bent down and picked it up.

Jacobus Jonker could not believe his eyes. The rock was the biggest diamond he had ever seen.

Jonker sold the diamond for a fortune. Soon, it was bought by a New York diamond merchant named Harry Winston. Winston called it the Jonker Diamond and later had it cut into twelve different gems. Today, each of these gems is worth a lot of money. The Jonker Diamond is the largest diamond ever cut in the United States.

The Jonker Diamond as compared with a large hen's egg

510

Why Diamonds Are Valuable

Diamonds are rare, beautiful, and also quite useful. They are the hardest substance found in nature. That means a diamond can cut any other surface. And only another diamond can make a scratch in a diamond.

How Diamonds Are Made

Diamonds are made from carbon. Carbon is found in all living things, both plant and animal. Much of the carbon in the earth comes from things that once lived.

Scientists know that the combination of extreme heat and pressure changes carbon into diamonds. Such heat and pressure exist only in the hot, liquid mass of molten rock deep inside the earth. It is thought that millions of years ago this liquid mass pushed upward through cracks in the earth's crust. As the liquid cooled, the carbon changed into diamond crystals.

Where Diamonds Have Been Found

There are only four areas where very many diamonds have been found.

The first known area was in India, where diamonds were found thousands of years ago. In the 1600's, travelers from Europe brought back these beautiful stones from India. Diamonds became very popular with the kings and queens of Europe.

In the 1720's, diamonds were discovered in Brazil. This discovery came at a good time, too. India's supply of diamonds was finally running out after 2,500 years of mining the stones.

In the 1800's, two other important areas were found in the Soviet Union and South Africa. Today, most diamonds used in industry come from the Soviet Union.

Most diamonds used as gems come from South Africa. Only 25 percent of all diamonds mined are good enough for cutting into gems.

In the United States, diamonds have been mined in Murfreesboro, Arkansas. The mine is now a tourist attraction run by the state. Tourists can hunt for diamonds and keep whatever they find.

Diamonds are still rare today, but there are more of them than in the 1600's. Diamonds are not found just in the crowns of kings and queens. Many people can afford them. In the U. S. and other places, a diamond is the traditional stone of an engagement ring.

How Diamonds Are Mined

Most of the diamonds in India were found in stream beds. People would pick up handfuls of gravel from the bottom of the streams and sort out the diamonds. These diamonds were probably carried from where they were formed to India by great sheets of moving ice that covered parts of the earth 20,000 years ago. As the ice melted, it left behind tons of rocks and precious stones it had scraped up from the earth.

Most diamonds today are not found in stream beds, however. They are mined from rock formations deep inside the earth called *pipes*. Scientists believe that these are parts of volcanoes that were formed when molten rock pushed upward through the earth's crust. The hard rock in which diamonds are found is called *blue ground* for its bluish appearance.

In diamond mining, long shafts are sunk into the earth near the pipes. Tunnels lead from the shafts into the blue ground. The blue ground is blasted into large pieces of rock which are carried to the surface by elevators. Then the rocks are carefully crushed so that the diamonds are not destroyed. Next, the crushed material is taken over to washing tables. Here, it flows over boards thickly coated with grease. Since diamonds stick to grease, they are left behind by the rock and mud which flow down the tables.

Diamond mining takes patience and hard work. Only a few tiny diamonds are likely to be found in several tons of earth.

Diamonds, as they are found, do not look very impressive. They are gray, greasy-looking pebbles. Experienced diamond miners can tell a diamond immediately. But some people have carried around an unusual pebble for weeks before finding out that they had stumbled upon a diamond.

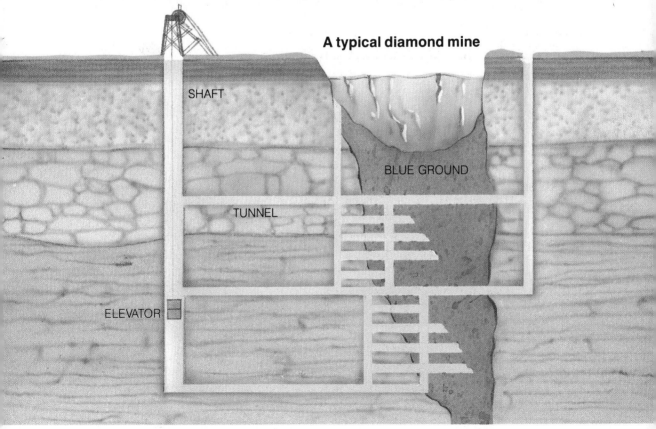

A typical diamond mine

SHAFT

BLUE GROUND

TUNNEL

ELEVATOR

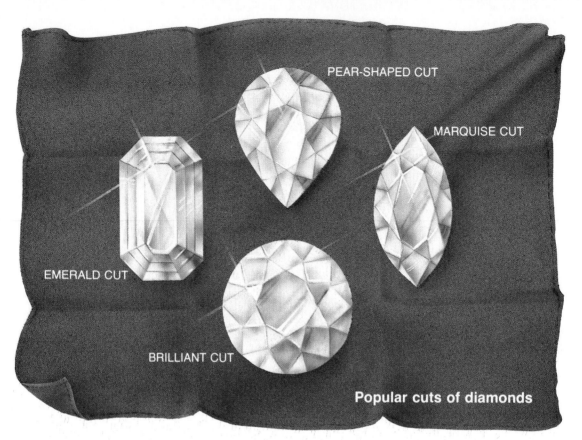

PEAR-SHAPED CUT

MARQUISE CUT

EMERALD CUT

BRILLIANT CUT

Popular cuts of diamonds

The "4 C's"

The value of a diamond is determined by the "4 C's." They are *carat, cut, color,* and *clarity.*

Carat is a unit of weight used for gems. One carat is equal to 1/142 of an ounce. This means that 142 carats weigh an ounce. The average diamond weighs a little less than one carat. Yet some diamonds are much larger.

The Jonker Diamond was 726 carats or about 5 ounces. The Cullinan, the largest diamond ever found, weighed a whopping 3,106 carats or about 1 pound, 6 ounces. It was discovered in South Africa.

The second "C" is *cut.* It is the cutting of the diamond that turns the gray, greasy-looking stone into a dazzling gem.

Diamond cutting takes a lot of skill. First the diamond cutter finds the diamond's lines of *cleavage*. These are the places where a diamond will divide leaving two flat and even surfaces. Then the cutter makes a groove on a line of cleavage. A thin, dull knife is stuck in the groove, and the knife is sharply tapped. If the cutter makes the groove in the wrong place, the diamond could shatter into bits.

The cut of a diamond gives it its beauty. Cutting the stone increases the number of faces or *facets*. If the facets are cut well, then the white light entering the diamond through the top of it will bend right back to the light source. As this occurs, the white light is separated into all the colors of the spectrum: red, orange, yellow, green, blue, indigo, and violet. This is what makes a diamond sparkle. In a poorly cut gem, the light entering through the top of the gem leaves through its sides or bottom.

One popular way of cutting diamonds is called the *brilliant cut*. This gives the gem a round shape with fifty-eight facets.

Light enters and leaves through the top of a diamond.

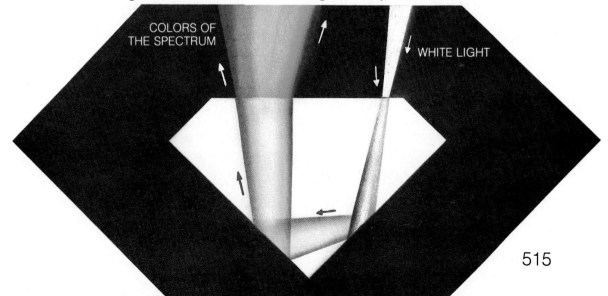

COLORS OF THE SPECTRUM

WHITE LIGHT

515

The last two "C's" are *color* and *clarity*. A good diamond will have brilliant color. The most common colors are yellow and brown. Diamonds that are colorless, blue, red, green, or black are rarer.

A good diamond should also have clarity. Sometimes, diamonds are a little cloudy or dull. If a diamond has good color and is clear, it is called *flawless*. This means that it is without mistakes or flaws.

Diamonds in Industry

Diamonds are widely used in industry. Since they are the hardest substance in nature, diamonds can cut any other material. Small diamonds are put into machines to make them strong cutting implements. Diamonds are also ground and baked into industrial tools.

Diamonds are used to cut out metal parts for cars and airplanes. They are also used in dentists' drills and in the tips of phonograph needles. A diamond needle lasts much longer than one made of anything else.

The diamonds used in industry are not of gem quality. Usually, they are flawed or have poor color. Still, they are expensive, and there is an increasing demand for them.

In the 1950's, scientists figured out how to make diamonds for industrial use. Recreating the conditions inside the earth, they placed carbon under extreme heat and pressure. The result was a rock as hard as a diamond but not of gem quality.

Imitation Diamonds

Scientists also can make imitation diamonds. They are man-made diamonds used as jewels. Although they are not as hard as real diamonds, they look and sparkle like the real thing. A trained eye, however, can spot the difference immediately. Imitation diamonds are much cheaper than real ones.

A few years ago, jewelers came up with a new slogan to advertise diamonds. The beauty of these gems and the spell they cast proves the truthfulness of that slogan: "Diamonds are forever."

THINK ABOUT IT

1. From what substance in the earth are diamonds made?
2. Where are most diamonds of gem quality found today?
3. What are the "4 C's"?
4. Name two uses of industrial diamonds.
5. Why do you think Jacobus Jonker was able to tell that the rock he found was a diamond?
6. Can an imitation diamond make a scratch in a real diamond? How do you know?
7. What would you do if you found a diamond like the one found by Jacobus Jonker?

WRITE AND READ
ABOUT IT

ONE

The Toothpaste Millionaire, 14-29

✎ *The Toothpaste Millionaire* is a full-length book. In the pages that follow the selection you have just read, Rufus is a guest on a popular TV talk show. On the show, he describes his toothpaste and tells how people can order it. Soon, orders for the toothpaste pour in.

Tell what steps you think Rufus will have to take to fill the orders for his toothpaste. Who will make the toothpaste? Where will it be made? How will Rufus deliver his product? Use your imagination to answer these questions in a paragraph.

📖 *Good Cents: Every Kid's Guide to Making Money* by the members of the Amazing Life Games Company (Houghton Mifflin Co.). This book contains lots of suggestions for goods and services that young people can market.

No More "No Money" Blues, 33-35

✎ Almost everyone knows what it is like to feel sad about not being able to buy something. But have you ever wondered what it would be like to have an endless supply of money? Imagine having a magic wallet that is always filled with money, no matter how much you spend.

Tell what you would buy with your endless supply of money. Give reasons why you would buy these things. Do you think you would enjoy the things you buy? Why or why not? Do you think it is possible to have the "too much money" blues? Write one or two paragraphs that contain your answers to these questions.

📖 *How to Turn Lemons Into Money: A Child's Guide to Economics* by Louise Armstrong (Harcourt Brace Jovanovich). Beginning with a story about a girl and her lemonade stand, this book goes on to explore the interesting and important subject of economics.

. . . and now Miguel, 38-47

✎ In ". . . and now Miguel," Miguel Chavez tells how sheep farmers deal with orphan lambs. Imagine what it would be like to be one of the orphan lambs on Miguel's farm. You look for your mother, but she is nowhere to be found. Miguel picks you

519

up and begins to feed you with a baby bottle. Soon, you are following him. For an entire summer, you go everywhere Miguel goes.

Write a few paragraphs from the point of view of an orphan lamb. Tell what you see and hear on the sheep ranch and explain how Miguel takes care of you. Describe your journey, with Miguel as your shepherd, to the Sangre de Cristo Mountains.

📖 . . . and now Miguel by Joseph Krumgold (Thomas Y. Crowell). To find out whether or not Miguel ever reaches the Sangre de Cristo Mountains, read the rest of this award-winning book.

The Mesa, 48-58

✎ In "The Mesa," Kate carefully describes what it is like to go to her grandmother's house every summer. Do you have a grandmother, a grandfather, an aunt, an uncle, or a parent you visit often? If so, what do you like most about this person? Does this person have a special hobby or interest? What do you like most about this person's house or apartment? What do you like best about the neighborhood that you visit?

Write two paragraphs telling why you like to visit this person. The first paragraph should tell about the person you visit. The second should tell about the house and neighborhood in which this person lives. Be sure to answer the questions on the previous page in your paragraphs.

📖 *Annie and the Old One* by Miska Miles (Atlantic Monthly Press). This is a story about a young Native-American girl named Annie who lives with her grandmother. Annie learns to accept and understand the cycle of life and death.

The Boy Who Voted for Abe Lincoln, 59-81

✏️ "The Boy Who Voted for Abe Lincoln" is historical fiction. The story contains some facts from history that are true. It is fictional because it contains many made-up details.

Use the following setting and characters to write a scene from a historical-fiction story about Abe Lincoln. You may want to get more facts for your story from an encyclopedia.

> The year is 1818, and the place is Hardin County, Kentucky. You live in a log cabin in the woods. Your nearest neighbors—more than a mile away—are the Lincoln family. Their son, ten-year-old Abe, is your best friend. Tell about what you do together.

Use facts in the scene you write, but make up details and conversations so that your writing will be interesting and dramatic.

📖 *Me and Willie and Pa* by F. N. Monjo (Simon & Schuster). This is a delightful account of life in the White House with Abe Lincoln.

TWO _____

My Side of the Mountain, 88-95

✎ In the selection from *My Side of the Mountain* that you have just read, Sam Gribley prepares for a snowstorm. Pretend a major storm is about to hit your hometown. The storm could be a blizzard, a hurricane, or very heavy rains and wind that cause flooding. Tell how you and your family prepare for the storm.

As the storm rages around you, tell how you feel. Explain what you see and hear outside. Then explain what you see around your home and neighborhood when the storm is over. Tell what people have to do to clean up after a storm.

📖 *Time of Wonder* by Robert McCloskey (The Viking Press). This poetic description of a summer storm tells how people prepare for it and what happens as a result of the storm.

Other People's Weather, 98-107

Febold Feboldson was famous for interfering with the weather and climate of the Great Plains. Choose one of the following situations to write another tall tale about Febold and Big Steve:

1. Febold and Big Steve dig a tunnel to the North Pole. They want to bring in cold air so that they can cool off in the summer. But the temperature gets too cold for the crops and for everything else, too.

2. The people in Nebraska need rain, so Febold decides to bring them some rain clouds. Using ropes and nets, he carries the clouds from the Atlantic Ocean to Nebraska. Getting the right amount of rain in the right place proves to be a problem, though.

Make your tale humorous by exaggerating people and events. Febold and Big Steve should be able to do the "impossible" easily. Of course, the problems that result from their actions should also be larger than life!

Heroes in American Folklore by Irwin Shapiro (Messner). Some of the tall-tale heroes you'll meet in this book are Casey Jones, John Henry, Joe Magarac, and Steamboat Bill. One tale seems taller than the other!

Super Power, 108-114

✎You have just discovered the ideal solar collector. It is small, inexpensive, and easy to install. It produces huge amounts of electricity for only pennies a day. With your invention, all homes will be heated and lit with solar power. Cars, trucks, and factories will also be powered with sunlight.

Write a letter to your local newspaper telling why your invention is good and necessary. Explain that making, selling, and installing the solar collectors will create many new jobs. The air will be cleaner, too, and people will have more money to spend on other things. Try to persuade the readers of your letter that everyone will live better as a result of your invention.

📖*Solar Energy* by John Hoke (Franklin Watts). Some of the many possible uses of the sun's energy are described in this book. There are also some practical projects for you to do using the sun and household materials.

The Mystery of Lyme Regis, 118-124

✎In this story we read that the word *ichthyosaurus* is formed from Greek root words meaning "fish lizard." The names that scientists have given to other famous dinosaurs are listed below. Read the meanings of these names, and then write why you think the creatures were given these names. Later, check your guesses in an encyclopedia or other reference.

anatosaurus—goose lizard; *triceratops*—three-horned face; *tyrannosaurus rex*—king tyrant lizard; *stegosaurus*—roofed lizard; *apatosaurus*—unreal lizard; *ankylosaurus*—stiff lizard

Dinosaurs and Other Prehistoric Animals by Tom McGowen (Rand McNally & Company). This book contains complete descriptions of every dinosaur, as well as full-color pictures.

Dar Tellum, 128-139

Telekinesis is the ability to move objects by thinking hard about them. In "Dar Tellum," Ralph Winston was given the power of telekinesis by Dar Tellum of the planet, Sidra. If you were given this power, how would you use it?

Tell about three incidents in which you use telekinesis. First, tell how you use your power to play a harmless trick on a friend. Add details to make the incident funny. Next, tell how you use telekinesis to make your life more comfortable. Finally, tell how you use it to prevent an accident in your school or town. You might use your power to move an object so that danger is eliminated. Tell how the people around you react to your mysterious powers.

A Wrinkle in Time by Madeleine L'Engle (Farrar, Straus, & Giroux). Meg and her friends are contacted by beings from another world. These beings take Meg to their world where she has many adventures.

THREE

Sarah Caldwell: Magician of Opera, 142-150

You have just read an interview with Sarah Caldwell, a famous conductor of operas. You, too, can write an interview. Here's how.

First, choose a friend, neighbor, or relative who has interesting or unusual opinions or ideas. Write an introduction of one or more paragraphs. Tell who the person is and why you are interviewing him or her. The introduction to the interview with Sarah Caldwell is on pages 142-144.

Next, make up a list of questions. Think of interesting questions that will make the person you are interviewing want to talk. Think of questions that will need more than a yes or no answer.

Write down the person's answers to your questions. Make sure you write the person's exact words. It helps to have a tape recorder with you. Try to end the interview with a question and answer that sums up the person's feelings and ideas.

📖 *Stories of Favorite Operas* by Clyde Robert Bulla (Thomas Y. Crowell). This book tells and illustrates the stories of twenty-three of the most popular operas.

The Magic Guitar, 151-160

✎ What do you think was magical about Juan's guitar? It seemed ordinary enough, yet Juan used it to make some magical-sounding music. He also used it to make some friends, and friends often have a special magic between them.

The word *magic* means different things to different people. Write five sentences that tell what magic means to you. You might write sentences such as these: (1) *Magic is a white rabbit in a black top hat.* (2) *Magic is knowing what someone else is thinking.* (3) *Magic is a rose in bloom.* (4) *Magic is a dream come true.*

📖 *My Book of Guitar* by Andres Segovia (Collins). This book will give the beginning guitar player information about the guitar and how to play it. It is written by a renowned guitarist.

527

The Sultan's Perfect Tree, 161-172

✎ A *synopsis* gives the main points of the plot of a story. It should mention briefly the major characters and the setting of the story. It should be short and clear. A synopsis of "The Three Bears" might look like this:

> A girl named Goldilocks went into a house belonging to three bears. Although the bears weren't home, Goldilocks ate their cereal, sat in their chairs, and slept in their beds. When the bears did come home, they were angry to find Goldilocks there and chased her away.

Write a one-paragraph synopsis of "The Sultan's Perfect Tree." Remember to tell the important points of the story in complete sentences.

📖 *Transfigured Hart* by Jane Yolen (Thomas Y. Crowell). Richard and Heather see a pure-white hart, or deer, in the Five Mile Wood. Sure that it is a unicorn, they are determined to save it from hunters.

Where's Robot? 180-191

✎ Robot's discovery of an important archaeological treasure in France is big news. Imagine that you are a reporter from the biggest newspaper in Paris. You have been sent to cover the story of the Cro-Magnon cave in the Vézère Valley. First, make up a headline for your story. It should state the main idea of the story in a few words. Next, write a lead paragraph for your story. The lead paragraph should give the important facts of the story. It should answer the *Wh* questions: *Who? What? Where? When? and Why?*

The rest of the story should give details that support the lead paragraph. For example, describe the paintings in the cave and tell what Abbé Breuil thought about them. The last paragraph should sum up and tell why the discovery is important.

☐ *The First Artists* by Dorothy and Joseph Samachson (Doubleday). This book shows and describes cave paintings and carvings from around the world.

The Lonely Silence, 192-205

✎ Trying to keep her parent's deafness a secret, Bina Hall must have been very lonely. She was afraid to have friends over to her house because she didn't want them to laugh at her.

Bina might have felt better if she had written about her secret in a *diary*. A diary is a book in which a person writes about what happens in his or her life daily. The word *diary* means "daily." People write whatever they want to in their diaries—thoughts, feelings, and facts.

529

Try to write an entry for a diary. Write about what you did yesterday and what you were thinking about. Begin by writing yesterday's date. You might want to start writing in a diary every day.

📖 *A Dance to Still Music* by Barbara Corcoran (Atheneum Publishers). A fourteen-year-old girl becomes deaf after an illness. To make matters worse, she had just moved to a new community. Read how she deals successfully with both her problems.

FOUR

The Prophecy, 212-217

✎ As a character in a tall tale, Paul Bunyan is larger than life. By exaggerating or overstating the truth, the author has made the story funny. For example, Paul is so big he can put a full-grown bear in his hat and fit six deer in his pocket.

Use exaggeration to describe a day in Paul Bunyan's life. First, tell about Paul's house. Describe how big it is and what it has inside it. Then describe how Paul helps or causes problems for one of his normal-sized neighbors. If you make your descriptions larger than life, you should have a funny tall tale.

📖 *Legends of Paul Bunyan,* edited by Harold W. Felton (Alfred Knopf). Legends about Paul Bunyan sprung up among loggers in Michigan, Minnesota, Wisconsin, the Northwest, and Canada. Finally, they were recorded. You can read them in this book.

Amelia and the Bear, 218-226

✎ An author of a story decides from whose *point of view* a story will be told or, *narrated.* In "Amelia and the Bear," the author is the *narrator.* The narrator seems to know everything about the plot, setting, and characters of the story. She tells the story from an *"all-knowing" point of view.*

Other stories are told from a *personal point of view.* A character in the story is the narrator and tells the story from his or her point of view. The character uses the pronouns, *I, me,* and *my.*

Reread the scene on pages 223-224 in which Amelia fights off the bear. Pretend you are Amelia. Rewrite the passage from the personal point of view. The pronoun *she* should become *I,* and *her* should become *me* or *my.* For example, *Amelia grabbed the pole and crawled toward the pen on her hands and knees* would become *I grabbed the pole and crawled toward the pen on my hands and knees.* Make any other changes you think will help the reader know Amelia is telling the story.

📖*Wolf Run: A Caribou Eskimo Tale* by James Houston (Harcourt Brace Jovanovich). A young Eskimo boy has a run-in with a pack of hungry wolves as he hunts caribou for his hungry family.

Why Don't You Get a Horse, Sam Adams?
227-235

✎An outline is a good way to organize information before you begin to write. An outline lists the information you want to include in your writing in the order it should appear.

Use the following outline to write a brief biography of Sam Adams. Start a new paragraph for each topic listed next to a Roman numeral. Be sure to cover each of the points listed in the outline.

I. Sam Adam's early life
   A. Born in Boston, September 27, 1722
   B. Entered Harvard College at age 14
      1. Graduated in 1740
      2. Received Master's degree in 1743
   C. Fails in his first business
   D. Fails in his first political office as tax collector in Boston
II. Sam Adams, revolutionary and patriot
   A. Led protest and revolt against the Stamp Act in 1764
   B. Elected to Massachusetts House of Representatives in 1765

C. As a lawmaker, made many fiery speeches against Great Britain
 1. Became chief revolutionary spokesman
 2. Demanded that British troops leave the town of Boston
D. Succeeded in having the troops removed after the Boston Massacre in 1770
E. Wrote newspaper articles demanding more liberty in the colonies
 1. Writings led to the Boston Tea Party
 2. Barely escaped arrest by the British

III. Sam Adams, political leader
A. Elected to the First and Second Continental Congresses in 1774 and 1775
B. Voted for and signed the Declaration of Independence in 1776
C. After the Revolutionary War, became governor of Massachusetts (1793–1797)
D. Accomplished the great goal of his life in Philadelphia on July 4, 1776

☐ *Mr. Revere and I* by Robert Lawson (Little, Brown). Sam Adams was famous for not riding a horse. Paul Revere, another leader of the American Revolution, became famous by riding a horse. In this book, his horse, Scheherazade, tells what it was like to make that famous midnight ride. The horse also creates a very interesting picture of the events leading up to the war for independence.

Ananse and the Globe of Light, 236-251

✎ Try to imagine "Ananse and the Globe of Light" presented on stage with sound effects, lighting, and actors. Pretend you are a drama critic for a local newspaper. You see and review plays. Tell what you think about the play performance of "Ananse and the Globe of Light" in a review for tomorrow's newspaper.

Begin your review by telling where and when you saw the play. (You can make up these details.) Then write a short paragraph that tells what the play is about. Be sure not to give away the ending. Next, list a few things you didn't like, too. End your review by telling whether or not people should go and see the play themselves.

📖 *Plays for Folktales of Africa and Asia* by Barbara Winther (Plays, Inc.). All the plays in this collection contain trickery and adventure. There are lots of helpful hints on how to produce the plays for an audience.

Arthur the Author, 254-264

✎ "Arthur the Author" is a short story, but it could easily be a play. Rewrite as a scene from a play Arthur's discussion with the newspaper editors that appears on pages 259-262.

First, make up a list of the characters in the scene. Tell a little bit about each character next to his or her name. Then, describe the setting of the scene—a newspaper editor's office. Use the picture on pages 260-261 to help you.

When rewriting the conversation as the lines of a play, remember to place a colon (:) after a character's name. Write his or her lines after the colon. Stage directions, words that tell what a character does as he or she speaks, should be written in parentheses. Sound effects and lighting effects can also be placed in parentheses.

You can follow the story exactly in your play scene or you can change it. Try to make it funny.

You Can Act by Lewy Olfson (Oak Tree Press). This book is filled with suggestions on how to produce interesting plays, puppet shows and pantomimes. There are ideas and suggestions on how to play a part creatively.

archy hunts a job, 265-267
"archy hunts a job" is a poem, but you can rewrite it as a story. All you have to do is write it in paragraphs, using capital letters and punctuation where necessary.

Start the story on page 265, beginning with the words, *well boss*. Capitalize the first word of each sentence you write and the pronoun *I*. End each sentence with a period, a question mark, or an exclamation point. Enclose the exact words of each speaker in quotation marks (" "). Start a new paragraph each time the speaker changes during the conversation. Here are some sentences to get you started:

> "Well, boss, I went up to the circus the other day and tried to hire out."
> "What do you want?" they asked me. "A job as an animal or a job as an artist?"
> "An artist," said I.

📖 *Listen, Children, Listen* edited by Myra Cohn Livingston (Harcourt Brace Jovanovich). This is a collection of many of the best-known and best-loved children's poems ever written.

The Flowering Peach Tree, 268-285

✎ Tu Thuc found out that one year on Mount Nam-Nhu is equal to one hundred years on earth. Suppose you and your family were to go to Mount Nam-Nhu. After enjoying the sights and sounds of the magic mountain for a year, you decide to return home. But as you make the return trip, you realize something is wrong. Futuristic cars soar above you, and the superhighways are more super than ever. When you reach your town or city, you are not sure you are in the right place.

Tell what your town will look like 100 years in the future. Are your house and school still there? What do they look like? What are people in the town doing? What do they have to say to you? End your description by telling whether you will stay in town or return to Mount Nam-Nhu.

📖 *Rip Van Winkle* by Washington Irving (J. B. Lippincott Company). Rip Van Winkle fell asleep in the Catskill Mountains of New York State and didn't wake up for twenty years. Find out what happened when he returned home.

_____ **FIVE**

Island of the Blue Dolphins, 288-303

✎ Imagine Karana, all alone on the Island of the Blue Dolphins. During the day, she struggles to find food. At night, she listens to the growling of the wild dogs and the pounding of the waves.

The feelings we have for Karana could be expressed in poetry. One type of poem is called a

537

cinquain. It has five lines, each of which has a certain number of syllables. The first line has two syllables; the second line has four syllables; the third line has six syllables; the fourth line has eight syllables; and the last line has two syllables. The lines of a cinquain do no have to rhyme. A cinquain about Karana might look like this:

Alone (2 syllables)
Karana waits (4 syllables)
Through sun and winter storms (6 syllables)
Watching the blue sea
  and wild dogs (8 syllables)
Alone (2 syllables)

Try to write another cinquain that expresses how you feel about Karana's lonely life on the Island of the Blue Dolphins.

Zia by Scott O'Dell (Houghton Mifflin). In this adventure, Karana's niece Zia attempts to rescue her aunt from the Island of the Blue Dolphins.

Vision Without Sight, 304-311
The *main idea* of a paragraph is what the paragraph is all about. Often the main idea of a paragraph is stated in one sentence called the *topic sentence.* The other sentences in the paragraph give details that tell about (or support) the main idea.

Look at this paragraph from "Vision Without Sight." The topic sentence is underlined. Notice that the other sentences contain details that develop it.

> <u>Here is how echolocation works.</u> First, the dolphin sends out a series of sound waves ahead of it. If the sound waves hit an object, such as a rock or a fish, they bounce back to the dolphin. Otherwise, the sound waves keep moving through the water. When the sound waves bounce back, the dolphin hears them and knows that something is ahead. If they don't bounce back, the dolphin knows that the path is clear.

Choose one of the following topic sentences. Find information and details in the selection that support the topic sentence. Use the topic sentence and information to write a paragraph.

1. Arthur McBride discovered echolocation when he tried to catch dolphins in nets.
2. Dolphins seem to like helping people and performing for them.
3. Echolocation depends on sound, and a dolphin is equipped to make and control sound waves.

📖 *Here Come the Dolphins* by Alice E. Goudey (Charles Scribner's Sons). This book tells about the fascinating lives of dolphins.

Bo of the Island, 312-323

✎Pretend that you are Buddy Carson. You lost your dog Bo months and months ago on Isle Royale. You never expect to see Bo again. One day, two men knock on your door. You answer the door and see that the men have Bo on a leash.

Using this situation, write a new ending for "Bo of the Island." Try to describe the feelings of Buddy Carson and her family. Use quotation marks to show the exact words of the Carsons and the two men. Tell how Bo reacts to his old home.

📖*Lassie Come Home* by Eric Knight (Holt, Rinehart & Winston). This story tells of a dog that returns home after being gone several months.

Featherwoman, 324-333

✎The article "Featherwoman" is a detailed account of how Helen Naha produces her beautiful pottery. All the steps for pottery-making are contained in the article. Can you find them, number them in correct order, and write them clearly? Here are the first two steps:

1. Dig up white chalky clay from the clay pits in the desert.
2. Spread out the clay in the sun and let it dry for two or three days.

540

Continue through the article, listing all the necessary steps. The total number of steps will depend on how you organize your directions. Do not include unimportant details.

Potterymaking by Virginie Fowler Elbert (Doubleday). If you'd like to make pots, bowls, tiles, jewelry, boxes, or figures out of clay, this book will tell you how.

American Indian Art, 334-337

The selection you have just read, "American Indian Art," is a photo essay; photographs are used to express a theme or an idea. The pictures are the main part of a photo essay. The words which make up the text support and develop the theme.

You can make your own photo essay. First, you'll need a theme and photographs. It might be a good idea to choose a broad theme such as "My Family." Then you will be able to use family snapshots. You could also use magazine pictures to illustrate a theme such as "Places I Want to Visit."

Your text should identify the pictures and tell what is special about them. It should also link the pictures together to form a unified photo essay. The photographs should be the most important part of the essay.

541

Indian Arts by Robert Hofsinde (Morrow). This book shows examples of Indian works of art done in horn, bone, shells, clay, wood, stone, copper, and silver.

The Golden Apples, 340-345

If you were a radio announcer covering the race between Atalanta and Hippomenes, what would you say? How would you describe the excitement of the race? What would you say about the golden apples Hippomenes uses to win the event?

Write a moment by moment account of the race. It should be clear, so that a person listening to it on the radio would understand what is happening.

Book of Greek Myths by Ingrid and Edgar D'Aulaire (Doubleday). This is a brightly-illustrated collection of well-known myths from ancient Greece.

The Race, 346-355

When writers *compare* two or more objects, they tell what the objects have in common. When writers *contrast* objects, they tell how they are different.

Think about the race that Atalanta and Hippomenes ran. Then think about the race that Atalanta and Young John were in. Of course, the races were alike in some ways, but they were also different.

Write a paragraph that contrasts the two races. Name five ways in which the two races were different. Begin your paragraph with a topic sentence.

📖 *Track and Field for Young Champions* by Robert J. Antonacci and Jene Barr (McGraw-Hill). This book tells the history and rules for all track events. It also gives tips, drills, and exercises for distance running, relay races, hurdling, jumping, and throwing events.

_____ **SIX**

Sona Goes Sailing, 358-369

✏️ A short, friendly letter is a nice way to say thank-you to someone who has taken you on a special trip or invited you into their home. Write one of the letters described below.

1. You are Sona Baronian. Nana has asked you to write to Mr. Jerry O'Brien. Nana wants you to thank him for inviting you out on his sailboat. Although you got seasick, thank Mr. O'Brien.
2. You are Tommy O'Brien. Nana asked you and your uncle to Sunday dinner, and you accepted. Write to Nana, thanking her for the meal. Explain why you enjoyed the dinner.

Your letter should have the date at the upper right. The *greeting*—Dear Mr. O'Brien or Dear Mrs. Baronian—should be at the left, followed by a comma. The body of your letter should follow the greeting. End with a *closing*—Yours truly, Sincerely, etc.—and your signature.

Sailing by Tony Gibbs (Frankling Watts). This is an introduction to sailing. There is important information on the parts of a sailboat, how to sail, boat care, and water safety.

Skyscraper, 372-377

In "Skyscraper," the author describes a building as though it were a living thing. First he likens it to a plant, then to an animal.

In what ways other than those described in the story is a building like a plant or an animal? Write a paragraph comparing a building either to a plant or to an animal. The building does not have to be a skyscraper. Name at least three ways that the building and the plant or animal are *alike*.

A Skyscraper Goes Up by Carter Harman (Random House). Photographer/writer Carter Harman watched the construction of the Exxon Building in New York City. In this book, Harman describes what he saw.

The Lost Umbrella of Kim Chu, 380-393

✎Does Kim Chu get her umbrella back? "The Lost Umbrella of Kim Chu" leaves us wondering.

Write an ending for the story that tells how Kim Chu tries to get her umbrella back from the millionaire man. Your ending should contain a solution to Kim Chu's problem.

📖 *The Witch Family* by Eleanor Estes (Harcourt Brace Jovanovich). The witch family is a crayon creation of two girls whose imaginations work overtime as Halloween nears.

Zeely, 396-409

✎A simile is a comparison of two dissimilar things that uses the word *like* or *as*. The author of "Zeely" uses similes to describe Miss Zeely Tayber. She is said to be "thin and deeply dark *as* a pole of Ceylon ebony." The author also writes, "Zeely's long fingers looked exactly *like* bean pods left a long time in the sun." In the first simile, a woman is compared to a wooden pole. In the second simile, fingers are compared to bean pods.

Write a description of a character using similes. The character you write about can be someone you know or a made-up character. Using the word *like* or *as*, compare a body part or character trait to something that is unlike it.

545

📖 *M.C. Higgins, The Great* by Virginia Hamilton (Macmillan). Not only is M.C. great, but so are his exciting adventures!

SEVEN _____

Sasha, My Friend, 414-435

✎ In a way, writing is like taking a photograph. Describing something in words can put a picture of it in someone else's mind.

Choose one of the following illustrations from "Sasha, My Friend" to write about. Imagine that you are describing the picture to someone who has not seen it. Describe what you see in detail.

1. Describe Dr. Meyers's house, barn, and outbuildings as shown on pages 420-421.
2. Describe Sasha, the fawn, and their surroundings as shown on page 426.

📖 *Silver Wolf* by Paige Dixon (Atheneum). Read about the struggles of a wolf living in the wild.

An Introduction to Veterinary Medicine, 436-443

✎ Pretend you are head veterinarian at a large city zoo. Choose one of the following situations. Write a humorcus account of how it developed and what you did to solve the problem.

1. Whitey, a slightly unfriendly polar bear, has developed frostbite on its front paws.
2. Spouter, a porpoise, has something clogging its spout. You must clear the spout in order for Spouter to expel air and water normally.

Animal Hospital by Melvin Berger (John Day). The activities of veterinarians and their assistants are highlighted in this book.

Do Bananas Chew Gum? 446-471

Not being able to read or write well, like Sam Mott, can create problems. Choose one of the following situations. Tell what might happen to Sam as a result of his disability.

1. One summer, Sam has the chance to work in the dinosaur exhibit of a large museum. First, however, he must complete a 3-page application. Sam wants this job badly.
2. For his birthday, Sam got a small home computer. Sam can't wait to use it, but he is having trouble reading the instructions manual.

Ramona the Brave by Beverly Cleary (Morrow). Although young Ramona has no trouble reading, her behavior causes lots of problems for her in school. See how she solves them in this book.

The Vikings, 472-479

About the year 982, Eric the Red was outlawed from Iceland because of his involvement in several quarrels. He and his family got into a ship and sailed west from Iceland across the unknown ocean in the hope of finding another land. When he first landed on the continent he later named Greenland, he thought it was all ice. But traveling southward, he came upon greener country.

Pretend that you are Eric the Red. Write about the problems you met at sea and how you felt when you first spotted land. Explain what you had to do to survive in the new land.

Vikings Bold: Their Voyages and Adventures by Samuel Carter III (Crowell). Find out more about Viking life on land and sea.

The 21 Balloons, 484-509

In "The 21 Balloons," William Waterman Sherman describes his adventures to members of the Explorer's Club. This is a real organization that has had some of the world's greatest explorers and adventurers as members. The club has given help and money to explorers who have plans for special exploration or adventure.

Write a short speech to give to the Explorers' Club, describing a plan for an exploration you would like to make. Tell what you hope to accomplish. Persuade the club members that your plan is a good one and that you deserve their help.

Kon-Tiki by Thor Heyerdahl (Junior Version by Rand McNally). Thor Heyerdahl was a real-life member of the Explorer's Club. This book tells of his trip across the Pacific Ocean on a small raft.

Diamonds, 510-517

Diamonds are the source of countless anecdotes, stories, and legends. Now it's time to write your own diamond story. Choose one of the following story ideas, or make up one of your own.

1. You are a diamond cutter. You are about to begin shaping a huge diamond into a pear shape. The stone is worth a fortune, and one slip of your wrist could destroy it.
2. You know that diamonds are very valuable, so you are thrilled when you find a bag of them in the street. Tell what you do with them.

Diamonds by Sara Hannum Chase (Franklin Watts). Read this book to find out everything you ever wanted to know about diamonds and their history.

HELP WITH WORDS
(Glossary)

How to Use HELP WITH WORDS

HELP WITH WORDS is your glossary. It was written to help you under-stand certain words found in the stories and articles in this book. It is shorter than a full dictionary. However, it has many of the helps you will find in dictionaries.

Alphabetical Order

The words that begin with **a** come first in HELP WITH WORDS. Those that begin with **b** come next, and so on. you may need to check beyond the first letter of the word you want if another word begins with the same letter or letters. For example, in these word pairs, which word comes first in the dictionary:

1. **alias** or **algae**?
2. **grating** or **gravel**?
3. **intrigue** or **interview**?
4. **relate** or **relative**?

Guide Words

Look at the words **abreast** and **animalculae** at the top of page 554. These two words are called "guide words" because they help you find the words you want. The left guide word on each page is the same as the first word explained on that page. The right guide word is the same as the last word explained on that page.

Entry Words

Find the word **absorb** on page 554. Notice that it is printed in heavy black type. Such a word is called an "entry word." HELP WITH WORDS does not list entry words for names of people and places. It does list prefixes like **inter-** and suffixes like **-age.**

Help with Spelling and Writing

Here is the entry for **affect:**

> **af·fect** (ə fekt′) *v.* to act on or
> change something (What you
> eat *affects* your health.)

How is **affect** spelled? In HELP WITH WORDS, the centered dots show where you may break a word at the end of a line in writing. After what letters may you break the word **affect**?

All dictionaries give you help with forms of words if there is a spelling change before **-ed, -ing, -er, -est, -s,** or **-es.** Note the entry word **cascade** on page 557. Why do the forms **cascaded** and **cascading** also appear?

Help with Meanings

A full dictionary gives all the meanings for a word. HELP WITH WORDS gives the meaning of the word as it is used in your book. For some words, it also gives other common meanings. The different meanings of a word are numbered so that you can find them quickly.

For help in understanding meanings, example sentences are sometimes given. For some entry words, pictures are used to help explain the meaning. A blue dot (●) appears after the meaning for each word that is pictured.

In HELP WITH WORDS you will sometimes find that an entry has exactly the same spelling as the entry that follows it. Look at parts of the entries for the word **ebony.**

eb·o·ny¹. . . a hard, black wood   **ebony²**. . . like ebony, especially in color; black

Words that are spelled alike but that are different in origin or meaning are called "homographs." After each homograph in HELP WITH WORDS you will find a small raised numeral.

Study the full entries for the homograph **ebony:**

eb·o·ny¹ (eb′ə nē) *n.* **1** a hard, black wood (The black keys on the piano are made of *ebony.*) **2** the tree that produces this wood (*Ebony* grows in Asia and Africa.)

ebony² *adj.* like ebony, especially in color; black (The color of Gary's hair is *ebony.*)

Which entry is a noun? Which is an adjective? After each entry an abbreviation tells you how the word is used: for example, as a noun (*n.*) or as a verb (*v.*). The abbreviations for singular (*sing.*) and plural (*pl.*) are also used.

Look at the part of the entry for the word **reckon:**

reck·on . . . (*chiefly dialect*)

The usage label in parentheses tells you that **reckon** is used in a particular area or by a certain group of people.

Help with Pronunciation

The pronunciation is given right after the entry word:

af·fect (ə fekt′)

The symbols after the entry word show how the word **affect** is pronounced or spoken. These symbols sometimes look a lot like the entry word:

throb (throb)

Often, however, they look different:

ex·ten·sion (iks ten′chən)

When there is more than one way to pronounce a word, HELP WITH WORDS shows the pronunciations this way:

balmy (bä′mē *or* bäl′mē)

Look once again at the pronunciation symbols for **extension:**

(iks ten′chən)

Notice that (ten′) is followed by a heavy mark called an "accent mark." This shows which part of the word **extension** is accented, or said more loudly. In some words a lighter, secondary accent mark is also shown for a syllable that is said somewhat less loudly:

(kyùr′ē os′ə tē)

All the pronunciation symbols used in HELP WITH WORDS are shown on this page. Some of these symbols are also shown in the key at the bottom of every right-hand page.

Study the symbols on this page carefully. Some look just like the letters of the alphabet: (a). Others have marks that make them look different from letters: (ā). The important thing to remember about both kinds of symbols is that they do not stand for letters; they stand for sounds.

Full pronunciation key

The pronunciation of each word is shown: just after the word, in this way:
ab·bre·vi·ate (ə brē′vē āt).
The letters and signs used are pronounced as in the words below.
The mark ′ is placed after a syllable with primary or heavy accent, as in the example above.
The mark ′ after a syllable shows a secondary or lighter accent, as in **ab·bre·vi·a·tion** (ə brē′vē ā′shən).

a	hat, cup	i	it, pin	p	paper, cup	v	very, save
ā	age, face	ī	ice, five	r	run, read	w	will, woman
ä	father, far			s	say, yes	y	young, yet
		j	jam, enjoy	sh	she, rush	z	zero, breeze
b	bad, rob	k	kind, seek	t	tell, it	zh	measure, seizure
ch	child, much	l	land, coal	th	thin, both		
d	did, red	m	me, am	ŦH	then, smooth		
		n	no, in			ə	represents:
e	let, best	ng	long, bring	u	cup, butter		a in about
ē	equal, be			u̇	full, put		e in taken
ėr	term, learn	o	hot, rock	ü	rule, move		i in pencil
		ō	open, go				o in lemon
f	fat, if	ô	order, all				u in circus
g	go, bag	oi	oil, voice				
h	he, how	ou	house, out				

Grammatical key

adj.	adjective	*n.*	noun
adv.	adverb	*prep.*	preposition
conj.	conjunction	*pron.*	pronoun
interj.	interjection	*v.*	verb
sing.	singular	*pl.*	plural

553

Aa

abreast (ə brest′) *adv.* in a row across; side by side (to march four *abreast*)

ab·sent·ly (ab′sənt lē) *adv.* as if lost in thought (Ellen looked at the door *absently*.)

ab·sorb (ab sôrb′) *v.* to drink in; to take in (Paper towels *absorb* water quickly.)

ac·cus·tomed to (ə kus′təmd tü) *adj.* familiar with; used to (City people are *accustomed to* noise.)

af·fect (ə fekt′) *v.* to act on or change something (What you eat *affects* your health.)

-age a noun suffix that means **1** "things thought of together or as a whole" (*mileage; plumage*) **2** "an action, process, or result" (*breakage*) **3** "rate of" (*percentage*) **4** "place of" (*orphanage*) **5** "rank" (*peerage*) **6** "fee" (*postage*)

al·gae (al′jē) *n. pl.; sing.* **al·ga** (al′gə) plants without true roots, stems, and leaves that grow mostly in water, as seaweeds (Some *algae* can be used as food.) ●

ali·as (ā′lē əs) *adv.* otherwise called; also known as (His name is Franklin, *alias* "Frank the Crank.")

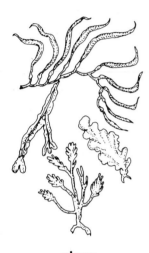

algae

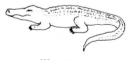

alligator

al·le·giance (ə lē′jəns) *n.* loyalty or service to one's country or to a cause (I pledge *allegiance* to the United States of America.)

al·li·ga·tor (al′ə gā′tər) *n.* a large water animal with a broad head, four short legs, and a long tail (An *alligator* looks like a giant lizard.) ●

almond-shaped (ä′mənd shāpt′ *or* am′ənd shāpt′) *adj.* having the narrow, slanted shape of the almond nut

aloof (ə lüf′) *adv.* at a distance; withdrawn (The shy child stood *aloof* from the group.)

al·ti·tude (al′tə tüd) *n.* height (the plane flew at a high *altitude*.)

an·ces·tor (an′ses′tər) *n.* a person from an earlier time from whom one is descended

an·ces·try (an′ses′trē) *n.* **an·ces·tries** the persons or animals making up a line of descent

an·i·mal·cu·lae (an′ə mal′kū lē) *n. pl.; sing.* **an·i·mal·cu·lum** (an′ə mal′kū ləm) tiny animals that are invisible or nearly invisible to the naked eye (The *animalculae* were seen with a microscope.)

an·tic·i·pa·tion
(an tis′ə pā′shən) *n.* the act of eagerly awaiting (The children awaited their grandparents' arrival with *anticipation*.)

ar·chae·ol·o·gist *or* **ar·che·ol·o·gist** (är′kē ol′ə jist) *n.* an expert in the study of the people, customs, and life of the times before historic records were kept

ar·is·to·crat·ic (ə ris′tə krat′ik) *adj.* possessing the tastes, views, and manners of the upper classes (We met an *aristocratic* family.)

as·bes·tos *also* **as·bes·tus** (as bes′təs) *n.* a material that will not burn (The walls of the safe were covered with *asbestos*.)

at·tempt (ə tempt′) *n.* the act of trying to do something (Jack's first *attempt* at doing a backward flip was a failure.)

aware (ə wer′ *or* ə war′) *adj.* knowing; realizing (Dad was *aware* that something was wrong with the car when it wouldn't start.)

awe (ô) *n.* a feeling of wonder inspired by great beauty, majesty, or power

Bb

bal·lot (bal′ət) *n.* paper slip or other method of marking used in secret voting (How will you mark the *ballot*?)

balmy bä′mē *or* bäl′mē) *adj.* **balm·i·er; balm·i·est** gentle; mild (a *balmy* breeze.)

bal·us·trade (bal′əs trād′) *n.* a row of upright supports and the railing on them ●

bam·boo (bam bü′) *adj.* of a tough, treelike grass with hollow stems used for fishing poles, furniture and huts ●

bam·boo·zle (bam bü′zəl) *v.* to mislead or cheat by trickery (He *bamboozled* us into buying a TV that didn't work.)

ban·yan tree (ban′yən trē) *n.* a large East Indian tree related to the fig tree and whose branches send out shoots that hang down, root in the ground, and start new trunks (The forest began with a single *banyan tree*.) ●

balustrade

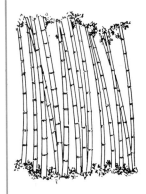

bamboo

banyan tree

a	hat	ō	open	sh	she
ā	age	ô	order	th	thin
ä	far	oi	oil	ᴛʜ	then
e	let	ou	out	zh	measure
ē	equal	u	cup		a in about
ėr	term	u̇	put		e in taken
i	it	ü	rule	ə =	i in pencil
ī	ice	ch	child		o in lemon
o	hot	ng	long		u̇ in circus

555

bellows

beret

boar

bask (bask) *v.* to enjoy warmth (to *bask* in the sun)

bay·o·net (bā′ə nit *or* bā′ə net′) *n.* a knife or dagger made to fit on the end of a rifle

beck·on (bek′ən) *v.* to signal with a motion of the hand or a nod (The police officer *beckoned* us to cross the street.)

bed (bed) *n.* the ground or bottom of a body of water (The stream *bed* was filled with valuable stones.)

bee·line (bē′līn′) *n.* the straightest way from one place to another (to make a *beeline* for the toy store)

bel·lows (bel′ōz *or* bel′əs) *n. sing.* or *pl.* a device spread apart and then pressed together for producing a stream of air to make a fire burn more brightly. •

be·ret (bə rā′ *or* bər′ā) *n.* a soft, round, flat cap (The wind blew Carmen's *beret* off her head.) •

be·wil·dered (bi wil′dərd) *adj.* confused or mixed up (The *bewildered* dog howled at the scarecrow.)

bi·car·bon·ate (bī kär′bə nit *or* bī kär′bə nāt) *n.* a kind of white salt used in making baking powder, in cooking, and in medicine

birch-bark (bėrch′bärk′) *adj.* made of smooth, thin papery layers of bark from a birch tree (Some American Indians built a *birch-bark* cover on the framework of their canoes.)

blem·ish (blem′ish) *n.* a mark that spoils the looks of something (The long scratch on the new table is a *blemish.*)

bluff (bluf) *n.* a high cliff (We could see a mountain goat on the *bluff* munching on tall, brown grass.)

blur (blėr) *v.* **blurred; blur·ring** to make less clear; to dim (The wind blew so hard from the sea that tears flowed and *blurred* my eyes.)

boar (bôr *or* bōr) *adj.* of or relating to a wild hog •

boost (büst) *v.* to lift or push up from below (Ann tried to *boost* me up the tree.)

boun·ti·ful (boun′tə fəl) *adj.* more than enough; plentiful (We bought a *bountiful* supply of coal for the winter.)

breed (brēd) *v.* to produce or beget (Germs *breed* diseases.)

bris·tle (bris′əl) *n.* a short, stiff hair, as on the back of some animals or on a brush (The *bristles* of a hair brush are frequently taken from the hide of a boar.)

bro·ker (brō′kər) *n.* a person who buys and sells goods for other people (We sold our house through a *broker*.)

bud·get (buj′it) *n.* a plan for spending money based on what you have (Their *budget* did not allow them to buy a car.)

Cc

ca·hoots (kə hüts′) *slang, n.* in partnership with someone (John was thought to be in *cahoots* with the gang.)

cal·i·co (kal′ə kō) *adj.* **1** made of calico, a cotton cloth with a colored pattern printed on one side **2** spotted in colors (Several *calico* dresses were on sale.)

cal·loused (kal′əst) *adj.* having calluses; hardened (Many carpenters have large, *calloused* hands from handling rough building materials.)

can·ter (kan′tər) *n.* a horse's gentle gallop (The horse crossed the field at a *canter*.)

car·bon (kär′bən) *n.* a chemical substance found in nature and which can also be produced artificially (*Carbon* is found in all living things.)

car·bon di·ox·ide (kär′bən dī ok′sīd) *n.* a colorless, odorless, tasteless gas (*Carbon dioxide* produces the fizz in some soft drinks.)

care·free (ker′frē′ *or* kar′frē′) *adj.* free from worry; happy (We spent a *carefree* weekend playing and resting.)

cas·cade¹ (kas kād′) *n.* **1** a steep, usually small, waterfall **2** something that falls or rushes forth •

cascade¹ (1)

cascade² *v.* **cas·cad·ed; cas·cad·ing** to fall or pour forth, as in a cascade (Water from the burst dam *cascaded* into the valley.)

case·ment (kās′mənt) *n.* a window that opens on hinges like a door; in poetry, used to mean any window (The glass *casement* was cracked.) •

casement

cat·a·log (kat′l ôg) *n.* a list of items in a book or collection of some sort

a	hat	ō	open	sh	she
ā	age	ô	order	th	thin
ä	far	oi	oil	ŦH	then
e	let	ou	out	zh	measure
ē	equal	u	cup		a in about
ėr	term	u̇	put		e in taken
i	it	ü	rule	ə =	i in pencil
ī	ice	ch	child		o in lemon
o	hot	ng	long		u in circus

chaf·ing (chā′fing) *n.* rubbing; friction (Ted's neck was red from the *chafing* of the stiff collar.)

chaise (shāz) *n.* an open carriage, usually with a top that folds (We took a long ride in the country in our antique, horse-drawn *chaise*.) •

chaise

chem·i·cal (kem′ə kl) *adj.* of or relating to simple substances and the changes that occur when they combine to form other substances (*Chemical* changes are going on inside our bodies all the time.)

chick·a·dee (chik′ə dē′) *n.* a small, lively olive-gray and white bird with a dark head and throat •

chickadee

chief·tain (chēf′tən) *n.* the leader of a group (The *chieftain* told his crew to steer the ship northward.)

chis·el (chiz′əl) *n.* a cutting tool with a sharp edge at the end of a blade used to chip away or shape stone, wood, or metal (Mom worked with a *chisel* to shape her marble statue of the deer and the fawn.)

cir·cu·late (sėr′kyə lāt) *v.* to pass from person to person or from place to place; to move around (A library *circulates* books)

clar·i·ty (klar′ə tē) *n.* clearness (The diamond had remarkable *clarity*.)

clasp (klasp) *v.* to hold firmly with the hand (Jon *clasped* the hammer and hit the nails hard.)

cleat (klēt) *n.* a wooden or metal object around which a rope can be tied

clot (klot) *v.* **clot·ted; clot·ting** to become or cause to become a thick mass

clove (klōv) *n.* a dried flower bud of a tropical tree used to season food (Ham is often seasoned with *cloves*.)

cock·roach (kok′rōch′) *n.* a common household insect pest that is active chiefly at night

col·ic (kol′ik) *n.* sharp pains in the stomach (The vet gave the horse medicine for its *colic*.)

col·o·niz·er (kol′ə nīz ər) *n.* a person who settles an area with others (The *colonizers* suffered hardships their first winter.)

col·um·nist (kol′əm nist *or* kolə′mist) *n.* a person who writes on a special subject for a newspaper

com·et (kom′it) *n.* a heavenly body that appears to have a fuzzy head around a bright center and often has a long, shining tail (A bright *comet* can be seen during the day and without a telescope.)

com·mo·tion (kə mō′shən) *n.* great confusion; disorder (The fox caused a *commotion* in the chicken house.)

com·pli·ment (kom′plə ment) *n.* a flattering remark; something good said about someone or someone's work (The artist received many *compliments* for her fine paintings on display at the art gallery.)

con·cen·trate (kon′sən trāt) *v.* **con·cen·trat·ed; con·cen·trat·ing 1** to focus **2** to reduce in bulk by removing something, as water (Frozen orange juice is *concentrated*.)

con·fer·ence (kon′fər əns) *n.* a meeting of people to discuss something (My teacher had a *conference* with my parents regarding my musical talents.)

con·fi·den·tial (kon′fə den′shəl) *adj.* secret; private (Don't tell anyone what I told you; it's *confidential*.)

con·front (kən frunt′) *v.* to meet face to face (When *confronted* by the people, the newspaper editor agreed to a meeting.)

con·scious·ness (kon′shəs nis) *n.* the ability to know and feel (to loose *consciousness* from a blow on the head)

con·ti·nent (kont′n ənt) *n.* a large body of land (After being at sea for several weeks, the explorers were glad to finally sight the *continent*.)

con·tri·bu·tion (kon′trə byü′shən) *n.* the act of giving to or sharing in something (I made a *contribution* to the book fund.)

cove (kōv) *n.* a small sheltered bay

crack·lings (krak′lingz) *n. pl.* the crisp remainder after the frying or roasting of pork or goose skin

craft (kraft) *n.* a type of work requiring special skill, such as carpentry (The young woman learned her *craft* at a trade school.)

crane (krān) *n.* a machine that has a long, swinging arm for lifting and moving (The *crane* seemed to lift the heavy steel beams with ease.) •

crane

a	hat	ō	open	sh	she
ā	age	ô	order	th	thin
ä	far	oi	oil	ŦH	then
e	let	ou	out	zh	measure
ē	equal	u	cup		a in about
ér	term	ù	put		e in taken
i	it	ü	rule	ə =	i in pencil
ī	ice	ch	child		o in lemon
o	hot	ng	long		u in circus

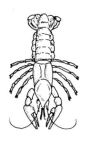

crawfish

craw·fish (krô′fish′) *n.* a spiny, small lobster (We had *crawfish* for dinner.) •

cri·sis (krī′sis) *n.* **cri·ses** (krī′sēz′) the turning point for better or worse (The fever broke, and the *crisis* was over.)

croc·o·dile (krōk′ə dīl) *n.* a large water animal with thick skin, webbed feet, a long, narrow head, and a long tail (A *crocodile* looks much like an alligator.)

crop (krop) *n.* a product grown or gathered for food or fibre (Three big *crops* of the United States are wheat, corn, and cotton.)

cru·el·ty (krü′əl tē) *n.* **cru·el·ties** painful or unkind act or acts (We can't excuse his *cruelty* in mistreating his horse.)

crys·tal·lized (kris′tl īzd) *adj.* formed into crystals (Diamond is pure *crystallized* carbon.)

cu·ra·tor (kyü rā′tər) *n.* one in charge, especially of a museum or zoo

cu·ri·os·i·ty (kyùr′ē os′ə tē) *n.* **cu·ri·os·i·ties 1** an eagerness to learn; an interest leading to inquiry (Lisa went to the zoo to satisfy her *curiosity* about snakes.) **2** something unusual

cur·ry *also* **cur·rie** (kėr′ē) *n.* **cur·ries** a mixture of powdered seasonings with a sharp flavor (The stew was prepared with *curry*.)

Dd

de·ceive (di sēv′) *v.* **de·ceived; de·ceiv·ing** to mislead; to lie (The magician was unable to *deceive* us easily.)

dec·la·ra·tion (dek′lə rā′shən) *n.* a public statement, or a written or printed paper used as proof of something (*declaration* of peace)

de·flat·ed (di flāt′id) *adj.* collapsed due to the release of air or gas (The *deflated* balloon crashed into the water.)

dense (dens) *adj.* thick; not easily entered into or cut through (The plane couldn't take off because of *dense* fog.)

de·scend (di send′) *v.* **1** to come down from a higher place (The gas balloon *descended*.) **2** to spring from (The Clark family is *descended* from the Pilgrims.)

des·per·ate·ly (des′pər it lē) *adv.* without hope; with extreme anxiety (The fire fighters fought the blaze *desperately*.)

de·vot·ed (di vō′tid) *adj.* completely loyal or dedicated to

de·vour (di vour′) *v.* to eat hungrily

dex·ter·i·ty (dek ster′ə tē) *n.* **dex·ter·i·ties** physical skill (*dexterity* on the high wire)

di·ag·nose (dī′əg nōs′) *v.* to identify a disease by its signs or symptoms (The doctor prepared to *diagnose* the illness.)

di·am·e·ter (dī am′ə ter) *n.* **1** a straight line through the center of a circle, cutting the circle in half **2** the distance through the center of an object from one side to the other; thickness (the *diameter* of a log) •

di·men·sion (də men′shən) *n.* **1** measurement of length, width, or thickness **2** size **3** importance (When the scenery was in place, the play took on new *dimensions*.)

di·plo·ma (də plō′mə) *n.* a written or printed paper showing graduation from a school or college or completion of a course of study (I have a *diploma* from the course.) •

dis·in·te·grat·ed
(dis in′tə grāt id) *adj.* broken up into small pieces

dol·phin (dol′fən) *n.* a long-nosed sea animal like a small whale

drawl (drôl) *v.* to speak slowly

Ee

eaves·drop·per (ēvz′drop′ər) *n.* one who listens secretly to talk not supposed to be heard

eb·o·ny¹ (eb′ə nē) *n.* **1** a hard, black wood (The black keys on the piano are made of *ebony*.) **2** the tree that produces this wood (*Ebony* grows in Asia and Africa.)

ebony² *adj.* like ebony, especially in color; black (The color of Gary's hair is *ebony*.)

edel·weiss (ā′dl vīs) *n.* a small plant growing high in the Alps and having nobs of tiny, yellow flowers in the center of several pointy, fuzzy leaves •

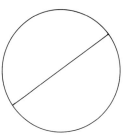

diameter (1)

diploma

edelweiss

a	hat	ō	open	sh	she
ā	age	ô	order	th	thin
ä	far	oi	oil	₮H	then
e	let	ou	out	zh	measure
ē	equal	u	cup		a in about
ér	term	ů	put		e in taken
i	it	ü	rule	ə = { i in pencil
ī	ice	ch	child		o in lemon
o	hot	ng	long		u in circus

ed·i·ble (ed′ə bəl) *adj.* safe to be eaten (The green apples are *edible*.)

EEG *n.* the abbreviation for the scientific term that means the tracing of a patient's brain waves. Doctors use a special machine for this purpose.

em·bark (em bärk′) *v.* to enter into an undertaking; set out; start (After leaving high school, Sue will *embark* on a college education.)

en·hance (en hans′) **en·hanced; en·hanc·ing** *v.* to make greater; to add to (Flowers often *enhance* the beauty of a room.)

en·tranc·ing (en trans′ing) *adj.* delightful; charming (The steady rhythm of the music and the crashing of waves against the shore were both so *entrancing*.)

ewe (yü) *n.* a female sheep ●

ex·haust·ed (eg zôst′id) *adj.* tired; worn out (Most of the boys and girls were *exhausted* after the long hike.)

ex·ot·ic (eg zot′ik) *adj.* strangely beautiful; from another country (The zoo has many *exotic* parrots.)

ex·port (ek′spôrt) *n.* goods sent from one country to another for purposes of trade (Grain is a major *export* of the United States.)

ex·ten·sion (iks ten′chən) *n.* the act of extending or adding on (The Gonzalez family was glad when Mr. Gonzalez got an *extension* on his vacation.)

ex·traor·di·nary (ek strôr′də ner′ē *or* ek′strə ôr′də ner′ē) *adj.* very unusual; remarkable (The colors of the sky at sunset were *extraordinary*.)

Ff

fade (fād) *v.* **fad·ed; fading** to grow dim or faint (After many washings, the color in the pants *faded*.)

fend (fend) *v.* to try to get along without help (The young birds had to *fend* for themselves.)

fer·vent·ly (fėr′vənt lē) *adv.* with great feeling; earnestly (She asked them *fervently* to give to the charity.)

fe·ver·ish·ly (fē′vər ish lē) *adv.* marked by great activity (The boys and girls worked *feverishly* for the party.)

ewe

fi·brous (fī′brəs) *adj.* made up of threadlike parts

fi·nan·cial (fə nan′shəl *or* fī nan′shəl) *adj.* having to do with money (The bank helped our club with *financial* matters.)

fla·men·co (flə meng′kō) *n.* a fast rhythmic dance style of the Andalusian Gypsies of Spain

flex (fleks) *v.* to bend (I can *flex* my stiff knee slowly.)

fo·cus (fō′kəs) *v.* to center; to direct; fix (*Focus* your camera and then take the picture.) ●

fol·ly (fol′ē) *n.* **fol·lies** a foolish idea or act (At first, the steamboat was called "Fulton's *folly*.")

for·lorn (fôr lôrn′) *adj.* **1** neglected; forgotten; **2** feeling sad and lonely because of neglect (At last the *forlorn* kitten had found a home.)

fruit·less (früt′lis) *adj.* useless; coming to nothing (a *fruitless* attempt to escape)

Gg

ga·lore (gə lôr′ *or* gə lōr′) *adj.* plentiful; in abundance (flowers *galore*)

game (gām) *adj.* brave; having courage (The bear was a *game* fighter; she would let no one near the cub.)

gan·der (gan′dər) *n.* a male goose

gan·gly (gang′glē) *adj.* **gan·gli·er; gan·gli·est** tall, thin, and awkwardly built (That tall, well-built man was once a *gangly* youth.)

gaunt (gônt) *adj.* very thin and bony (A long illness made my uncle *gaunt*.)

gem (jem) *n.* a precious stone that has been cut and polished for use as a jewel (Many came to see the rare *gems* on display at the museum.)

gnarled (närld) *adj.* knotted; twisted (a *gnarled* oak tree) ●

gnaw (nô) *v.* to trouble; to torment (The feeling of guilt *gnawed* at his conscience for weeks.)

(to) **focus**

gnarled

a	hat	ō	open	sh	she
ā	age	ô	order	th	thin
ä	far	oi	oil	ŦH	then
e	let	ou	out	zh	measure
ē	equal	u	cup		a in about
ėr	term	u̇	put		e in taken
i	it	ü	rule	ə = { i in pencil
ī	ice	ch	child		o in lemon
o	hot	ng	long		u in circus

563

gore (gôr) *v.* **gored; gor·ing** to stab with a horn or tusk

gorge (gôrj) *n.* a narrow, deep-walled valley, as between two mountains

gourd (gôrd) *n.* fruit related to the pumpkin and melon (The hard-shelled *gourds* were hollowed out and used as bowls and drinking cups.) ●

gourd

grat·ing (grāt'ing) *adj.* **1** unpleasant **2** harsh in sound (The *grating* sound of the rusty swing was annoying.)

grave (grāv) *adj.* serious (By not following directions, the student had made a *grave* error on the test.)

grav·el (grav'əl) *n.* loose rounded bits of rock coarser than sand

grime (grīm) *n.* dirt; soot (The man washed the *grime* from the window.)

grove (grōv) *n.* a group of trees standing together (We stood under a *grove* of cherry trees.)

gun·ny·sack (gun'ē sak) *n.* a sack or bag made out of a strong, coarse fabric (The travelers carried their belongings in a *gunnysack.*)

Hh

hand·i·cap (han'dē kap) *n.* an unfavorable condition that makes progress or success for a person more difficult (A broken toe would be a *handicap* to anyone, but especially to a runner.)

haunch·es (hônch'əz) *n. pl.* the back part of an animal (The fox sat on its *haunches* and waited.)

hay·mow (hā'mou') *n.* the upper part of a barn where hay is stored; hayloft (Hallie loved to climb up on the *haymow* and watch the sky through the cracks in the barn.)

hedge (hej) *n.* a row of bushes or trees planted as a fence or boundary (The farmer was surprised when the horse jumped over the *hedge.*)

hoist (hoist) *v.* to lift up or raise (Several crew members helped to *hoist* the sails of the large ship.)

hub (hub) *n.* the center of a wheel (The *hub* of the wheel became loose.) ●

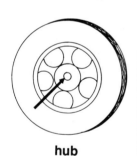

hub

hur·ri·cane (hėr'ə kān) *n.* a storm with violent wind and usually very heavy rain (The *hurricane* knocked down trees and caused severe flooding in the small town.)

Ii

idly (īd′lē) *adv.* in a lazy manner (They sat on the porch, chatting *idly* about their trip to the Rocky Mountains.)

ig·nore (ig nôr′) *v.* **ig·nored; ig·nor·ing** to pay no attention to (The pupil *ignored* the instructions and did the wrong lesson.)

il·lu·mi·nate (i lü′mə nāt) *v.* **il·lu·mi·nat·ed; il·lu·mi·nat·ing** to make light; to light up (The full harvest moon *illuminated* my room.) •

im·pa·tient (im pā′shənt) *adj.* not willing to put up with delay (Terry was *impatient* to go home.)

im·pa·tient·ly (im pā′shənt lē) *adv.* showing lack of patience; crossly (The officer directing the traffic answered the young driver's question *impatiently*.)

im·ple·ment (im′plə mənt) *n.* a tool (The dentist needed a special *implement* for grinding the patients' teeth.)

im·pose (im pōz′) *v.* **im·posed; im·pos·ing** to put a charge on something as a punishment, or a tax, or burden (The judge *imposed* a fine of $50 for driving through a red light in a busy intersection.)

im·pulse (im′puls) *n.* a strong, sudden feeling that one should do something (an *impulse* to run)

in·cense (in′sens) *n.* a material that smells sweet when burned (The burning *incense* smelled like peppermint.)

in·dig·nant·ly (in dig′nənt lē) *adv.* angrily because of unfair treatment (He reacted *indignantly* when he wasn't invited to the party.)

in·fec·tion (in fek′shən) *n.* a disease that is caused by germs entering the body (The *infection* began to clear up with medicine.)

in·fe·ri·or (in fir′ē ər) *adj.* of poorer quality; not of high grade (Reused yarn is sometimes *inferior* to new wool.)

in·flate (in flāt′) *v.* **inflated; inflating** to puff up or swell with air or gas (The gas station attendant *inflated* the truck's tires with air.)

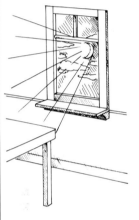

(to) **illuminate**

a	hat	ō	open	sh	she
ā	age	ô	order	th	thin
ä	far	oi	oil	ŦH	then
e	let	ou	out	zh	measure
ē	equal	u	cup		a in about
ėr	term	u̇	put		e in taken
i	it	ü	rule	ə =	i in pencil
ī	ice	ch	child		o in lemon
o	hot	ng	long		u in circus

in·flu·ence (in′flü əns) *v.* to affect or alter someone's thoughts, feelings, or actions (That movie *influenced* me to become a doctor.)

in·let (in′let) *n.* a narrow strip of water extending from the ocean into land (The people living around the *inlets* were mostly traders and fishermen.)

in·sult (in′sult) *n.* a rudeness; an abuse (The fact that I wasn't asked to join the club was a grave *insult* to me.)

inter- a prefix that means **1** "carried on between or among" (*international; intercommunicate*) **2** "shared by one with the other" (*interlock; interlace*)

in·ter·com (in′tər kom′) *n.* any means, such as microphones or loudspeakers, with which staff members of an office, or people on a ship, plane, etc. can communicate with each other (The captain gave orders to his crew through the newly-installed *intercom*.)

in·ter·view (in′tər vyü) *n.* a meeting face to face for the purpose of talking over something special or obtaining information (A reporter had an *interview* with my aunt about the robot she invented to perform simple tasks.)

in·trigue (in trēg′ *or* in′trēg′) *n.* secret planning or plotting (There was much *intrigue* among the spies.).

-ion a noun suffix that means **1** "act or process" (*construction*) **2** "result of an act or process" (*regulation*) **3** "state or condition" (*perfection*)

ir·ri·gate (ir′ə gāt) *v.* **ir·ri·gat·ed; ir·ri·gat·ing** to supply land or crops with water by such means as pipes and flooding (Farmers *irrigate* the land so that their crops will grow.)

-ity a noun suffix that means "state or quality of being" (*curiosity; purity; intensity*)

Jj

jib (jib) *n.* a small three-cornered sail in front of the foremast ●

jun·co (jung′kō) *n.* **jun·cos** *or* **jun·coes** a small, mostly gray American finch. (The members of the bird watcher's club grabbed their cameras to take pictures of the *juncos*.) ●

Kk

kelp (kelp) *n.* a large, tough, brown seaweed (*Kelp* grows in the ocean.)

jib

junco

knead (nēd) *v.* to mix and work over by pressing, folding, and stretching with the hands into a mass (to *knead* dough) •

Ll

lad·en (lād'n) *adj.* filled or loaded with something (The ships *laden* with oil were quickly unloaded.)

lass (las) *n.* a girl or young woman

lat·i·tude (lat'ə tüd) *n.* the distance north or south of the equator, measured in degrees (The map showed that the island was located at 65 degrees north *latitude.*)

league (lēg) *n.* a measure of distance of about three miles (We went many *leagues* by canoe.)

lee (lē) *n.* a side or part that is sheltered or away from the wind (the *lee* of a ship)

lev·er (lev'ər *or* lē'vər) *n.* **1** a bar used to move something firmly fixed **2** in machinery, a bar that turns on a support and is used for changing force and motion (A car has a gearshift *lever* for speed and power.)

loot·er (lüt'ər) *n.* a person who robs or steals, using force (The *looters* returned to their country with silk and precious gems.)

lop·sid·ed (lop'sīd'id) *adj.* awkwardly leaning to one side; unevenly balanced (The paintings hanging on the wall appeared to be *lopsided.*)

lurch (lėrch) *v.* to make a sudden, jerky movement (The train carrying livestock and coal was *lurching* slowly past us.)

lure (lür) *v.* **lured; lur·ing** to attract by offering something attractive (We tried to *lure* the scared rabbit back into its hutch with a carrot.)

lus·ter *or* **lus·tre** (lus'tər) *n.* a bright shine; brightness (My new beads have a fine *luster* to them.)

lynx (lingks) *n.* **lynx** *or* **lynx·es** a wildcat with tufted ears, a short tail, and fairly long legs (The *lynx* slept peacefully in its forest cave.) •

(to) **knead**

lynx

a	hat	ô	open	sh	she
ā	age	ô	order	th	thin
ä	far	oi	oil	ᵺ	then
e	let	ou	out	zh	measure
ē	equal	u	cup		a in about
ėr	term	ù	put		e in taken
i	it	ü	rule	ə =	i in pencil
ī	ice	ch	child		o in lemon
o	hot	ng	long		u in circus

Mm

main·sail (mān′sāl′ *or* mān′səl) *n.* the large sail on the mainmast of a ship (The *mainsail* captured the wind and set the ship on a northern path.)

mal·a·dy (mal′ə dē) *n.*
mal·a·dies a disease or illness (A strange *malady* swept the continent and killed several thousand heads of cattle.)

mal·oc·clu·sion (mal ə klü′shən) *n.* a bad bite; the condition in which the teeth in the upper and lower jaws come together poorly when biting (The child's severe *malocclusion* was corrected with braces.)

man·da·rin (man′də rən) *n.* a high-ranking official in the former Chinese Empire

man·dib·u·lar (man dib′yə lər) *adj.* of or pertaining to the jaw, especially the lower jaw

man·za·ni·ta (man′zə nē′tə) *n.* an evergreen shrub or small tree that grows in western North America

mat·ted (mat′id) *adj.* roughly tangled (The dog's hair was *matted* with mud and leaves.)

mea·ger *or* **mea·gre** (mē′gər) *adj.* hardly enough; scanty (a *meager* meal of a few nuts and berries)

mer·chan·dise (mėr′chən dīz) *n.* goods for sale (The truck delivered new *merchandise* at the local toy store.)

mer·chant (mėr′chənt) *n.* a person who buys and sells goods to make money (The *merchant* made a high profit on the diamonds he sold.)

mes·quite (me skēt′) *n.* a small tree or shrub in the southwestern U.S. and Mexico that grows in thick clusters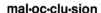

mock·ing (mok′ing) *adj.* making fun of by imitating (*mocking* sounds and gestures)

mol·ten (mōl′tn) *adj.* melted into liquid by extreme heat (The bubbling *molten* lava poured out of the volcano that had been inactive for so long.)

mon·as·tery (mon′əs ter′ē) *n.* a building where monks or nuns live and lead a religious life

monk (mungk) *n.* a man who devotes his whole life to his religion, usually living apart from the rest of the world in a special building with others like himself.

mesquite

moth·er·of·pearl
(muTH′ər əv pėrl′) *n.* the hard, shiny lining of certain seashells, used for buttons and other ornaments

mur·mur (mėr′mər) *v.* to speak in a soft, low voice that can hardly be heard (The busy storekeeper *murmured* a hello as I entered her store.)

mush·room (mush′rüm *or* mush′rùm) *v.* to spring up suddenly or grow quickly (The storm *mushroomed.*)

mute (myüt) *adj.* not speaking; silent (No one spoke; they were *mute* on the matter.).

mut·ton (mut′n) *adj.* of or relating to sheep meat

Nn

ne·on (nē′on) *n.* a chemical element that flows when electricity passes through it

nurs·ery (nėr′sər ē) *n.*
nurs·er·ies a place where plants are grown for replanting elsewhere or for sale

nut·hatch (nut′hach′) *n.* a small insect-eating bird that creeps along tree trunks and branches •

nu·tri·tious (nü trish′əs *or* nyü trish′əs) *adj.* nourishing, as food that is good for a person (Milk and eggs are *nutritious.*)

Oo

ob·long (ob′lông) *adj.* longer than wide (A loaf of bread is often *oblong.*)

of·fend·ing (ə fen′ding) *adj.* displeasing; having an unpleasant effect (The *offending* spots of dirt were washed off the wall.)

or·chard (ôr′chərd) *n.* a place where fruit or nut trees are grown (The *orchard* should bear good apples this year.)

or·der·ly (ôr′dər lē) *n.* a hospital attendant who performs routine tasks

orth·odon·tist (ôr′thə don′tist) *n.* a dentist that specializes in straightening teeth

nuthatch

a	hat	ō	open	sh	she
ā	age	ô	order	th	thin
ä	far	oi	oil	ŦH	then
e	let	ou	out	zh	measure
ē	equal	u	cup		a in about
ér	term	ù	put		e in taken
i	it	ü	rule	ə =	i in pencil
ī	ice	ch	child		o in lemon
o	hot	ng	long		u in circus

ot·ter (ot′ər) *n.* a fish-eating animal with webbed feet and dark-brown beaverlike fur (The *otter* swam on its back and floated on the waves.) ●

out·build·ing (out′bil′ding) *n.* a small building near the main building

ox·y·gen (ok′sə jən) *n.* a colorless, odorless, tasteless gas found in the air and necessary to human and most animal life (Fire will not burn without *oxygen.*)

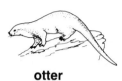

otter

Pp

pa·go·da (pə gō′də) *n.* an Oriental temple with many stories, each of which has a roof that curves upward at the edges and corners (*Pagodas* are found in Japan and other Asian countries.) ●

pal·ate (pal′it) *n.* the roof of the mouth (The steaming food burned my *palate.*)

pa·py·rus (pə pī′rəs) *n.* a kind of writing paper made from the pith of the papyrus plant

parch·ment (parch′mənt) *n.* a writing material made from the skin of a sheep or goat (A secret runic message was written on the ancient *parchment.*)

pagoda

par·tic·i·pa·tion (pär tis′ə pā′shən) *n.* act of taking part (The *participation* of students in the book sale was excellent.) ●

ped·es·tal (ped′i stəl) *n.* a base; support of something, such as a statue, vase, or lamp (The statue fell off the *pedestal.*)

per·suade (pər swād′) *v.* **per·suad·ed; per·suad·ing** to win over by argument or earnest request (We tried to *persuade* her to come along.)

pierc·ing (pir′sing) *adj.* loud, shrill (The night's quiet was broken by a *piercing* cry.)

pig·ment (pig′mənt) *n.* the material that gives color to other materials, as a powdered material mixed with a liquid to give color (The red *pigment* was made of three minerals.)

pig·my or **pyg·my** (pig′mē) *adj.* very small or dwarfish (*Pigmy* plant life flourished on the island.)

pi·ña·ta (pēn yät′ə) *n.* in Mexican tradition, a decorated container filled with candies, fruits, and small gifts that is hung from the ceiling and broken during the celebration of Christmas (We hit the *piñata* three times before it finally broke.)

570

pitch (pich) *n.* a thick, black sticky material made usually from tar to fill the seams of wooden ships and to cover roofs and roads

pity (pit′ē) *n.* a feeling of sadness for someone (Kay felt *pity* for the cold and hungry puppy.)

plague (plāg) *n.* a dreaded disease that spreads quickly and usually causes death

poll (pōl) *v.* to cast a vote

polling place (pōl′ing plās) *n.* the building or place where voters cast their ballots in an election (The city residents flocked to their *polling places* to cast their ballots for mayor.)

pol·lute (pə lüt′) *n.* **pol·lut·ed; pol·lut·ing** to make dirty; unclean (The waste from the paint factory *polluted* the river.)

prac·ti·cal·ly (prak′tik lē) *adv.* almost but not quite; nearly (The store is only two blocks away, so we are *practically* there.)

pre·his·to·ry (prē his′tər ē) *n.* the time before histories were written

prem·is·es (prem′is əz) *n. pl.* **1** a house or building and its grounds **2** a tract of land with its buildings

prof·it (prof′it) *n.* the money left from a business undertaking after all the expenses have been paid (Our successful cookie sale showed a large *profit.*)

proph·e·cy (prof′ə sē) *n.* **proph·e·cies** a telling of future events

pur·sue (pər sü′) *v.* **pur·sued; pur·su·ing** to follow in order to catch; to chase (The police *pursued* the robber.)

Qq

quar·ry (kwôr′ē) *n.* **quar·ries** a hole where stone for building is dug or blasted out of the ground ●

queer (kwir) *v.* to spoil; to ruin (*queer* one's travel plans)

quench (kwench) *v.* to stop; to put an end to (*quench* one's thirst)

quarry

a	hat	ō	open	sh	she
ā	age	ô	order	th	thin
ä	far	oi	oil	ŦH	then
e	let	ou	out	zh	measure
ē	equal	u	cup		a in about
ér	term	ů	put		e in taken
i	it	ü	rule	ə =	i in pencil
ī	ice	ch	child		o in lemon
o	hot	ng	long		u in circus

Rr

raid·er (rād'ər) *n.* a person who invades a territory to take what is valuable

ram·page (ram pāj') *v.* **ram·paged; ram·pag·ing** to rush or storm wildly (The raging floodwaters *rampaged* across the countryside.)

re·ac·tion (rē ak'shən) *n.* a feeling or action brought about by some force or influence (My *reaction* to a funny story is to laugh.)

re·bound·ing (rē'boun'ding *or* ri boun'ding) *adj.* springing back (The girl hit every *rebounding* ball on the court.)

reck·on (rek'ən) *v.* **1** to regard; consider **2** *(chiefly dialect)* to think; to suppose (I *reckon* they won't win.)

re·cline (ri klīn') *v.* **re·clined; re·clin·ing 1** to lie down **2** to lean back

rec·og·nize (rek'əg nīz') *v.* **rec·og·nized; rec·og·niz·ing** to know or identify from past experience or knowledge (Joe *recognized* the dog because of its floppy ears.)

red·wood (red'wud') *n.* a tall evergreen tree of California that often grows to a height of 300 feet

reptile

re·hearse (ri hėrs') *v.* **re·hearsed; re·hears·ing** to practice a play, part, etc. (They *rehearse* their parts for the show every day.)

re·late (ri lāt') *v.* **re·lat·ed; re·lat·ing** to give an explanation of; to tell a story (He *related* the story to me.)

rel·a·tive (rel'ə tiv) *n.* a person who belongs to the same family by blood or marriage (Cousins are *relatives*.)

rel·ic (rel'ik) *n.* a thing left from the past (*relics* of an ancient civilization)

rep·tile (rep'təl) *n.* any of a group of cold-blooded, air-breathing animals having a backbone that crawl on their bellies or on short legs (A snake is a *reptile*.) ●

re·search (ri sėrch' *or* rē'sėrch') *n.* a careful hunting for facts in order to discover new information (*Research* has led to many medical cures.)

re·sume (ri züm') *v.* **re·sumed; re·sum·ing** to begin again; go on (Jan went back home to *resume* writing her story.)

rick·et·y (rik'ə tē) *adj.* shaky; not sturdy (We climbed the *rickety* staircase.)

rind·less (rīnd′les) *adj.* without a firm outer covering (A peeled orange is *rindless*.)

riv·ets (riv′its) *n.* metal bolts used to hold metal or wood pieces together

Ss

sa·gua·ro (sə gwär′ō) *n.* a giant cactus of the southwestern United States

sands·pit (sand′spit′) *n.* a small piece of land running into a body of water and made of sand and gravel left behind by waves and the flow of water

sap·ling (sap′ling) *adj.* of or pertaining to a young tree

sap·phire (saf′īr) *adj.* a deep purplish blue

satch·el (sach′əl) *n.* a small bag with a flat bottom for carrying clothes, books, papers (Mom packed her tax papers into the *satchel*.)

scam·per·ing (skam′pə ring) *n.* a light or quick movement or running (The dogs' wild *scampering* caught my attention.)

schol·ar (skol′ər) *n.* a learned person

scroll (skrōl) *n.* a roll of paper or parchment used for writing (Ancient *scrolls* are on display in the museum.) •

scythe (sīŦH) *n.* a long curved blade on a handle for cutting tall grass or grain (He cleared the weeds in the lot with a *scythe*.) •

sep·a·rate (sep′ə rāt′) *v.* **sep·a·rat·ed; sep·a·rat·ing** **1** to divide into parts or groups (to *separate* into reading groups) **2** to part (The teacher *separated* two talkative pupils.)

shaft (shaft) *n.* a vertical passageway sunk deep into the earth for mining various substances

shard (shärd) *n.* a piece of broken pottery •

skit·tery (skit′ər ē) *adj.* (of a horse) uneasy and easily frightened; high-spirited and unwilling to stand at ease

slack (slak) *adj.* loose (a *slack* line)

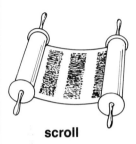

scroll

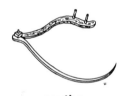

scythe

shard

a	hat	ō	open	sh	she
ā	age	ô	order	th	thin
ä	far	oi	oil	ŦH	then
e	let	ou	out	zh	measure
ē	equal	u	cup		a in about
ėr	term	u̇	put		e in taken
i	it	ü	rule	ə =	i in pencil
ī	ice	ch	child		o in lemon
o	hot	ng	long		u in circus

slith·er (sliⱯH′ər) *v.* to slide (A snake *slithered* across the road.)

smid·gen *or* **smid·geon** *or* **smid·gin** (smij′ən) *n.* a tiny bit; a small amount (I'll have just a *smidgen* of pie.)

sneaker·shod (snē′ker shod) *adv.* wearing canvas shoes with rubber soles (Jane played tennis *sneaker-shod*.)

snug (snug) *adj.* **snug·ger; snug·gest** comfortable; cozy (a *snug* shelter)

so·ber·ly (sō′bər lē) *adv.* quietly; calmly (He accepted the bad news *soberly*.)

so·cia·ble (sō′shə bəl) *adj.* friendly; liking people (Our club has *sociable* people.)

so·ci·ety (sə sī′ə tē) *adj.* of fashionable people and their activities

sock·et (sok′it) *n.* a hollow place into which something fits (an eye *socket;* a light bulb *socket*)

so·nar (sō′när) *n.* a device for finding objects under water by means of sound waves

spec·tac·u·lar (spek tak′yə lər) *adj.* showy; making a grand display (The fireworks were *spectacular*.)

spec·trum (spek′trəm) *n.* the colors formed when a beam of white light is separated into all the colors that make it up. The colors of the spectrum are red, orange, yellow, green, blue, indigo, and violet. The naked eye cannot see all the colors of the spectrum.

spray (sprā) *n.* small drops of liquid flying through the air (The *spray* from the hose sent everyone scurrying.)

spurt (spėrt) *v.* to gush forth in a jet or stream

squash¹ (skwosh) *v.* to crush (*squash* a banana)

squash² *n.* a large green or yellow vinelike plant, the fruit of which is eaten as a vegetable or used as filling for pie ●

starch (stärch) *n.* a white, tasteless, odorless food matter found in potatoes, wheat, rice, and corn

state·room (stāt′rüm) *n.* a private room for passengers on a boat, ship, or railroad train

stim·u·lat·ing (stim′yə lāt ing) *adj.* exciting; causing to move or act (The *stimulating* music captivated the audience.)

squash²

574

struc·ture (struk′chər) *n.* the way parts of something are arranged (the *structure* of a plant or animal)

stut·ter (stut′ər) *v.* to speak with sounds repeated unwillingly (Whenever I was nervous I *stuttered*.)

sul·tan (sult′n) *n.* a king or ruler (The people obeyed the *sultan*.)

surge (sėrj) *v.* **surged; surg·ing** to rise suddenly (The stock market dropped yesterday but *surged* today.)

sus·pi·cious·ly (sə spish′əs lē) *adv.* feeling that something may be wrong; distrustfully (She looked about the house *suspiciously* when she found the doop open.)

swarm (swôrm) *n.* a large number or group of animals or people moving together (A *swarm* of bees chased the bear.)

swatch (swoch) *n.* **1** a sample piece of fabric or other material **2** a patch (a *swatch* of color)

swerve (swėrv) *v.* **swerved; swerv·ing** to turn to the side suddenly from a straight line or course

swiv·el chair (swiv′l chãr) *n.* a chair that can turn round on its base

Tt

tack (tak) *n.* the direction of a sailboat (We sailed across the bay on one *tack*.)

ta·ran·tu·la (tə ran′chə lə) *n.* a large, hairy, European spider having a painful bite. People once thought that its bite caused an urge to dance.

tel·e·scope (tel′ə skōp) *n.* an instrument with lenses for viewing far-off objects and especially for observing the heavenly bodies

teth·er (teᴛʜ′ər) *n.* a rope or fastening by which an animal's movements are limited (The grazing horse pulled at the *tether*.) •

tether

thaw (thô) *v.* to melt (The directions say to *thaw* the frozen food before cooking it.)

a	hat	ō	open	sh	she
ā	age	ô	order	th	thin
ä	far	oi	oil	ᴛʜ	then
e	let	ou	out	zh	measure
ē	equal	u	cup		a in about
ėr	term	ù	put		e in taken
i	it	ü	rule	ə =	i in pencil
ī	ice	ch	child		o in lemon
o	hot	ng	long		u in circus

the·a·ter *or* **the·a·tre** (thē'ə tər) *n.* a place where plays or motion pictures are presented

theme (thēm) *n.* **1** a subject or topic in an art form (Ruth's paintings all have a nature *theme*.) **2** a written work (My *theme* is due on Monday.)

thread (thred) *v.* to make one's way carefully; go on a winding course (The conductor *threaded* his way through the crowded train.)

threat (thret) *n.* an expression of intent to do harm; a warning

thresh (thresh) *v.* to separate the seeds or grain from the wheat, etc. by beating

throb (throb) *v.* **throbbed;** **throb·bing** to beat, pound, or vibrate (Ken's heart *throbbed* with excitement.)

throng (thrông) *v.* **1** to crowd into (*throng* a stadium) **2** to crowd together in great numbers (Thousands *thronged* to watch the parade.)

til·ler (til'ər) *n.* a handle used to turn the rudder of a boat from side to side ●

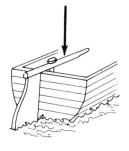

tiller

tor·na·do (tôr nā'dō) *n.* **tor·na·does** *or* **tor·na·dos** a strong and destructive whirlwind with a funnel-shaped cloud ●

tornado

tor·rent (tôr'ənt) *n.* a rushing stream, as of water (The waterfall poured from the cliff in a roaring *torrent*.)

tow (tō) *n.* the fact or condition of being pulled along behind (The man had his children in *tow*.)

tract (trakt) *n.* a stretch of land (Our house is on a wooded *tract*.)

tra·peze (trə pēz') *n.* a swing that hangs from a ceiling or frame high above the ground, used in circuses and for exercises (He soared gracefully across the tent on his silver *trapeze*.)

tre·men·dous (tri men'dəs) *adj.* very great; large (A *tremendous* wave knocked me down at the beach.)

trench (trench) *n.* a long narrow ditch or groove (A *trench* was dug for the pipes.)

tri·um·phant·ly (trī um'fənt lē) *adv.* victoriously or successfully (The winning army marched *triumphantly* into the deserted city.)

Uu

un·der·cut (un'dər kut') *n.* a cut, or cutting away, underneath so as to leave an overhang

-ure a noun suffix that means "an act, a process, or a being" (*departure; pressure; moisture*)

Vv

ven·i·son (ven′ə sən *or* ven′ə zən) *n.* the flesh of a wild animal killed by hunting and suitable for eating (deer *venison*)

vent (vent) *n.* an opening used to release air, a gas, or a liquid; an outlet (The cat's carrying case has air *vents*.)

vi·brate (vī′brāt) *v.* **vi·brat·ed; vi·brat·ing** to shake; to move with slight motion

vig·or·ous·ly (vig′ər əs lē) *adv.* in a strong, forceful way

vo·cal cords (vō′kl kôrds) *n. pl.* either of two pairs of membranes in the throat that produce sound when they vibrate from air passing between them

vol·un·teer (vol′ən tir′) *n.* a person who serves without pay

Ww

wash (wosh *or* wôsh) *n.* stretch of land sometimes covered with water and sometimes dry

watt (wot) *n.* an amount (unit) used to measure electric power (a 60 *watt* bulb)

wea·sel (wē′zəl) *n.* a small, active animal with a long, slender body and short legs that is related to the mink

wick (wik) *n.* the loosely woven or twisted cotton tape or cord in the center of a lamp or a candle that draws up oil or melted wax to be burned; the part of a candle or oil lamp that is lit (The *wick* ran nearly the entire length of the candle.)

Yy

yoke (yōk) *n.* **1** a wooden frame fitted around the necks of two working animals **2** two animals joined together by a yoke (a *yoke* of oxen) ●

yuc·ca (yuk′ə) *n.* a plant growing in dry regions with stiff, pointed leaves at the base of a tall spike ●

yoke

yucca

a	hat	ō	open	sh	she
ā	age	ô	order	th	thin
ä	far	oi	oil	ŦH	then
e	let	ou	out	zh	measure
ē	equal	u	cup		a in about
ér	term	ù	put		e in taken
i	it	ü	rule	ə =	i in pencil
ī	ice	ch	child		o in lemon
o	hot	ng	long		u in circus

PHONICS HANDBOOK

VOWEL SOUNDS

The Long Sound /ā/a

THINK ABOUT THIS:

Say these words. Listen to the sound the underlined letters stand for.

play   shade   brain   nation   weight

These words all have the long a vowel sound. Look at the words above to see some of the ways this vowel sound can be spelled.

DO THIS:

Say the first word in each row. Find and write the other word in the row that has the same vowel sound *and* spelling. Underline the letter or letters that stand for the vowel sound.

1. gray   yellow   loyal   payment
2. famous   feature   navy   blanket
3. main   explain   among   mansion
4. sleigh   wiggle   freight   height
5. escape   scarf   regret   cascade

The Short Sound /a/a

THINK ABOUT THIS:

Say these words. Do all of these words have the same vowel sound?

attic   mask   blanket

All of these words have the short a vowel sound. How is the short a vowel sound spelled in each word? Notice where the letter a appears in each word.

DO THIS:

Read the words below. Find and write the words that have the short a vowel sound. Tell where the letter that stands for this vowel sound appears in each word. For example, you can write the following: The a in *patch* appears between the letters p and t.

1. patch   3. advance   5. gnaw
2. bamboo   4. raven   6. alligator

578

The Long Sound /ē/e

THINK ABOUT THIS:

Say these words. Listen to the sound the underlined letters stand for.

she   east   sleep   duty   brief   valley

These words all have the long e vowel sound. Look at the words above to see some of the ways this vowel sound can be spelled.

DO THIS:

Say the first word in each row. Find and write the other word in the row that has the same vowel sound *and* spelling. Underline the letter or letters that stand for the vowel sound.

1. me   metal   female   measure
2. study   plenty   yesterday   stallion
3. plead   plaid   trample   breathe
4. knee   knit   steeple   never
5. thief   grief   threat   fixture
6. monkey   kitten   yonder   honey

The Short Sound /e/e

THINK ABOUT THIS:

Say these words. Do both have the same vowel sound?

smell   steady

Both *smell* and *steady* have the short e vowel sound. How is the short e vowel sound spelled in each word? Notice where the letters e and ea appear in the words.

DO THIS:

Read the words below. Find and write the words that have the short e vowel sound. Tell where the letters that stand for this vowel sound appear.

1. thread 2. museum 3. vent 4. pleasure 5. clever 6. theme

The Long Sound /ī/i

THINK ABOUT THIS:

Say these words. Listen to the sound the underlined letters stand for.

write   rely   kind   mighty   lie

These words all have the long i vowel sound. Look at the words above to see some of the ways this vowel sound can be spelled.

Write the five words given on page 579 as headings on your paper. Then put each of the following words under the heading that has the same spelling for the long *i* sound.

1. quite   4. blind   7. tighten
2. despite   5. invite   8. die
3. tonight   6. climb   9. occupy

The Short Sound /i/*i*

THINK ABOUT THIS:

Say these words. Do all of these words have the same vowel sound?

image   dish   glisten

All of these words have the short *i* vowel sound. How is the short *i* vowel sound spelled in each word? Notice where the letter *i* appears in each word.

DO THIS:

Read the words below. Find and write the words that have the short *i* vowel sound. Tell where the letter that stands for this vowel sound appears in each word.

1. river   3. hitch   5. tiller
2. frighten   4. media   6. little

The Long Sound /ō/*o*

THINK ABOUT THIS:

Say these words. Listen to the sound the underlined letters stand for.

drove   throat   moment   crow   hold

These words all have the long o vowel sound. Look at the words above to see some of the ways this vowel sound can be spelled.

DO THIS:

Write the five words given above as headings on your paper. Then put each of the following words under the heading that has the same spelling for the long o vowel sound.

1. stroke   4. motion   7. goal
2. soda   5. arrow   8. follow
3. sparrow   6. croak   9. told

The Short Sound /o/o

THINK ABOUT THIS:
Say these words. Do all of these words have the same vowel sound?

    hop   odd   clock   comic

All of these words have the short *o* vowel sound. How is the short *o* vowel sound spelled in each word? Notice where the letter *o* appears.

DO THIS:
Read the words below. Find and write the words that have the short *o* vowel sound. Tell where the letter that stands for the vowel sound appears in each word.

    1. honest 2. obvious 3. devote 4. throttle 5. copy 6. closet

The Long Sound /yü/*u*

THINK ABOUT THIS:
Say these words. Listen to the sound the underlined letters stand for.

    fuse   uniform

These words all have the long *u* vowel sound. Notice that there are only two common spellings for this vowel sound. What are they?

DO THIS:
Say the first word in each row. Find and write the other word in the row that has the same vowel sound *and* spelling. Underline the letter or letters that stand for the vowel sound.

1. useful	sugar	mutter	cube
2. human	future	hunter	mayor
3. tribute	refuse	assert	mustard
4. union	understand	refuel	opinion

The Short Sound /u/*u*

THINK ABOUT THIS:
Say these words. Listen to the sound the underlined letters stand for.

    scrub   mother   country   none

These words all have the short *u* vowel sound. How many *different* spellings do you see for this sound? All of the other short vowel sounds you've worked with have only one or two common spellings. The short *u* vowel sound has four!

DO THIS:
Say the first word in each row. Find and write the other word in the row that has the same vowel sound *and* spelling. Underline the letter or letters that stand for the vowel sound.

1. j<u>u</u>dge   public   jingle   because
2. c<u>ou</u>ple   people   double   couch
3. c<u>o</u>lor   brother   collar   locker
4. s<u>o</u>mething   mister   stone   become

Some Spellings for /ü/

THINK ABOUT THIS:
Say these words. Listen to the sound the underlined letters stand for.

wh<u>o</u>   sm<u>oo</u>th   thr<u>ew</u>   bl<u>ue</u>   ass<u>u</u>me

These words all have the same vowel sound. Your glossary uses the symbol /ü/ to show this sound. Look at the words above to see some of the ways this sound can be spelled.

DO THIS:
Write the five words given above as headings on your paper. Then put each of the following words under the heading that has the same spelling for the vowel sound /ü/.

1. spool   4. undue   7. include
2. movie   5. loop   8. conclude
3. scoot   6. strew   9. flew

Some Spellings for /ů/

THINK ABOUT THIS:
Say these words. Listen to the sound the underlined letters stand for.

br<u>oo</u>k   w<u>ou</u>ld   p<u>u</u>ll

These words have the same vowel sound. Your glossary uses the symbol /ů/ to show this sound. Look at the words above to see the ways this sound can be spelled.

Say the first word in each row. Find and write the other word in the row that has the same vowel sound *and* spelling. Underline the letter or letters that stand for the vowel sound.

1. cr<u>oo</u>k   croak   spool   soot
2. c<u>ou</u>ld   should   destroy   cloud
3. b<u>u</u>sh   busily   union   sugar

Two More Vowel Sounds /ou/ and /oi/

THINK ABOUT THIS:
Say these words. Listen to the sound the underlined letters stand for.

r<u>ou</u>nd   sc<u>ow</u>l

These words both have the same vowel sound. Your glossary uses the symbol /ou/ to show this sound. Look at the words above to see two common spellings for this sound.

Now say these words. Again, listen to the sound the underlined letters stand for.

destr<u>oy</u>   p<u>oi</u>nt

These words both have the same vowel sound. It is NOT the vowel sound you hear in *round* and *scowl*. Your glossary uses the symbol /oi/ to show the vowel you hear in *destroy* and *point*.

DO THIS:
Write the symbols /ou/ and /oi/ as headings on your paper. Then put each of the following words under the symbol that stands for the vowel sound you hear in the word or in the unaccented syllable.

1. avoid   3. boiler   5. prowl   7. allow
2. coin   4. annoy   6. pound   8. counter

Some Spellings for /ô/

THINK ABOUT THIS:
Say these words. Listen to the sound the underlined letters stand for.

w<u>a</u>ll   th<u>ough</u>t   l<u>o</u>st   cr<u>aw</u>l   t<u>augh</u>t   bec<u>au</u>se   st<u>a</u>lk

These words all have the same vowel sound. Your glossary uses the symbol /ô/ to show this sound. Look at all the different ways that this sound can be spelled. You must think: How AWful!

Letters are missing from certain words in the sentences below. The missing letters stand for the /ô/ sound. Write each word—spelled correctly—on your paper. Use a dictionary to help you.

1. If you will go, I will go _lso.
2. Josh threw the ball; I c_ _ _ _t it.
3. There was fr_st on the windowpane.
4. If you y_ _n, it's a sign you are sleepy.
5. Some people jog; others prefer to w_ _k.
6. The general shouted, "H_lt!"
7. I've br_ _ _ _t you some flowers!
8. A yellow light signals c_ _tion.

Four Spellings for /ôr/

THINK ABOUT THIS:
Say these words. Listen to the sound the underlined letters stand for.

short   store   pour   warm

Most people hear the same vowel sound when they say these words. Your glossary uses the symbol /ôr/ to show this sound.

The sound /ôr/ can be spelled *or, ore, our,* and *ar.* You know that the letter *r* is not usually thought of as a vowel letter. But when the letter *r* follows a vowel letter, it often influences the sound that the vowel letter stands for. For this reason, we sometimes call a sound like /ôr/ an "*r*-controlled" vowel sound.

DO THIS:
Say the first word in each row. Find and write the other word in the row that has the same *r*-controlled vowel sound *and* spelling. Underline the letters that stand for the *r*-controlled vowel sound.

1. sore	adore	molar	remote
2. course	coward	fourth	certain
3. storm	force	reword	curtain
4. war	wander	rawhide	award
5. fourth	youth	squirm	court
6. explore	chore	errand	frontier
7. torn	round	burst	morning
8. quarter	swarm	earthen	beard

Another *r*-Controlled Vowel Sound /ėr/

THINK ABOUT THIS:
Say these words. Listen to the sound the underlined letters stand for.

whirl   worse   burst   hurry   concern   earn

All of these words have the same *r*-controlled vowel sound. Your glossary uses the symbol /ėr/ to show this sound. Look at the words above to see some of the ways this sound can be spelled.

DO THIS:
Write the six words given above as headings on your paper. Then put each of the following words under the heading that has the same spelling for the *r*-controlled vowel sound.

1. skirt	4. world	7. curl
2. alert	5. pearl	8. scurry
3. earthen	6. purpose	9. research

More *r*-Controlled Vowel Sounds /īr/, /er/, and /ir/

THINK ABOUT THIS:
Say these words. Listen to the sound the underlined letters stand for.

wire   desire

Both of these words have the same *r*-controlled vowel sound. Your glossary uses the symbol /īr/ to show this sound. The letters *ire* are usually used to spell this sound.

Here is another *r*-controlled vowel sound. What letters are used to spell this sound?

berry   errand

Your glossary uses the symbol /er/ to show this sound.

Now say these words. Listen to the sound that the underlined letters stand for.

sneer   clear   fierce

These three words have the same *r*-controlled vowel sound. Your glossary uses the symbol /ir/ to show this sound. What letters can be used to spell this sound?

Say the words in each row. Then find and write the two words in the row that have the same *r*-controlled vowel sound. Underline the letters that stand for the *r*-controlled vowel sound.

1. empire   retire   curtain   soldier
2. terrible   fairy   ferry   alert
3. stair   deer   pioneer   parlor
4. spear   pearl   large   rear
5. cashier   frontier   barrier   horrid
6. barrel   dairy   fear   beard

Still More *r*-Controlled Vowel Sounds /är/ and /ar/

THINK ABOUT THIS:
Say these words. Listen to the sound the underlined letters stand for.

dark   heart   sergeant

These three words have the same *r*-controlled vowel sound. Your glossary uses the symbol /är/ to show this sound. What letters can be used to spell this sound?

Now say these words. Again, listen to the sound the underlined letters stand for.

tariff   marry

These two words have the same *r*-controlled vowel sound. Your glossary uses the symbol /ar/ to show this sound. What letters can be used to spell this sound?

DO THIS:
Say the words in each row. Then find and write the two words that have the same *r*-controlled vowel sound. Underline the letters that stand for the *r*-controlled vowel sound.

1. hear   cart   stark   pearl
2. tarry   board   furry   narrow
3. farmer   artist   fork   spare
4. stare   harbor   startle   tore
5. barrel   bear   warm   carrot

586

The Schwa Sound /ə/

THINK ABOUT THIS:

Say these words. First listen for the number of syllables in each word. Then listen for the vowel sound in the unaccented syllable.

about   open   wagon   bargain   circus   pencil

The underlined letter or letters in the unaccented syllable of each of these words stand for the same vowel sound. The dictionary and your glossary use the symbol /ə/ (called the *schwa*) to show this vowel sound.

DO THIS:

Copy and say the words below. Find the schwa sound in the unaccented syllable or syllables in each word and underline the letter or letters that stand for this sound.

1. parade	4. among	7. imagine	10. status
2. moment	5. diet	8. above	11. family
3. villain	6. galore	9. apron	12. bonus

The *r*-Controlled Schwa Sound /ər/

THINK ABOUT THIS:

Say these words. Listen for the number of syllables in each word. Then listen for the *r*-controlled *schwa* sound in the unaccented syllable.

winter   favor   molar   murmur   picture

Your glossary uses the symbol /ər/ to show this sound. Look at the words above to see some of the ways this sound can be spelled.

DO THIS:

Copy and say the words below. Find the /ər/ sound in the unaccented syllable in each word and underline the letters that stand for this sound.

1. over	4. miller	7. pleasure
2. miner	5. horror	8. sugar
3. sulfur	6. harbor	9. culture

CONSONANT SOUNDS

Clusters with r

THINK ABOUT THIS:

Say these pairs of words. Listen to the sounds the underlined letters stand for.

race—brace	rail—frail	ray—tray
rate—crate	reed—greed	rush—thrush
rag—drag	ride—pride	rub—shrub

In the first word of each pair, you heard only one consonant sound at the beginning. But in the second word, you heard two consonant sounds together at the beginning. We call such sounds *consonant clusters.*

DO THIS:

Use each word below to make other words by writing a consonant letter before the letter *r.* For example, using the word *ray,* you can make the words *bray, dray, fray, gray, pray,* and *tray.*

1. rock   3. rust   5. rill
2. room   4. rake   6. rip

NOW THINK ABOUT THIS:

Say these words. Listen to the sounds the underlined letters stand for.

sprout   scratch   straw

When you say these words, you hear three different consonant sounds together at the beginning of each word.

AND DO THIS:

Say the words in each row. Then find and write the two words in the row that have the same beginning consonant sounds. Underline the letters that stand for these sounds.

1. sprain	spread	pressed	splender
2. craggy	screen	scribble	sprout
3. trouble	stretch	stealthy	strength

588

Clusters with _l_

THINK ABOUT THIS:
Say these pairs of words. Listen to the sounds the underlined letters stand for.

leak—bleak   lee—flee   lug—plug
loud—cloud   land—gland   lid—slid

In the first word of each pair, you heard only one consonant sound at the beginning. How many consonant sounds did you hear at the beginning of the second word? What consonant letter stayed the same at the beginning of these words?

The letter _l_ is also used in a three-letter consonant cluster, as in _spl_urge and _spl_ice.

DO THIS:
Use each word below to make other words by writing a consonant letter before the letter _l_. For example, using the word _lot,_ you can make the words _blot, clot, plot,_ and _slot._

1. lank   3. late   5. lash
2. lit   4. lap   6. lay

Some Other Beginning Clusters

THINK ABOUT THIS:
Say these words. Listen to the sounds the underlined letters stand for.

dwell   swamp   twirl

These consonant clusters all use the letter _w._

DO THIS:
Copy and say the first word in each row. Then find and write the other word in the row that has the same beginning sounds. Underline the letters in both words that stand for these sounds.

1. swift   smash   swirl   sugar
2. dwarf   twenty   drawing   dwelling
3. twilight   trouble   tumult   twinge

589

Clusters That Begin with s

THINK ABOUT THIS:

Here are some consonant clusters that you've already studied. What do these clusters have in common?

<u>s</u>ling <u>s</u>wamp <u>s</u>prout <u>s</u>cratch <u>s</u>treak

These clusters all begin with the letter s. Here are some other clusters with the letter s:

<u>s</u>care <u>s</u>kimp <u>s</u>mart <u>s</u>nail <u>s</u>pare <u>s</u>till

And here is one more cluster that you should know:

<u>s</u>quirt <u>s</u>queeze <u>s</u>quabble

Can you think of some other words that begin with these clusters?

DO THIS:

Write each word below on your paper. Then write the letter s before the word. Say the new word, and write a sentence using that word.

1. kit 2. tack 3. nap 4. camp 5. peak 6. mile

Clusters at the End

THINK ABOUT THIS:

A consonant cluster can occur at the beginning of a word. It can also occur in the middle or at the end of a word. Here are some common final consonant clusters:

ma<u>st</u> mea<u>nt</u> dri<u>ft</u> bo<u>lt</u> stri<u>ct</u>

What do these clusters all have in common?

Here are some other clusters you should know:

sco<u>ld</u> sta<u>nd</u> bri<u>nk</u> stu<u>mp</u>

DO THIS:

Say the words in each row. Then find and write the two words in the row that have the same final consonant sounds. Underline the letters that stand for the final consonant sounds.

1.	scald	chant	thump	vent
2.	shrink	trench	flank	trust
3.	fend	bland	think	fold
4.	hoist	waft	thrift	fact
5.	mend	ramp	colt	slump

590

Some Special Sounds at the Beginning

THINK ABOUT THIS:

Say these words. Listen to the sounds the underlined letters stand for.

chant   shoal   thaw   they   phase

In each word, you hear only one sound at the beginning. But two letters are used to spell each sound. What consonant letters stand for the beginning sound in each word?

DO THIS:

Say the words in each row. Then find and write the two words in the row that have the same beginning sound *and* spelling. Underline the letters that stand for this sound.

1. chore   cease   challenge   bleach
2. shock   thigh   thunder   trigger
3. chariot   smother   shower   shudder
4. phony   piano   phantom   frequent

Some Special Sounds at the End

THINK ABOUT THIS:

Say these words. Listen to the sounds the underlined letters stand for.

beach   brush   tooth   bring   laugh

In each word, you hear only one sound at the end. But two letters are used to spell each sound. What consonant letters stand for the final sound in each word?

DO THIS:

Say the words in each row. Then find and write the two words in the row that have the same final consonant sound *and* spelling. Underline the letters that stand for this sound.

1. church   thrush   past   cash
2. path   scratch   truth   roof
3. swung   think   king   gain
4. brag   cough   count   enough
5. reach   marsh   much   truck

Cover, Front Matter, Unit Openers designed by *Thomas Vroman Associates, Inc.* Illustrators: Melanie Arwin, pp. 151-160; Edgar Blakeney, pp. 436-438, p. 441; Judith Cheng, pp. 472-479; Gil Cohen, pp. 227-235; Olivia Cole, pp. 30-35; Pat Cummings, pp. 14-29, 396-409; Diane de Groat, pp. 206-208; Susan Detrich, pp. 370-371; William Pène du Bois, pp. 484-509; Marian Ebert, pp. 96-97, 174-177, 252-253; Allan Eitzen, pp. 236-250; 358-369; Joy Troth Friedman, pp. 324-333; Will Harmuth, pp. 59-81; Michael Hostovich, pp. 86-95; Yee Chea Lin, pp. 268-285; Al Lorenz, pp. 480-481; Bertrand Mangel, pp. 188-190; Sal Murdocca, pp. 265-267; Ann Neumann, pp. 510-517; Tom Newsom, pp. 128-139, 180-187, 446-471; Louis Pappas, p. 110, 117, pp. 304-311, 482-483; Diane Patterson, pp. 254-264; Howard Post, pp. 118-124; Albert John Pucci, pp. 48-58, 192-205, 218-226, 412-435; H. Tooter Randall, pp. 142-150, 178-179; Charles Robinson, pp. 380-393; Laurie Simeone, pp. 340-344; Jerry Smath, pp. 161-173, 212-217, 346-355; SN Studios, pp. 36-37, 104-114, p. 116, pp. 125-127, 394-395; Freya Tanz, pp. 288-303, 444-445; Kyuzo Tsugami, pp. 38-47; Tom Vroman, pp. 378-379; Ron Wolin, pp. 82-83; Lane Yerkes, pp. 98-107.

Photo Research: Diana Bourdrez, Elyse Rieder, Tobi Zausner; Photo Credits: Peter B. Kaplan, cover and pp. 1, 8, 9, 11, 12, 13; Flip Schulke, Black Star, pp. 84-85; Tom McHugh, Photo Researchers, p. 112 (top); Russ Kinne, Photo Researchers, p. 112 (bottom); Daniel Brody, Editorial Photocolor Archives, p. 113; Charles Belinky, Photo Researchers, p. 115; Lawrence Schiller, Photo Researchers, pp. 140-141; Frederick Eberstadt, p. 142; Elliott Erwitt, Magnum, p. 143; J. Heffernan, p. 145; Thomas Bloom, Courtesy Opera Company of Boston, pp. 148, 149; Susan McCartney, Photo Researchers, pp. 210-211; Frank Miller, Photo Researchers, pp. 286-287; Museum of the American Indian, Heye Foundation, New York City, pp. 334, 335, 336; Nelson Gallery—Atkins Museum, Kansas City, Missouri (Gift of Mr. Paul Gardner through The Friends of Art), p. 339; U.S. Dept. of Housing and Urban Development, p. 372; George E. Jones III, Photo Researchers, p. 373; U.S. Dept. of Housing and Urban Development, p. 374; Bjorn Bolstad, Photo Researchers, p. 376; Stan Pantovic, Photo Researchers, Inc., pp. 410-411; Earth Scenes/L.L.T. Rhodes, p. 439; Bruce Buchenholz, p. 440; Richard B. McPhee. Courtesy of Dodd Mead & Company, p. 442.

ACKNOWLEDGMENTS

Every reasonable effort has been made to trace the owners of copyright materials in this book, but in some instances this has proven impossible. The publishers will be glad to receive information leading to more complete acknowledgments in subsequent printings of the book, and in the meantime extend their apologies for any omissions.

To the Antioch Press for "On Watching the Construction of a Skyscraper" by Burton Raffel. Copyright © 1961 by the Antioch Press. First published in the *Antioch Review*, Volume 20, No. 4. Reprinted by permission of the editors.

To Atheneum Publishers for "Gravel Paths" from *Catch Me a Wind* by Patricia Hubbell, copyright © 1968 by Patricia Hubbell; for "The Lost Umbrella of Kim Chu" By Eleanor Estes, adapted Chapter Six "Mae Lee" from *The Lost Umbrella of Kim Chu* by Eleanor Estes (A Margaret K. McElderry Book), copyright © 1978 by Eleanor Estes; for "The Mesa" from *The Spider, the Cave, and the Pottery Bowl* by Eleanor Clymer, copyright © 1971 by Eleanor Clymer; and for "Sasha, My Friend" adapted text excerpt from *Sasha, My Friend* by Barbara Corcoran. Copyright © 1969 by Barbara Corcoran (New York: Atheneum, 1969). Used by permission of Atheneum Publishers.

To Brandt & Brandt Literary Agents, Inc. for "Nancy Hanks" by Rosemary & Stephen Vincent Benét, taken from *A Book of Americans* by Rosemary & Stephen Vincent Benét, copyright 1933, by Rosemary & Stephen Vincent Benét. Copyright © renewed by Rosemary Carr Benét. Reprinted by permission of Brandt & Brandt Literary Agents, Inc.

To *The Christian Science Monitor* for "Unfolding Bud" by Naoshi Koriyama from *The Christian Science Monitor*, 7/13/57. Reprinted by permission from *The Christian Science Monitor*, copyright © 1957, The Christian Science Publishing Society. All rights reserved.

To Coward, McCann & Geoghegan, Inc. for "The Mystery of Lyme Regis" from *Mary's Monster* by Ruth Van Ness Blair, text copyright © 1975 by Ruth Van Ness Blair; and for "Why Don't You Get a Horse, Sam Adams?" adapted from *Why Don't You Get a Horse, Sam Adams?* by Jean Fritz, text copyright © 1974 by Jean Fritz. Reprinted by permission of Coward, McCann, & Geoghegan, Inc.

To *Cricket* Magazine for "Featherwoman" by Elaine de Bree, reprinted from *Cricket* Magazine, © 1978 by Open Court Publishing Company.

To Thomas Y. Crowell, Publishers for ". . . and now Miguel" adapted text excerpt from *. . . and now Miguel* by Joseph Krumgold, copyright 1953 by Joseph Krumgold; for "Where's Robot?" from *Deep Down: Great Achievements in Cave Exploration* by Garry Hogg, copyright © 1962 by Garry Hogg, a Criterion book; and for "Sky Day Dream" from *Seeing Things: A Book of Poems* by Robert Froman, lettered by Ray Barber. Copyright © 1974 by Robert Froman. By permission of Thomas Y. Crowell, Publishers: New York.

To Cunard Line, Ltd. for their courtesy in supplying information on the Queen Elizabeth 2.

To Dodd, Mead & Company, Inc. for "The Flowering Peach Tree," adapted from *Fairy Tales from Viet Nam*, retold by Dorothy Lewis Robertson. Copyright © 1968 by Dorothy Lewis Robertson. Reprinted by permission of Dodd, Mead & Company, Inc.

To Doubleday & Company, Inc. for "archy hunts a job" from *Archy Does His Part* by Don Marquis copyright 1927 by Doubleday & Company, Inc.; and for "The Waking," copyright 1953 by Theodore Roethke, from the book *The Collected Poems of Theodore Roethke*. Reprinted by permission of Doubleday & Company, Inc.

To Dresser, Chapman & Grimes, Publishers for "Tall City" by Susan Nichols Pulsifer from *The Children Are Poets*, copyright © 1963 by Dresser, Chapman & Grimes. Reprinted by permission of the publisher.
(Continued on page 592)